HAVOC

THE AUXILIARIES IN IRELAND'S WAR OF INDEPENDENCE

To my wife, Marian, and daughter, Bláthnaid,
this book is affectionately dedicated.

HAVOC

THE AUXILIARIES IN IRELAND'S WAR OF INDEPENDENCE

Waterford City and County
Libraries

PAUL O'BRIEN

The Collins Press

First published in 2017 by
The Collins Press
West Link Park
Doughcloyne
Wilton
Cork
T12 N5EF
Ireland

A CIP record for this book is available from the British Library.

Paperback ISBN: 978-1-84889-306-1
PDF eBook ISBN: 978-1-84889-620-8
EPUB eBook ISBN: 978-1-84889-621-5
Kindle ISBN: 978-1-84889-622-2

Typesetting by Carrigboy Typesetting Services
Typeset in AGaramond
Printed in Poland by Drukarnia Skleniarz

Contents

Cry 'Havoc,' and let slip the dogs of war;

(Act III, Scene 1, *Julius Caesar* by William Shakespeare)

Abbreviations

ADRIC	Auxiliary Division of the Royal Irish Constabulary
ASU	Active Service Unit
BMH	Bureau of Military History
CB	Companion of the Order of the Bath
CMG	Companion of the Order of St Michael and St George
COIN	Counter-insurgency Operations
CP	Command Post
CRB	Central Raid Bureau
DCM	Distinguished Conduct Medal
DFC	Distinguished Flying Cross
DI	District Inspector
DSO	Distinguished Service Order
DMP	Dublin Metropolitan Police
DORA	Defence of the Realm Act
EOD	Explosive Ordnance Disposal
FOB	Forward Operating Base
GHQ	General Headquarters
HO	Home Office
HVI	High-value Individual
IED	Improvised Explosive Device
IRA	Irish Republican Army
KBE	Knight Commander of the Order of the British Empire
MC	Military Cross
O/C	Officer Commanding
PRO	Public Records Office
ROIA	Restoration of Ireland Act
RIC	Royal Irish Constabulary
T/Cadet	Temporary Cadet
VC	Victoria Cross

Glossary

Blue on Blue
Relating to an attack in which soldiers, etc., are killed or injured by their own army or by soldiers on the same side as them

Dual monarchy
Two separate kingdoms that are ruled by the same monarch, follow the same foreign policy and have similar if not the same customs along with combined military strengths but are otherwise self-governing.

Havoc
The military order 'Havoc' was a signal given to the English military forces in the Middle Ages to direct the soldiery to create chaos.

Lewis machine gun
A squad automatic weapon that has the capability of firing 550 rounds per minute.

Mufti
Refers to plain or ordinary clothes, especially when worn by one who normally wears a military or other uniform.

Picquet (picket)
A soldier or small group of soldiers performing a particular duty, especially one sent out to watch for the enemy

Platoon
A military unit typically composed of more than two squads/sections/patrols. Platoon organisation varies depending on the country and the branch, but typically consists of around 15 to 30 soldiers.

R & R
Rest and recuperation

Shoot and Scoot
Firing on a target and then moving away from the location

Section/Squad
Eight to twelve soldiers commanded by a sergeant

Tender
Manufactured by Crossley Motors, Manchester, England, these personnel carriers were capable of high speeds and traversing rough terrain making them suitable for operations in Ireland.

Preface

The military order 'Havoc' was a signal given to belligerent English forces in the Middle Ages to direct the soldiery to create chaos. During the period 1919 to 1921, the Irish War of Independence was a brutal and bloody conflict of insurgency and counter-insurgency operations conducted in every county in Ireland, leaving death and chaos in its wake.

The British government failed to contain this insurgency, and having tried to bolster its police force, the Royal Irish Constabulary, it decided to recruit a specialist Division to operate in the most hostile counties in the country. The Auxiliary Division of the Royal Irish Constabulary (ADRIC), considered by many to be the world's first anti-terrorist unit, came into being on 23 July 1920. In the months that followed, Companies of Auxiliaries were deployed throughout Ireland in an attempt to stem the tide of republican insurgency that was sweeping the island.

The British government made the ADRIC a part of the Royal Irish Constabulary, its Temporary Cadets (T/Cadets) adopting the rank structure, insignia and general look of a police force. It may have been seen by many as essentially a quasi-military organisation, but the ADRIC was created and managed by politicians. The responsibility for its creation, tasking and general conduct lay not with Dublin Castle, the headquarters of policing in Ireland, but with the British cabinet in London. The ADRIC did not report through normal police channels but reported directly to Major General Henry Hugh Tudor, Police Adviser to the Dublin Castle administration via their commandant Brigadier General Frank Percy Crozier, CB, CMG, DSO.

However, the Auxiliaries did not limit themselves to what police procedure dictated. As former soldiers, these men were not police constables or detectives. They had been trained for swift, surgical assaults, relying on extreme violence to seek out and destroy their enemy. This period in Irish history was a vicious and violent affair that resulted in the deaths of hundreds of people, both combatants and non-combatants. Many of the engagements have gone undocumented by both sides but the stories that have emerged are remarkable, consisting of high-risk operations and intense ruthlessness.

Living in isolated outposts under austere conditions, the Auxiliaries carried out counter-insurgency operations that involved small groups of men in asymmetric warfare. By capturing key insights from these operations, the various actions described in these pages take the reader through a variety of daily operations from intelligence gathering to counter-insurgency patrols and intense firefights.

The stereotypical view of this unit being 'guns for hire' is not the case, as their formation and deployment is much more complex. Inaccurate and often sensational press reporting and the IRA propaganda of the time has to this day created a bogeyman out of the force that still exists in the minds of many. In order to understand this period in Ireland's history, a dispassionate study must be conducted of the events and of those involved from both sides in this brutal conflict of insurgency and counter-insurgency warfare.

My aim is not to make the Auxiliary Cadets look good or bad, but unlike many popular histories, neither does this book attempt to gloss over the inherently brutal and dehumanising nature of counter-insurgency warfare. Nothing unflattering or upsetting has been edited out, nor do I seek to make Auxiliaries or their actions acceptable as an unquestioned means to an end. This is not an exhaustive account of every mission carried out during this period, but rather the fullest account possible of a selection of operations conducted by the ADRIC on successive assignments.

Drawn from a number of resources and reconstructing the actions they were involved in, the types of tactical and operational challenges that faced the Auxiliaries reveal the complex and challenging nature of conducting counter-insurgency warfare in Ireland from 1920 to 1921.

Introduction

As Irish nationalists continued their struggle for independence into the twentieth century, the peaceful political agitation of the latter part of the nineteenth century slowly gave way to militancy and armed insurrection. Though the Rising of 1916 did not achieve an independent Irish republic, it did regenerate the ideas of independence and encourage others to continue the struggle against British rule in Ireland. After a period of reorganisation, republican forces launched a guerrilla campaign against the British Crown in Ireland. The Irish Republican Army (IRA) considered the regular police to be legitimate targets, deemed agents of a foreign oppressor. Though a number of these police officers were Irishmen, often members of local communities, many were killed in ambushes and assassinations in an attempt to intimidate British supporters and to lessen British authority throughout Ireland.

While Irish forces continually referred to the increasing violence in Ireland as a war, the British government refused to acknowledge that fact. Prime Minister Lloyd George ordered that the trouble in Ireland be crushed whatever the cost, but without acknowledging that they were actually in a war, and when asked by the viceroy, Lord French, if he would declare war, the Prime Minister replied, 'You do not declare war against rebels.'[1]

In the aftermath of the Great War and the conclusion of the Versailles peace talks in 1919, the British Empire found itself overstretched by ever-increasing demands to police its interests in places such as Germany, the Middle East, India and Ireland. The government was concerned that the unrest in Ireland would have a domino effect and spread to Britain's other colonies. The authorities were unprepared and under-equipped to deal with the large number of nationalists demanding independence, and the possibility of increased numbers of violent and bloody insurgencies that might occur. In Ireland the government depended on the civil administration based in Dublin Castle and the Royal Irish Constabulary to deal with the situation.

Because of this, the government only deployed the army in a supportive role to the police in Ireland, as they believed any show of military force would cause alarm and possible panic among colonialists.

In London, Sir Henry Wilson, a supporter of the Curragh mutineers in 1914 and now Chief of the Imperial General Staff, captured the thoughts of many loyalists when he wrote, 'I said that the measures taken up to now had been quite inadequate, that I was terrified at the state of the country, and that in my opinion, unless we crushed out this murder gang this summer we shall lose Ireland and the Empire.'[2]

The recruitment and arrival of Auxiliaries during July 1920, and their aggressive tactics, brought a new dimension to the conflict in Ireland. These Temporary Cadets, as they were titled, waged a campaign in which the old rules of warfare were torn up and a devastating new style of operations emerged: that of counter-insurgency (COIN). While the regular police largely waited for the IRA to attack them, the Auxiliaries were intended as an elite force tasked with taking the battle to the insurgents. The British military had encountered similar tactics during the Boer War in South Africa but the new army that was raised during the Great War was very different from the army that had adapted to fight the Boers.

The sprawling suburbs of Dublin, Cork and Limerick or the green fields of Counties Kerry, Waterford and Laois had little in common with the Western Front or Gallipoli where the British army had perfected its techniques. In a guerrilla war, there are no large battles. Instead there are many small skirmishes, raids and minor engagements involving a few men on either side. This was not a European battlefield but something altogether more alien: a confused battlefield with no front line and an unseen enemy that managed to appear and disappear, leaving death and chaos in its wake.

The ADRIC and their actions while stationed in Ireland are often mistakenly attributed to the Black and Tans, a completely separate unit.

'K' Company ADRIC arriving at Cork railway station, early December 1920. It was this unit that was involved in the burning of Cork city in retaliation for the killing of one of their colleagues.

This confusion arises because military and police officials as well as the general populace of both Ireland and England used the term 'Black and Tans' interchangeably when referring to the two units.

Though active at the same time as the Black and Tans, the reputation of the ADRIC by far exceeds that of the Tans. While the Black and Tans were hated, the Auxiliaries were feared by many in the IRA.

Speaking many years later, Commandant Tom Barry, former O/C of the IRA West Cork flying column, differentiated between the two paramilitary forces.

> The Black and Tans and the Auxiliaries came from two different strata of life, and the general feeling even here in Ireland at the time, was that the Black and Tans were the worst. I don't accept that at all. The Black and Tans included good and bad, like every

armed force you meet, and quite a number of them were rather decent men.

But the Auxiliaries were something else. There was no excuse for them. Every damned one of them had to be a commissioned officer and to have served on one or more fronts. They were far worse than the Black and Tans. They were a more efficient body because they had more experience and they were half mad with bloodlust. I've no doubt that there were a few amongst them that could pass as ordinary decent men, but the vast majority of these were the worst the British produced at any time. You have the SAS now up in the North, but they're not commissioned officers. Perhaps their experiences in France had driven them half mad. It must be said that the better quality British officer wouldn't join up to go over to Ireland to become a terrorist policeman, which is what they were. They were sent over here to break the people and they were a far more dangerous force than the Black and Tans.[3]

With their role ill defined and the frustration of fighting a guerrilla war, the Temporary Cadets gained a reputation for poor discipline, drunkenness and brutality, which made the force not only unpopular with Irish citizens but also with their police colleagues and the military. However, they also gained a reputation amongst republicans as ruthless and resilient fighters, giving and expecting no quarter in battle.

Though the idea of unconventional warfare made the British government uncomfortable, senior politicians realised that a specialist unit was needed to fight the insurgency that was spreading throughout the country. These men were hastily trained before being deployed into a war zone, with little or no understanding of the conflict or of the people of the region.

Though assigned to a government department and offering their skills for pay, is it possible that this elite force, in the guise of police officers, found themselves fighting the first counter-insurgency of the twentieth century? While historians have questioned the force's role as police cadets, few have examined their possible function as special forces operatives.

Tasked with hunting down the enemy, the Auxiliaries found themselves confined by political restraints, becoming an instrument of foreign policy by proxy. With no effective defence against the hit-and-run tactics of the IRA, the rules of engagement that constrained British forces in Ireland slowly began to disintegrate, resulting in havoc. Although it never numbered more than 2,263 operatives, the ADRIC left a bloody, indelible mark on Irish history.

Within their brief ten months of operational service, the force passed into legend, their deployment and their actions leaving a lasting legacy of bitterness and hatred amongst the Irish population that is still evident today.

I

A Policeman's Lot
Law Enforcement in Ireland

A police force may be defined as 'a constituted body of persons empowered by the state to enforce the law, protect property and limit civil disorder'.[1] As guardians of the peace, officers are considered trusted members of the community, honest and upright, willing to protect and serve those within that community.

Throughout history there have been honest men entrusted to keep the peace within society. The first centrally organised police force was created in Paris by King Louis XIV in 1667. The king created a force that was instructed to ensure the peace and quiet of the public and of private individuals, purging the city of what might cause disturbances and having everyone live according to their station and duties. The exercise proved successful and was to be copied by other countries in the decades that followed.

In England a police force was developed in the early nineteenth century to police the docks and prevent theft. The success of this group witnessed other forces being raised and when Sir Robert Peel was appointed as Home Secretary in 1822, a parliamentary committee was established to investigate the possibility of effective policing in London.

In 1829 Royal Assent to the Metropolitan Police Act was granted and the Metropolitan Police Service was established in London, the first modern and professional police force in the world.[2]

Watchmen or parish constables were entrusted to keep the peace in cities and towns throughout Ireland prior to the organisation of a recognised force. For large civil disturbances local militias were called upon to restore law and order. The Baronial Police Force was created in 1787 but its constables were considered undisciplined and often troublesome. The first organised police force in Ireland came through the Peace Preservation Act of 1814. This Peace Preservation Force could be dispatched to any area within the country to deal with a variety of criminal cases. The force consisted of many ex-soldiers who, due to the lack of a regular uniform, wore their military attire while on service. Later, in 1828, the County Constabulary, as they had become known, were issued with a standard uniform. The reorganisation of the Act in 1836 saw the consolidation of the Irish Constabulary and the Peace Preservation Force transformed into an Irish police force, the Constabulary of Ireland.

The Inspector General at Dublin Castle issued a standard code of rules and regulations for this new force that would police rural Ireland. Cities such as Belfast, Dublin and Derry would have their own police forces. The majority of constables were recruited from the same social class, religion and general background as the population that they would police, the greater number of recruits being the sons of farmers. Candidates were selected for their intelligence, good character and physique and, through a series of examinations and merit, could rise through the ranks to a certain level.

The organisation offered its rank and file a lifelong career, good pay, promotion and a guaranteed pension. Though the majority were Irishmen, there were a number of Englishmen, many of them ex-army officers who had experience within colonial police forces.

Distinctive in their dark green military-style uniforms, they were deployed throughout the country (except for some cities) and were subject to military drill and discipline. They were an armed force, each constable being equipped with a cavalry carbine and bayonet, while officers were issued with a revolver. They were trained along military lines and were taught skirmishing techniques, volley firing up to 1,500 yards and defence against a mounted assault. They lived in barracks rather than stations; the *Morning Post* newspaper described them as 'those little barrack forts that are the block houses of Imperial rule in Ireland'.[3]

Centrally controlled from Dublin Castle, the Constabulary training depot was located in the Phoenix Park. Considered one of the most competent police forces in the world at the time, the success of the force was based on its intensive training and examinations. Policing was mixed with the study of law, and local knowledge interspersed with a reputation of being tough but fair placed the police force at the centre of Ireland's rural community.

Rewarding their loyalty to the Crown after the suppression of the Fenian Rising of 1867, Queen Victoria granted the prefix 'Royal' to their name and the Royal Irish Constabulary (RIC) came into being.[4] The government believed that Ireland required an armed paramilitary force rather than civilian regulation, as was the case elsewhere in the British Isles. Its main task was the imposition of public order, but locally the RIC were considered the eyes and ears of the British government in rural Ireland, collecting information, reporting possible dissidents and applying force to impose Crown law on the local populace.[5]

In Dublin city, it was the job of the unarmed Dublin Metropolitan Police (DMP) to patrol the streets and keep the peace. Its G Division, with approximately 40 detectives, was tasked with the investigation of any political or subversive groups that were considered a threat to the Crown. The detectives worked with the RIC, all information relating to political suspects being sent to Dublin Castle and collated. Weekly reports containing county situation reports were submitted and those suspected of subversion were put under surveillance and a file created where every movement, associate and political thought was recorded.

Officers, many of them undercover, were stationed at railway stations, on boats and at the docks, watching and following suspects that arrived in or left the city. This intelligence network comprised not only the two police forces, but also a network of informers and spies. The forces liaised and information was shared with RIC officers assisting the city police with identification of suspects. Country stations telegraphed descriptions of suspects who were travelling to Dublin, who were then followed on their arrival in the city.

While the period from 1867 to 1914 was one of relative peace, the RIC gained widespread distrust from among the poor Catholic population after the enforcement of thousands of eviction orders during the land wars of the nineteenth century. By the beginning of the twentieth century, the RIC was firmly established, with 1,600 barracks and 11,000 constables spread around Ireland.

The force suffered a number of casualties during the Easter Rising of 1916, the majority during an engagement at Ashbourne, County Meath. In the aftermath of the Rising and in the years that followed, even though many constables were Irishmen, the RIC were seen by militant nationalists as agents of the Crown, and therefore as legitimate targets.

2

A Situation Report from Ireland

The year 1798 was a watershed in Irish and British history. Before that fateful year, none of the armed insurrections in Ireland were about severing the links with Britain; in fact, between 1689 and 1691, thousands of Irishmen fought (unsuccessfully) to restore James II to his throne. The failure of the 1798 rebellion set in motion a series of events that would, and still does, affect the whole country. When the rebellion erupted in Ireland, the British government considered the country to be a serious security threat as its main army was away fighting in Europe. The total military garrison in Ireland numbered just 12,000 troops and the British administration in Ireland employed local militias to put down the rebellion, which they did with considerable force and brutality.

Britain's involvement in the Napoleonic Wars against France between 1792 and 1815 had a detrimental effect on political and social affairs in Ireland. The threat of further uprisings in Ireland worried the British government. Whitehall decided that, to end instability in Ireland, direct rule from the Houses of Parliament in London had to be applied. Under-Secretary Edward Cooke wrote to William Pitt, the Prime Minister, in 1799, 'The Union is the only means of preventing Ireland from becoming too great and too powerful.'[1]

In 1801, Ireland's legal independence was removed by Westminster with the implementation of the Act of Union. While all Irish parliamentary members were Protestant, many did not agree with the Act but it was passed by 158 votes to 115. Ireland's Catholic majority were unrepresented in the British Parliament and even with the implementation of Catholic Emancipation in 1828, for the next hundred years Irish politics would be dominated by attempts to change or repeal that Act of Union.

Since 1885, Home Rule for Ireland had been part of the political agenda of the Liberal Party in England. However, the Bill was constantly blocked by the Conservative-dominated House of Lords. This constitutional crisis was ended in 1911 with the passing of the Parliament Act, which removed the House of Lords' power to veto legislation: it could only delay bills from becoming law for two years, after which time they would automatically pass into law. It meant that Home Rule should have become operational by 1914, but the opposition by the Ulster Unionists and the outbreak of the Great War prevented this. Constitutional nationalism had become discredited, leading to the rise of a number of armed groups who were willing to resort to violence to achieve their aims. While the Great War defused the possibility of a civil war in Ireland, many of the groups continued to plan for an insurrection and the possibility of an independent Irish republic. The 1916 Easter Rising was a failed attempt to overthrow British rule in Ireland. The insurrection was brutally put down, its leadership executed and the rank and file imprisoned. These actions changed popular opinion in Ireland and Britain and public anger against the rebels turned to public sympathy.

Realising that the situation in Ireland would remain tense, the newly elected Prime Minister, David Lloyd George, organised the release of many of the prisoners. The majority were released in August 1916, the remainder in December and convicted prisoners were freed in July 1917.

However, the Irish Republican Army had used the prisons as training grounds; while its members were incarcerated, they reorganised and trained in new strategies and tactics for a new war against British rule in Ireland.

Though Sinn Féin had nothing to do with the Rising, the two became synonymous because the British authorities incorrectly linked the organisation with the failed insurrection, branding any group that disagreed with constitutional politics as being Sinn Féin. Unfortunately, this led to the title becoming an umbrella term that encompassed all forms of Irish nationalism, both moderate and extreme. Arthur Griffith, the leader of Sinn Féin, realised that his organisation's political agenda would no longer satisfy national sentiment. His party never favoured military action, believing it to have little chance of success, but instead sought Home Rule under a dual monarchy. Sinn Féin adopted republicanism in 1917, not so much for the sense of being radical but to win international support. Griffith believed that Ireland could successfully assert its position by withdrawing from Parliament in London and establishing its own government in Dublin. On 26 October 1917, the Sinn Féin Ard Fheis took place where Arthur Griffith was replaced by Éamon de Valera as President of the organisation. This significant event was welcomed by many who saw it as increasing the militancy of the organisation. When Cathal Brugha was asked if Griffith had wholeheartedly accepted the idea of a Republic, he replied, 'He had to or walk the plank.'[2]

The party was divided over its monarchist and republican agendas but a compromise was reached where the people could decide if they wanted a republic or a monarchy, subject to the condition that no British Royal would be head of state. The first sign of the changing political climate occurred when in 1917 Count Plunkett, father of the executed 1916 leader, won the Roscommon by-election as an independent candidate and was again successful in the 1918 election. He refused to take his seat at Westminster and therefore became the first elected representative to implement Sinn Féin policy. Other by-elections were won on this policy of abstention from the House of Commons.

The huge losses sustained by the British army on the Western Front prompted the government to extend conscription to Ireland in April 1918. The proposal met with fierce opposition and many Irish men and women from various backgrounds united. An anti-conscription pledge was drawn up and was signed by thousands. Sinn Féin, the Irish Parliamentary Party, Labour and Church leaders came together in a rare show of unity. The Conscription Crisis increased the membership of Sinn Féin, who strongly opposed such a Bill, and resulted in the British government reintroducing internment and imprisoning most of the Sinn Féin leadership. The police were once again marginalised as they found themselves on the front line, clashing with protestors at recruitment meetings and anti-conscription demonstrations. The situation was defused only with the signing of the armistice in November 1918, when the idea of conscription in Ireland was finally shelved.

The general election held in December 1918 was plagued with difficulties for Sinn Féin because many of their candidates had been arrested and part of their election manifesto was censored.

The once-popular Irish Parliamentary Party now found itself the object of general dissatisfaction because of its inability to secure anything better than Home Rule with partition. The party gradually lost support and votes as the results of the election showed when Sinn Féin secured 78 seats, the Home Rule Party secured six and the Unionists 26. Sinn Féin had campaigned on a policy of withdrawing from Westminster and establishing an independent constituent assembly to be known as Dáil Éireann. The first Dáil convened at the Mansion House in Dublin on 21 January 1919 despite being banned by British authorities. Only 27 of the elected candidates were present as many were in prison, in hiding or on the run. The Dáil intended to pursue the original Sinn Féin policy of simply ignoring the British administration in Ireland and setting up its own government departments so that the British government would become increasingly irrelevant.

The RIC were responsible for maintaining over 1,300 barracks of various sizes and tasked with maintaining the peace with a force of 9,300 officers and men. In order to undermine the police force in Ireland, senior figures within the republican movement devised and supported an organised boycott against the RIC that consisted of economic, social, political and religious sanctions. Many officers were considered traitors for serving the Crown and came under increasing pressure to relinquish their ties with the regime. While the wording and methods of the campaign varied, its message was clear. A Dáil statement read:

> that the police forces must receive no social recognition from the people; that no intercourse except such as is absolutely necessary on business, be permitted with them; that they should not be saluted or spoken to in the streets or elsewhere nor their salutes returned; that they should not be invited to nor received in private houses as friends or guests; that they be debarred from participation in games, sports, dances and all social functions conducted by the people; that intermarriage with them be discouraged; that, in a word, the police should be treated as persons, who having been adjudged guilty of treason to their country, are regarded as unworthy to enjoy any of the privileges and comforts which arise from cordial relations with the public.[3]

This took a severe toll on the RIC's capacity to operate as they became ostracised from the communities they were meant to police, were shunned at Church services and were forced to travel to source supplies. The boycott also applied to their families, friends and anyone seen to collaborate with them.

The result was that the constabulary became isolated; many constables decided to resign or retire and recruiting dropped off dramatically. A military report on the situation stated that:

> The RIC were at this time distributed in small detachments throughout the country, quartered in 'barracks', which consisted, in the vast majority of cases, of small houses adjoining other buildings, quite indefensible and entirely at the mercy of disloyal inhabitants. The ranks of the force had already been depleted by murders, and many men, through intimidation of themselves or more often of their families, had been induced to resign. Although, in the main, a loyal body of men their moral [sic] had diminished, and only two courses were open to their detachments; to adopt a policy of *laissez faire* and live, or actively to enforce law and order and be in hourly danger of murder.[4]

The campaign against the RIC began to take its toll and by 1919 the force was considered 12 per cent under strength.

Michael Collins, Minister for Finance and Director of Intelligence, encouraged attacks on the police. This resulted in police barracks being attacked and destroyed, and law and order in rural Ireland slowly began to disintegrate. The initial strategy of the IRA was to intimidate Crown forces in Ireland until the country was ungovernable. Government buildings were destroyed and judges, magistrates and public servants were targeted for intimidation. In the House of Commons, Winston Churchill, then Minister for War and Air, stated that as a result of the deteriorating situation, the army was rushing more armoured vehicles and protective measures to Ireland.[5] However, with no state of war being declared against the Irish Republican Army, the task of combating the insurgents remained with the police.

On the same day as the first Dáil was meeting, 21 January 1919, two RIC officers, Constables James McDonnell and Patrick O'Connell, were detailed to escort a consignment of 168 lb of gelignite and 38 detonators from the magazine at the Military Barracks in Tipperary town to the quarry at Soloheadbeg, a journey of an estimated 2½ miles. The explosives were contained within three cases, each containing half a hundredweight of gelignite, and were being conveyed to the quarry via a horse and cart driven by Edward Godfrey. The detonators were carried in the pocket of a County Council employee, Patrick Flynn, who walked with the two officers behind the cart. The routine assignment had been carried out many times before and the two officers, with their rifles slung on their shoulders, expected no trouble. As the group neared their destination, Seán Treacy, Vice Brigadier of the IRA's South Tipperary Brigade, confronted the men and issued the challenge 'Hands up.'

Along with nine of his men, Treacy had the road covered. The officers, taken unawares, attempted to raise their weapons but Treacy opened fire, his initial shots followed by a barrage of gunfire that killed both constables. Volunteer Dan Breen moved out onto the road and secured the cart while the others seized the arms and ammunition from the dead police officers. The group made their getaway in different directions, leaving the two civilian witnesses in a state of shock. While the group made their escape with the gelignite, the detonators remained undetected in the pocket of Flynn. The opening shots of what was to become known as the Irish War of Independence had claimed the lives of two police officers, both Irishmen.

While the British government regarded the incident as a murderous attack by terrorists, Dáil Éireann considered it an act of war carried out by its military wing against enemy occupying forces in Ireland. The Irish War of Independence had begun.

3

The Aftermath of War
The Return Home

From the end of the Great War on 11 November 1918, the powers that had fought began demobilising their forces. The British government faced the problem of reintegrating 4 million men back into society and into the civilian workforce. During the following months, hundreds of thousands of young men, a large number of them officers, returned to Britain from the front line with little or no prospect of employment. Many of them had enlisted in their teens and, now in their early twenties, were unemployable, having few or no skills or pre-war work experience. Commissioned from the ranks as much of the earlier officer class had been expunged, these 'temporary gentlemen' had been trained to kill and had witnessed death and destruction on a scale never experienced before.

Almost every industry had been geared to meet the requirements of the war effort and not only would many factories have to convert to peace-time manufacturing, but large numbers of companies would no longer have any business as the government terminated military contracts. The war had put an enormous strain on Britain's resources. It emerged with much of its export trade lost, its capital equipment depleted and industrial system outdated. The structural roots of this crisis lay in the pre-war inheritance of a narrowly based and increasingly archaic export trade. This was exacerbated by the general decline in world markets. The war had stimulated wartime industries and agriculture, and ensured full employment. However, Britain now began paying the price for its underdeveloped markets with an over-reliance, since 1870, on imperial trade and its failure to encourage more technologically advanced industries, such as motor vehicles, machine tools and electrical goods.

Thousands of returning soldiers would face unemployment and hardship as they sought to reintegrate into society. Having fought for King and Country, they had returned not to 'a land fit for heroes', but to an economy in recession and a society that, though it remembered the war dead, was reluctant to lend assistance to those who had survived.

Then there were those who lacked income, had families to support and knew that their chances of finding employment along with millions of others were hopeless. 'There were those who were lucky and could get away to the Colonies but they were few. There were those who addressed envelopes for 5s. a thousand; those who turned hawker to sell matches or bootlaces and such things, in other words became beggars.'[1]

A London newspaper advertisement calling for ex-officers to manage coffee stalls for £2 10 shillings a week received 5,000 applicants.[2] Ex-soldier and winner of the Military Medal, George Coppard, wrote:

> I joined the queue for jobs as messengers, window cleaners and scullions. It was a complete let down for thousands of men like me, and for some young officers too. It was a common sight in London to see ex-officers with barrel organs, refusing to earn a living as beggars. Single men picked up twenty-one-shillings a week unemployment pay as a special allowance, but there were no jobs for the 'heroes' who had won the war.[3]

The end of the war had created a void and a generation of violent young men, many of them suffering from post-traumatic stress disorder. Many sought solace in alcohol to forget the horrors they had witnessed, the friends they had lost and the difficulty of adjusting to peacetime.

No doubt many of us had ideas above our station: we had been somebody during the war and we expected to continue to be somebody. Perhaps it was a good thing that I had not got that MC [Military Cross] or that captaincy, for I might have felt more like that myself. Perhaps also we contributed to the disillusionment ourselves by conforming unconsciously, that is to say, to the tradition of peacetime employment; the tradition of having an un-heroic cash nexus ... one did not strike in the army, for pay or anything else. It had probably never occurred to me that I was employed and for pay ... there *was* a nobility in being a soldier.[4]

Others, like Adrian Carton de Wiart, had enjoyed their time in the forces; they were adventurers who had lived on the edge and survived.

Frankly I enjoyed the war; it had given me many bad moments, lots of good ones, plenty of excitement, and with everything found for us. Now I had ample time for retrospection ... Far and away the most interesting and important lesson I had learned was on man. War is a great leveller; it shows the man as he really is, not as he would like to be, nor as he liked to think he is. It shows him stripped, with his greatness mixed with pathetic fears and weaknesses, and though there were disappointments they were more than cancelled out by pleasant surprises of the little men who, suddenly, became larger than life.[5]

One of the popular slogans of the time was 'A Home Fit for Heroes' but many on returning home found a very different scenario: inflation, labour strife, women's suffrage (which many at the time viewed in a dim light) and political unrest along with fighting in Russia, Persia, Africa and Afghanistan; all this weighed heavily on the British government and its exchequer.

In Ireland, the nationalists continued their struggle for independence against the British government, its forces now widely seen as an army of occupation. The Irish Republican Army, acting as the military wing of the newly proclaimed Irish government, embarked on a campaign of harassment that slowly began to escalate, resulting in the attack at

Soloheadbeg. In the aftermath of this attack there was an increase in republican activity, with a series of coordinated attacks on security forces. Initial targets were members of the RIC and their barracks throughout the country. These isolated stations were attacked at night, overwhelmed and captured. While the attacks were intended to seize much-needed arms and ammunition, the buildings were destroyed as a message to the authorities that the countryside was a no-go area for the police and army. While security measures, such as steel shuttering and the use of flare pistols to summon help if the phone lines were cut, were put in place, many police officers thought it safer for them to resign rather than risk death or endanger their families.

The barracks in isolated areas were abandoned as the force consolidated and concentrated the remainder of their forces in the population centres. A military intelligence officer wrote, 'Anyone passing a police barracks with its locked doors and seeing the constables looking through the barred windows will at once realise that no body of men could preserve its morale under such conditions.'[6] Small units could not effectively carry out their police duties and protect their barracks without the fear of ambush or attack. The writer Darrell Figgis recalled, 'that wherever one travelled in Ireland, one saw the roofless walls of burned-out police stations, sandbags still piled in the windows.'[7]

In September 1919, with the situation in Ireland steadily worsening, the then General Officer Commanding British forces in Ireland, Lieutenant General Sir Frederick Shaw, suggested that the police force be augmented by the recruitment of a special force consisting of British ex-servicemen.

With Michael Collins and his network of spies having infiltrated Dublin Castle, the British government in early 1920 commenced a shake-up of British administrative, military and police structures. A committee under Sir Warren Fisher, Head of the Civil Service, was established to review the Dublin administration.[8] The investigation revealed a serious lack of communication and unity between the police, military and civil administration. Dublin Castle was described as 'some thirty-six Departments, many of them hardly on speaking terms with each other and ... honeycombed with spies and informers who cannot be trusted'.[9] The findings of the committee on 12 May 1920 recommended the appointment of a senior civil servant to take control of the deteriorating situation. In a purge of the Dublin Castle administrative staff and senior civil servants, many of its ineffective administrators were dismissed and many incompetent civil servants were recalled to London. Sir Hamar Greenwood was appointed Chief Secretary of Ireland, giving him the overall responsibility for government administration in the country. General Sir Cecil Frederick Nevil Macready, a veteran of coal miners' and police strikes, was transferred from the Commissionership of Police in London to Commander of British Forces in Ireland, in April 1920, replacing Lieutenant General Sir Frederick Shaw.

Though the incoming civil and military administration were familiar with the security situation in Ireland, they were not given a clear mandate by Westminster, leaving those in Ireland to determine policies themselves at a local level, with disastrous results.

In response to the number of attacks on RIC officers in June 1920, the Divisional Police Commissioner for Munster, Lieutenant Colonel Gerald Bryce Ferguson Smyth, addressed a number of police constables at Listowel, County Kerry:

> Should the order 'Hands Up' not be immediately obeyed, shoot and shoot with effect. If the persons approaching carry their hands in their pockets, or are in any way suspicious-looking, shoot them down. You may make mistakes occasionally and innocent persons may be shot, but that cannot be helped, and you are bound to get the right parties some time. The more you shoot, the better I will like you, and I assure you no policeman will get into trouble for shooting any man.[10]

Many officers refused to carry out such an instruction and resigned in protest at this inflammatory speech. What little support London offered did not instil confidence amongst the rank and file. The Treasury secured a deal to purchase a large quantity of coffins for the RIC, at reduced prices![11]

In order to restore the RIC's ranks, the government launched a recruitment campaign in England for constables, an action that broke with tradition as the constabulary had traditionally been an Irish-dominated police force. Thousands of young, unemployed working-class men, many with military service, applied, attracted to the job by promises of promotion, steady work, good pay and a pension. Due to the lack of regulation police attire, the newly recruited constables wore a hybrid of dress that consisted of dark green police tunics and khaki military trousers. The appearance of this unusually attired quasi-military force in the villages and towns of Ireland gave rise to the sobriquet 'the Black and Tans', the name deriving from a pack of similarly coloured hounds from County Tipperary.

The new recruits were stationed within the existing RIC barracks where they immediately came under siege from republican units. Hurried into the front line of policing in Ireland, the Tans' lack of discipline, poor training and affinity for violent reprisals and looting proved a propaganda coup for Sinn Féin. One observer described the unit as follows: 'They had neither religion or morals, they used foul language, they had the old soldier's talent for dodging and scrounging, they spoke in strange accents, called the Irish "natives", associated with low company, stole from each other, sneered at the customs of the country, drank to excess and put sugar on their porridge.'[12]

Assaults by the police, the burning and destruction of property and the intimidation by state forces of the population enabled republicans to mobilise public opinion against the government. The new recruits were branded by the republican propaganda machine as the dregs of English prisons and pubs or maladjusted war veterans addicted to killing and mayhem, an untruth that was taken up by the British and international press.

In Ulster, a paramilitary police unit, the Ulster Special Constabulary, was established. An armed part-time force that could be called upon in times of emergency, consisting mainly of Protestants, it was sanctioned by the government and gave Ulster Unionists a sense of security when law and order in Ireland was rapidly deteriorating.

Members of 'Q' Company, T/Cadet Godfrey Hall and T/Cadet E. J. Alexander, photographed in Armagh in 1921. (Ernest McCall)

However, with the intimidation of and attacks on the police continuing unabated, the government came under pressure to curb the terror that was becoming prevalent in Ireland. Lloyd George decided that the most effective response was to implement a counter-terror strategy that of kill or capture the enemy.

On 11 May 1920, Secretary of State for War, Winston Churchill, who had always had a liking for special forces units, proposed at a cabinet meeting the formation of a Special Emergency Gendarmerie, which would become a branch of the Royal Irish Constabulary. While a gendarmerie is, in principle, a force tasked with conducting police duties amongst a civilian population, Churchill had a more aggressive role in mind for his scheme.

Major General Tudor (*centre*) at the Phoenix Park Depot, Dublin in 1920, in front of the Royal Irish Constabulary (*left*) and Black and Tans (*right*). Tudor was head of the two police forces in Ireland, the RIC and the Dublin Metropolitan Police (DMP), from 1920 to 1922. (RTÉ Archives)

General Sir Nevil Macready initially dismissed the idea but two months later, on 6 July, Major General Henry Hugh Tudor, Police Adviser to the Dublin Castle Administration, endorsed the scheme, advising the Under-Secretary, Sir John Anderson, that it would take too long to reinforce the regular police force. General Tudor had been commissioned in the Royal Horse Artillery and had extensive service

overseas. He was a close personal friend of Winston Churchill, and this ensured strong support for the counter-terror strategy in the British cabinet. On 15 May 1920, Tudor replaced Sir Thomas James Smith KBE, CBE, KPM as Chief of Police in Ireland.

Tudor devised a plan initially to recruit a force of 500 ex-officers to the ADRIC under the following terms of service:

(1) These ex-officers will be called Temporary Cadets.

(2) Terms of enlistment 1 year, terminable on one month's notice after the first four months, if the Temporary Cadet wishes to resign.

(3) Pay, £7 per week.

(4) To rank as Sergeants for discipline and allowances.

(5) Uniform Khaki, with RIC badges and buttons, or Sergeants' uniform, RIC, at will. When Khaki is worn the letters T.C., for Temporary Cadet will be worn on shoulders, instead of badges of rank or stripes.

(6) These Temporary Cadets will have priority of consideration for permanent appointment as officers of the RIC.[13]

Those who would make up the rank and file of the new force were required to have an exceptional service record. The RIC officer sent to London to oversee the recruitment of the Auxiliaries stated that 'A canard has been put about that we recruited criminals; deliberately … We had a police report on every candidate and accepted no man whose army character was assessed at less than "good". The assessment "fair" met automatic rejection.'[14]

The titles Temporary Cadet or Auxiliary Cadet were derived from the RIC, which had an officer class system with new recruits being T/Cadets on enlistment. When some officers were asked what the TC on their shoulder badges stood for, they replied, 'Tough Cunts'.

Sir John Anderson, Chief Secretary at Dublin Castle, received a memo from Tudor recommending that the T/Cadets be formed into companies, consisting of eight platoons of 25 men each, and that company and platoon commanders receive additional payments of fifteen shillings and seven shillings sixpence respectively. Anderson objected to these payments, considering them too high, which forced Tudor to reconsider the company organisation and submit a revised pay proposal. He recommended that Companies should consist of four platoons with Company commanders receiving ten shillings per day, their seconds in command (2I/C) receiving five shillings, Platoon Commanders four shillings and Section Commanders two shillings.

For the administration and catering needs of the unit, he suggested that a Depot staff be formed consisting of a Quartermaster and a Mess Caterer.

The unit was beginning to take shape on paper and, as a former soldier, Tudor brought a military mindset to the table and immediately began to address a number of problems. Having organised the Companies, he would concentrate his new force in strategic areas and arm the units with the latest weaponry available. He envisaged a highly mobile strike force and submitted requisitions for vehicles such as Crossley Tenders and Lancia armoured cars. This strike force would take the war to the Irish Republican Army and was given the task of making Ireland 'an appropriate hell for those whose trade is agitation'.[19]

A violent and bloody counter-insurgency was about to commence.

4

The Dogs of War
Recruiting a New Force

During July 1920, the following advertisement appeared in London, seeking former army, navy and air force officers to join a new unit being raised.

Join–The Corps d'élite
For Ex-Officers
Join the Auxiliary Division of the Royal Irish Constabulary. Ex-Officers with first-class record are eligible. Courage, Discretion, Tact and Judgment required. The pay is £1 per day and allowances. Uniform supplied. Generous leave with pay.
Apply now to
R.I.C.
RECRUITING OFFICES
Great Scotland Yard, London, W.

Men wishing to join were interviewed at Scotland Yard and those accepted were given a first-class one-way ticket to Ireland. Within the first two weeks, over 1,000 applications were received. At the interview, the service records of the ex-officers were examined for the highest

Brigadier General Frank Percy Crozier who commanded the ADRIC and resigned over controversial issues relating to the disciplining of his men. (Allen Library)

military and personal standards, both during and after demobilisation. They had to be physically fit and provide a number of referees. Applicants were informed that contracts for a period of twelve months would commence after a brief training course. Major Fleming, the senior recruiting officer for the force, stated:

> Applications were being received from ex-officers of every class from the West End clubmen to soldiers who were commissioned from the rank and file of the regular army. Quite a number of the applicants are Irishmen and many are well-to-do men who are taking on the job in a spirit of duty or adventure. There is no class bar against candidates. We are still open to take recruits and a man's social position will not affect his chances of acceptance.[1]

Recent research reveals that 10 per cent of the Auxiliaries were Irish-born but this number could be considerably higher, if on recruitment the men gave addresses in England as their place of residence instead of Ireland.[2] While Irishmen may have enlisted to escape unemployment, others may have joined up to serve the Crown as the security situation in the country worsened. They may have also felt safer back in the ranks as IRA intimidation of ex-soldiers and police increased. Recruits had the option to extend the initial twelve-month contract by a further six-

or twelve-month tour of duty. The average age of T/Cadets was twenty; 95 per cent had only one previous occupation, that of military officer.[3]

Other recruits were officers who had served within British regiments coming from Canada, New Zealand, Australia, South Africa and some Americans who had served with British regiments during the Great War.

The T/Cadets were under the command of Brigadier General Frank Percy Crozier who took up his position on 4 August 1920. Crozier was a career army officer, having served in the Boer War and West Africa before being forced to leave the army because of financial irresponsibility. In 1912, he became an officer in the Loyalist paramilitary Ulster Volunteer Force and when war broke out in 1914, he rejoined the army and fought on the Western Front until 1918. He became an Inspector-General in the Lithuanian army in 1919, but resigned within six months of his appointment.[4]

Crozier's second in command was Brigadier General E.A. Wood, another career officer who had seen service during the war on the Western Front and who had won the Distinguished Service Order three times and was recommended for the Victoria Cross twice.

As Tudor was taking up his appointment as Chief of Police, his old friend Brigadier General Sir Ormonde de l'Épée Winter KBE, CB, CMG, DSO, was appointed Deputy Chief of Police and Chief of British Army Intelligence in Ireland – Combined Intelligence Service. Commissioned into the Royal Horse and Royal Field Artillery in 1894, he spent his early military career in India. In 1903, while stationed in England, he was tried for manslaughter when he defended himself against a youth who had been throwing stones at his boat. He hit the boy with a scull, killing him. He was acquitted. During the War he served at Gallipoli and on the Western Front. He was to prove one of the most dangerous individuals that republican forces would have to contend with.

Thomas Girdwood Macfie was appointed Crozier's Adjutant. He had travelled extensively and had served in Africa, Canada and England. He was dismissed from the forces, having been court-martialled for attempting to embezzle military funds. He joined the South African Forces and received a commission in January 1918. He

Ormonde de l'Épée Winter, director of British Army Intelligence in Ireland. (Kilmainham Gaol)

was awarded an MC on the Western Front and later a DSO for service against the Bolsheviks in Russia.[5] It is worth noting that many of the misdemeanours of those holding senior posts within the force were overlooked when they applied for their positions.

The Auxiliary Division was to be maintained as an autonomous force and would be deployed into areas where the IRA was most active, with the mission of find, fix and destroy.

The first recruits arrived at the North Wall Dock, Dublin, from where they were transferred to Hare Park camp at the Curragh Training Camp in County Kildare. Here they underwent a brief training course in the rudimentary skills of policing. They also received a refresher course in weapons training, consisting of firing and bombing practice, for which they provided their own instructors. Recruit Bill Monroe wrote: 'We spent about six weeks messing about – what little we got of instruction had a very remote relationship to the work we had to do in the country. Theoretically we were put through a shortened police course, having impressed on us the meaning of a misdemeanour and a felony, our power of arrest, and what we could and could not do.'[6]

Little thought had been given to the organisation and administration of the force. When Crozier visited his new recruits at the Curragh Camp he found them disorganised and unruly. He wrote:

> … misery, inconvenience, and hard drinking could have been avoided had arrangements been made for the reception of these men, for their ordinary comfort – quartering, messing and discipline – but instead, the men were running about the Curragh as they liked. The original members of the division, which then had no name, had to arrange their own messing and canteens, and there was nobody in command. Conditions were appalling.[7]

The initial intake of recruits were formed into 'A' and 'B' Companies with Crozier and Major J.H.M. Kirkwood commanding 'B' Company.

The Curragh Camp also housed a large British military contingent and it is believed animosity between the two groups resulted in the new Auxiliary Cadets being relocated to Beggars Bush Barracks in Ballsbridge, Dublin, which eventually became Divisional Depot Headquarters. Companies were commanded by a divisional staff with each company being 100 men in strength. Though military in appearance, serving officers took their ranks from the police.

> The Company Commander was preferably held by a person with the military rank of Lieutenant Colonel who would be equivalent to an R.I.C. First Class District Inspector. He would have a Second Class District Inspector as the Company Second in Command (2I/C). Each of the four platoons would be commanded by a Third Class District Inspector and he would have two Head Constables in each platoon as Section Leaders. Within the platoon there would be two sections of Cadets including two section sergeants.[8]

(*L–r*): Colonel Johnson and Major General Sir Henry Tudor accompanying Field Marshall John French, Lord Lieutenant of Ireland, as he reviews T/Cadets at the Phoenix Park Depot, Dublin, 1920. (Allen Library)

There were 153 officers holding the rank of Platoon Commander with only eight of these T/Cadets being of Irish descent.[9] The men chosen to fill these command posts within a company were not picked because of any experience of the work but mostly by virtue of having held senior rank during military service. Company strengths were constantly changing due to transfers, termination of contracts, dismissals and resignations.[10]

By the end of August 1920, fifteen Companies had been formed and four were immediately deployed to areas of considerable insurgent activity in Counties Dublin, Kilkenny, Cork and Galway. In total there were to be 21 Companies, numbering between 40 and 80 T/Cadets, organised along military lines, deployed as an elite body to seek out and eliminate the IRA.

T/Cadet Ernest Lycett kept a diary and recorded his duties and experiences while on deployment in Ireland. He was stationed at Macroom Castle for a period.

> I was promoted to Assistant Superintendent of my Platoon. It was chiefly so that I could carry out the position of Mess President. I was responsible to the OC for the ordering of local supplies, food, wines, etc. which did not come under the authority of the Camp Quartermaster. I soon got to know local shop keepers, including the butcher, baker, grocer, greengrocers, wine stores and the Town Clerk and Chairman of the Town.
>
> I liked the work very much, but I still had to go on my duties with Patrols on the armoured cars and lorries. We had an area of country to patrol, covering about a 50 mile radius of Macroom. A programme and a roster of patrols and guards was prepared and put into operation from the second day we were at the Castle. We were on dangerous duty, which was to keep the highways and roads open to traffic. Every morning the patrols would leave the Castle gates at 8am with definite routes to be followed by the officer in charge. All in battle order and ready for trouble on the way, we took midday rations with us, also petrol to refuel if necessary. Notwithstanding the tension, it was very interesting, passing through the most beautiful country, but we never knew what was just around the bend. When passing through deep cuttings, sometimes we sent out scouts on either side ahead of us, for security against roadblocks etc.[11]

The arrival and deployment of the Auxiliaries around Ireland was raised in the House of Commons by Neville Chamberlain who asked the Chief Secretary of Ireland, 'In view of the confusion in the public mind as to the nature of the various forces responsible for law and order in Ireland, will he circulate for the information of members a statement showing the method of recruitment, organization and to the other forces of the Black and Tans and the ADRIC respectively?'[12]

Sir Hamar Greenwood replied, 'As I have previously explained the so-called Black and Tans are not a separate force but are recruits to the

Temporary Cadets, possibly from 'F' Company, at a sports event in Dublin in 1920. (Kilmainham Gaol)

permanent establishment of the R.I.C. The Auxiliary Division is also part of the R.I.C. but consists altogether of ex-officers of the army, navy and air force who have been recruited for temporary service only.'[13]

T/Cadets wore their military service dress tunics, trousers and puttees but without military insignia. Later the RIC uniform trousers were worn and the puttees were eventually discarded. Insignia consisted of RIC badges and buttons but with the addition of the shoulder title TC, which defined them as Temporary Cadets. A variety of military-issue overcoat was worn; in addition, there were light rain capes to protect men on patrol from the inclement Irish weather. Individual service ribbons worn on their tunics denoted awards such as the

Victoria Cross, the Military Cross, Military Medals and the Croix de Guerre. Many of the men had been promoted from the ranks, having received the Military Medal instead of (or in addition to) the officers' Military Cross. Not many T/Cadets received the Distinguished Service Order, revealing that the unit did not attract many ex-senior officers.[14]

The Auxiliaries were conspicuous for the type of headgear they wore, a British army officer-style khaki tam-o'-shanter or the later dark green Balmoral cap with the crowned harp insignia of the RIC. In relation to their dress, T/Cadet Monroe wrote: 'Really there were no uniform regulations and we could turn out in a mixture of army, RAF and Naval uniforms, provided we wore the regulation cap.'[15] A black ammunition bandolier with five 10-round pockets at the front was worn across the chest. All rifle ammunition was .303 which was held in five-round chargers. A black leather waist belt carried a scabbard, bayonet and a holster.

Each company had their own armoury where T/Cadets had access to a variety of weapons to choose from before they embarked on a patrol or raid. Arms consisted of the .303 Lee Enfield rifle and the .45 service revolver. Others chose to carry the Smith & Wesson and Colt revolvers, though many officers preferred the .45 Colt automatic pistol or the Webley .45 automatic. These weapons were carried in open-topped holsters for easy access, especially during close-quarters battle.

Patrols often included weapons such as Winchester pump-action shotguns and Winchester repeating rifles. T/Cadets were issued with a number of Mills hand grenades, a close-quarter pineapple-shaped explosive device with a seven-second fuse, which had proved its worth during the war for trench and building clearance. The squad automatic weapon was the Lewis .303 machine gun, capable of firing 500 rounds per minute.

Communications were very haphazard with each Company being assigned a number of naval ratings to operate battery wireless sets. These had a range of between 20 and 30 miles but the sets were unreliable as the batteries were unable to hold a charge for long periods. In order to replace the batteries, units would have to travel to the nearest city to have them recharged or replaced, a task that involved a lot of time and manpower. If the sets were down and an insurgent attack was imminent, Very flare pistols were used to summon help.

The Auxiliaries were a highly mobile force with a number of vehicles at their disposal. The transport for each Company consisted of five ordinary ex-Royal Air Force (RAF) Crossley Tenders, two caged or armoured Crossley Tenders and four Ford Tourers. The 20/25 hp Tenders were powered by a 4-litre, four-cylinder petrol unit.[16] The Tenders could each carry twelve men and were later armed with mounted Lewis machine guns, fore and aft.

Mobile fire support was provided to each Company by two Rolls-Royce or Peerless armoured cars. The main armament of the Rolls-Royce armoured car was a .303 water-cooled Vickers machine gun. The vehicle was heavily armoured, with 13mm thickness in certain areas. It was powered by a six-cylinder, water-cooled engine that ran with minimal vibration and noise, which assisted in reconnaissance and raiding operations. The American Peerless armoured car had a crew of four with two .303 Hotchkiss machine guns mounted in turrets with 10mm-thick armour. Reaching a speed of up to 16 mph, these cars gave the Auxiliaries a considerable amount of firepower if engaged.

Motor launches were also made available to certain units for patrolling the various waterways around Ireland. Because motor vehicles were a fairly new phenomenon, another unit within the ADRIC was formed, called the Veterans and Drivers Division. Classed as Temporary Constables, they specialised in driving and base security duties.

The republican intelligence network was vast and their communications lines were not easy to detect. Many women and children played vital roles, carrying messages, spying and relaying arms to caches or the transportation of weapons to and from attacks. In order to counteract this threat, a number of women Auxiliary officers were recruited. The Chief of British Army Intelligence in Ireland, Sir Ormonde, contacted the Women Police Service at Eccleston Square in London and enlisted a number of women constables for duties in Ireland. Their recruitment was designed to assist units in the questioning and searching of females. Before being deployed throughout the country, they received their orders: 'They were obliged to hold themselves in readiness, at any hour of the day or night, to accompany the Crown forces on raiding expeditions, whenever the presence of uniformed women was considered desirable. They were to assist in the search for firearms, military dispatches or any letters or papers likely to contain information useful to the Crown ...'[17]

An extract from Chief Inspector Campbell's diary reveals the women's first night in Dublin city:

> About midnight I was startled by the loud explosion of bursting bombs. The policewomen joined me in my room and from the window we saw a great fire burning, and heard shouting and the exchange of shots. Towards three o'clock the flames died down, and searchlights played over the town. On the following morning to our surprise, no mention of the occurrence was made by anyone at the hotel. We were made to realize forcibly enough that we were in a war zone. Two days later the young waiter who had served us at table was shot dead on the doorstep of the hotel.[18]

Counter-insurgency was a recent type of warfare that few governments or military forces had experienced. The deployment of the ADRIC was seen by many as the beginning of an offensive to retake the areas controlled by the IRA.

5

Strike Back
On the Offensive

As the first units of the ADRIC were being deployed, Depot Company, based in Beggars Bush Barracks, were actively seeking out the enemy. On 19 September 1920 they made contact with republican forces.

Kilmashogue, in the Dublin Mountains, in the district of Larch Hill, was the location of an Irish Republican Army training camp during the autumn of 1920. The 5th Battalion of the Dublin Brigade, an engineering unit that was in training for specialised work, was expecting a visit from a number of GHQ staff officers. A demonstration of a new explosive called 'War Flour' was to take place, followed by an inspection of the two engineering companies.

The area was considered secure and a number of sentries had been posted at various vantage points on the approach to the camp. A local Volunteer Company warned that British forces were active in the area but Company Commander M. McEvoy chose to ignore this information and ordered the exercises to continue.

Early on Sunday morning, 19 September, Rory O'Connor, Richard Mulcahy, Liam Archer and Jack Plunkett, accompanied by an armed escort, made their way to the demonstration area, a disused pit, which was located in Courtney's quarry. The explosive substances were packed into jam jars and detonated using electric detonators. Explosions shook the earth, the noise reverberating around the quarry. Large stones spewed upwards and clouds of dust enveloped the spectators. In between the detonation of several of these small charges, the men heard a number of shots emanating from the camp. Unknown to the Republican command, their position had been compromised.

The previous night, 18 September, at 22:00 hours, Depot Company of the Auxiliary Division of the RIC mounted a number of Crossley Tenders and drove at high speed out of Beggars Bush Barracks. Their destination, a closely guarded secret, was Kilmashogue Mountain. Acting on intelligence that a training session was planned for the following morning, Major George Vernon Dudley, DSO, MC, O/C, planned to encircle the camp and using surprise, speed and violence of action, kill or capture those within. His men, dressed in mufti, were armed with Lee Enfield Rifles and Webley revolvers.

Within a few hours the unit alighted from their vehicles in the grounds of St Columba's College in Whitechurch in south County Dublin, which they planned to use as their Forward Operating Base. Holding the gatekeeper at gunpoint, so he could not raise an alarm, the Auxiliaries waited until daybreak to launch their attack. Their Tactical Advance to Battle would take them to the rear of the Irish camp by crossing Ticknock Mountain, climbing the slopes of Kilmashogue Mountain, descending on the camp and surprising the enemy.

The T/Cadets trudged through the long grass, bracken and ferns, spaced about three yards apart, moving with stealth, weaving from cover to cover. On reaching the outskirts of the camp, the men took up static positions, crouching down in cover. Major Dudley divided his unit into three sections: an attacking force, a covering force and the third group providing overwatch with orders to round up anyone who managed to escape the net. The units spread out in tactical order, responding to the officers' well-drilled discipline. They formed a loose cordon around the area of operations, some training weapons on the camp, others facing outwards, covering all arcs of fire. It was carried out as precisely as a silent drill manoeuvre on the parade ground. From their vantage points, they watched as the Irish Volunteers milled around the camp preparing for the inspection.

A shrill blast on a whistle signalled the attack. Squads rushed the camp, shouting 'Surrender' and 'Put your hands up.' Those slow to comprehend what was happening or failing to comply with the order were brought to their senses by a rifle butt or swift kick. Some Volunteers chose to make a run for it towards a clump of trees. Shots were fired, prompting them to stop and surrender. As Major Dudley ordered his men to search the prisoners, a group of three Volunteers who had been manning an outpost entered the camp. On being challenged to halt, two men made a bid to flee while the third, Seán Doyle, raised his rifle and opened fire. The Auxiliaries returned fire, killing Doyle and wounding another. As a T/Cadet searched the dead body, a hand grenade was discovered in his pocket. Those who escaped the camp were captured near the road by the outer Auxiliary cordon. The raid was sudden, quick, unexpected and made from the rear of the camp, which the Volunteers had considered to be secure and impregnable.

The Volunteers making a run for it had distracted the Auxiliaries and amid the confusion, the men in the quarry split into a number of groups and proceeded to evade capture. Rory O'Connor and Richard Mulcahy took one route while Jack Plunkett and Liam Archer moved back towards the camp and, from a position of cover, witnessed their colleagues being escorted at gunpoint from the scene. The prisoners were marched back to St Columba's College and were kept under guard for four hours until they were removed in four lorries, which came for them from one of the military barracks in the city.

Two days later, on Tuesday 21 September, in the early hours of the morning, the prisoners were removed from the barracks and escorted to Mountjoy Prison.

Security forces had mounted a successful pre-emptive operation against insurgent forces in Dublin, resulting in the death of one insurgent and the capture of 40 prisoners from a specialised engineering battalion. This short operation was offensive and tactical, conducted in what many believed was an insurgent-controlled area. Acting on reliable intelligence, the ADRIC utilised speed and surprise in order to deploy their forces. This operation also resulted in the seizure of a large quantity of rifles, small arms, ammunition and explosives.

In the weeks that followed, the ADRIC acted with impunity, carrying out raids and searches throughout the country. Known IRA operatives, their families, friends and republican sympathisers were targeted in a wave of violence that spread across the island.

6

Chasing Shadows
Commencing Counter-insurgency Operations

'We will strike in our own way, in our own time. If we cannot, by force of arms, drive the enemy out of our country at the present moment, we can help to make his position impossible and his military activities futile'.[1] This strategy devised by the IRA was drawn up in the aftermath of the 1916 Easter Rising when a new form of warfare – a guerrilla war – was devised by republican prisoners incarcerated in an internment camp at Frongoch, Wales. Hit-and-run tactics not only inflicted heavy casualties on Crown forces but also affected their morale. Local knowledge and the support of the majority of the population compensated for the numerical superiority and firepower of the British military and police. Leading IRA operative Florrie O'Donoghue wrote: 'One thing they [the British] lacked which the IRA had in generous measure – the co-operation of the people and without it they were blind and impotent.'[2]

The modus operandi in every attack was similar. The first responders to the call of a missing police patrol were often greeted by the sight of detritus from an ambush strewn across the roadway: abandoned bicycles, their wheels buckled and their frames dented with the impact of bullets; spent brass cartridge casings littering the ground; discarded police caps in pools of congealed blood. Weapons and ammunition were missing, taken by the attackers after the ambush. The dead and wounded police officers lay where they had fallen, caught in a torrent of gunfire, with little or no chance of escape.

Just before noon on 25 October 1920, a regular mobile RIC patrol, consisting of a sergeant and eight constables stationed at Cliffoney Barracks, were ambushed between Grange and Ahanlish at Moneygold, 8 miles from Sligo town. They had been lured out from their barracks by a report of malicious damage. Three officers were killed outright, one died later and two were seriously wounded. Those killed were Sergeant Patrick Perry, a married man with ten children, Constable Patrick Laffey, married with five children, and Constable Patrick Keown, a single man from County Fermanagh. Constable Patrick Lynch succumbed to his wounds two days later. A married man, his death left a widow and two children. The wounded officers, Constables Clarke and O'Rourke, were transported to hospital in Dublin. All had been long-serving members of the constabulary and were well known in the area. Those who responded to the missing patrol found their dead, dying and wounded colleagues lying on the road. They were incensed at the death and carnage they discovered.

Major Dudley, O/C of 'E' Company Auxiliaries stationed at Coolavin House, County Sligo, opened the urgent communiqué that had been delivered to his headquarters. It was from the local District Inspector of the RIC requesting assistance in apprehending the killers of his men. Dudley called Section Leader Lieutenant G.H. Boddington and ordered him to assemble every available man. Within minutes, men were rushing through the building, grabbing their weapons and loading bandoliers full of ammunition. Leaving a small unit to guard their operations base, Major Dudley commanded six Tenders of Auxiliaries and headed towards the ambush site. On arrival they were briefed on the situation by the RIC and, with the army in support, they threw a cordon around the Grange area and spent two nights searching for the attackers.

Houses were raided, and the occupants interrogated as to the where-abouts of the ambushers. Buildings were turned over in the search for incriminating evidence that could be used to identify the perpetrators of the attack. Interrogation techniques were harsh, with punches, kicks and the butt ends of rifles being used on the locals. The police believed that many locals not only knew the IRA members in the area but also knew that the patrol was going to be ambushed. It was this fact that angered the Crown forces who were hell-bent on revenge.

On the night of 27 October, the Auxiliaries entered the village of Enniscrone. They raided many houses and arrested Matt Kilcawley, IRA Brigade Quartermaster and also a member of Dromore West District Council. Eamonn Hannon was also picked up and brought in for questioning.

It was discovered that the ambush had been planned and carried out by O/C Sligo Brigade of the Irish Republican Army Liam Pilkington and his 2I/C Seamus Devins. Their attack force consisted of 30 to 40 Volunteers armed with rifles, shotguns and pistols. Pilkington had used a young local man, Patrick McCannon, to glean information on the RIC patrol.

> He enquired what time I would be leaving the village for Sligo the next morning. I told him the time I usually left. He then told me not to leave until the R.I.C. would be leaving their bicycles outside the barracks in preparation for a journey to Grange and Sligo town. My instructions were to precede the R.I.C. on the road and when I arrived at the ambush position at Moneygold near Grange on the main Sligo–Bundoran road I was to report on the information re. strength of the force following me. As my home was very convenient to the barracks I kept it under observation until the appointed time and then proceeded on my journey. Knowing my mission, I cycled slowly to make sure I was not going to outpace those following me. This would enable me to give the exact position of the R.I.C. to the Volunteers in the ambush position. Preparations were then complete to carry out the ambush. A sergeant and four constables were killed. The survivors were disarmed and all booty captured.[3]

Amongst the ranks of the attackers, a young nurse named Linda Kearns administered first aid to the injured police officers in the immediate aftermath of the attack.

Reprisals by the authorities came in the form of burning houses that belonged to or were associated with known republicans. Ten houses were burned as well as a local Sinn Féin hall, a public house, a shop, Grange Hall and Ballintrillick Creamery. A lorry conveying the bodies of two of the dead police officers to Boyle had an inscription displayed in large letters which read, 'A Sinn Fein victory, three widows and seventeen orphans'.[4]

The arms taken in the ambush were recovered a month later when a car driven by Nurse Kearns was stopped by a combined police and military checkpoint. The occupants of the car – Nurse Kearns and three prominent Sligo IRA men, Devins, Gilbride and Andrew Conway – were arrested in possession of the weapons. They were interrogated and sent for trial but no witness to the ambush would testify against them for fear of reprisal.[5]

In the weeks that followed, increased Auxiliary patrols and retaliations continued to make it difficult for IRA units to operate. Arrests and arms seizures severely hampered operations.

An RIC report in December 1920 stated that 'the police are slowly but surely becoming masters of the situation ... they are absolutely confident that the battle will end in the complete rout of the revolutionary forces.'[6] The report also stated that confidential information received had resulted in two arrests at Ballisodare and the discovery of a substantial cache of arms, ammunition and explosives within the O'Connor tomb in Sligo cemetery.

However, even with these setbacks, small mobile groups of insurgents continued to operate in the area, their hit-and-run tactics continually posing problems for the authorities.

Liam Pilkington was never apprehended and like many members of his unit was constantly on the run. After the Treaty was signed with Britain, Pilkington became a prominent member of the Anti-Treaty Forces. After the Civil War he joined a Redemptorist Order and became known as Father William Pilkington. He served as a priest in Africa and Wales, retiring to Redemptorist House at Bishop Eton in Liverpool where he died in 1977.

The driving force behind the republican campaign was Michael Collins, a Cork man and veteran of the 1916 insurrection. Nominally the Minister of Finance in the Dáil, he also was the IRA Director of Intelligence. Along with his Chief of Staff, Richard Mulcahy, Collins made plans to launch a war of insurgency against the British Crown in Ireland. Collins was to become a 'high-value target' for British Intelligence during the Irish War of Independence. A bounty of £10,000 was offered for information that would lead to his capture.

While the Volunteers followed the British military concepts of brigades, battalions and companies on paper, they were never able to muster sufficient strengths in the field. Their lack of weapons and insufficient and inexperienced manpower greatly hindered IRA operations. Their initial attacks were against poorly manned rural RIC barracks in order to capture arms and ammunition. Stations were raided and officers were ambushed as they patrolled their districts.

As their arsenal grew, they began to target police bases in towns and cities as well as vulnerable patrols. Improvised Explosive Devices (IEDs) and mines were used to breach an entry with the element of surprise enabling the Volunteers to strike and withdraw with their captured weapons without engaging in a pitched battle with the police.

In the aftermath of the Soloheadbeg incident, IRA units increased their operations against the police in Ireland. Tactics varied from military-style attacks to the boycotting of police officers and their families.

As Director of Intelligence, Michael Collins realised the importance of denying information to the British authorities. He moved around from house to house and intercommunication between Collins and his operatives was maintained by a special messenger, Joe O'Reilly. His lieutenants were Liam Tobin and Tom Cullen. Intelligence staff consisted of Charles Dalton, Frank Thornton, Joe Dolan, Joe Guilfoyle, Paddy Caldwell, Frank Saurin, Charlie Byrne, Peter McGee, Dan McDonnell, Ned Kelleher, James Hughes, Con O'Neill, Bob O'Neill, Jack Walsh and Paddy Kennedy.[7]

This intelligence network infiltrated the DMP's G Division and other important branches of the British administration. Dossiers were compiled identifying high-value targets within G Division of the DMP and the Special Crimes Unit of the RIC. A hit squad (known as The Squad or the Twelve Apostles) was established in Dublin city in order to eliminate police detectives, spies and British agents. Between January 1919 and October 1920, over 100 RIC officers were killed, some in the line of duty, while others were targeted and shot while off duty, some in the presence of their families.

The police began to withdraw from rural stations and those posts that remained were reinforced and fortified against attack. Throughout 1919, the IRA's military campaign evolved, with attacks against mail trains, the blocking of roads and the targeting of military and civil service personnel.

The military acted in a supporting role to the civil powers but by January 1920 it was evident that the Defence of the Realm Act (DORA), which had been useful during the Great War, was insufficient to deal with the escalating crisis in Ireland. The British government was reluctant to impose martial law in Ireland, but under increasing pressure from individuals such as Sir Henry Wilson, Chief of the Imperial General Staff, Parliament passed an addition to DORA, the Restoration of Order in Ireland Act (ROIA). This Act came into force on 9 August 1920 and permitted the government to continue DORA in addition to some extra powers:[8] 'To the competent Military Authority the powers, previously vested in the police authorities and magistrates, of instituting and organizing action against the perpetrators of outrage and the organizers of lawlessness and to deport and intern under D.R.R. 14B, such persons on a warrant signed by the Chief Secretary of Ireland.'[9]

Criminal Courts were replaced by military courts, and military courts of inquiry replaced coroner's courts, the civilian juries of which had, in many cases, returned some politically embarrassing verdicts in relation to cases that involved the deaths of people at the hands of the security forces. Previously, suspects had evaded convictions in the courts as few people were willing to testify, but under the terms of this new Act, the police and the military were empowered to try a wide range of offences. The authorities could also withhold monetary grants from local governments to punish those they believed were aiding and abetting the insurgents. The judicial system was in disarray and in many parts of Ireland, British rule had ceased and republican forces had established a parallel government with their own courts and councils.

On the ground the Act enabled the security forces to stop and search suspects, to search houses for arms and to apprehend those committing outrages or arrest those where sufficient evidence was available to bring the suspects to trial. These new Acts still fell short of what the military wanted, which was the implementation of martial law in every county in Ireland. As the violence steadily increased, martial law was implemented on 10 December 1920 in Counties Cork, Kerry, Limerick, and Tipperary. In January 1921 it was extended to Clare and Waterford.

To restore law and order, the government, using these new laws, instructed the RIC and the newly formed Gendarmerie to root out the insurgents, destroy their network and retake the country. The Lord Privy Seal stated that:

> Dublin Castle needed emergency powers because peace and order had broken down, threatening the conditions of civilized society. The men responsible for this breakdown were common criminals. The very fact that an attempt is made to describe murder by another name, and to make excuses for it as if it were political action, must demoralize the whole life of any country where such excuses can be made. These gangsters do not represent the people of Ireland. The great mass of the Irish people, whatever their political views, however strong their desire for independence, would rejoice if this criminal conspiracy of murder was ended.[10]

An extract of the Martial Law proclamation read: 'Note Well: That a state of armed insurrection exists, that any person taking part therein or harbouring any person who has taken part therein, or procuring, inviting, aiding or abetting any person to take part therein, is guilty of levying war against His Majesty The King, and is liable on conviction by a military court to suffer DEATH.'[11] The enforcement of these new decrees meant that:

> The number of convictions steadily increased, running into 50–60 per week. The result of this was that the number of men 'on the run' grew week by week. The morale of the troops was greatly raised, and they began to show a good deal more cunning in dealing with attacks, in which the rebels suffered considerable casualties. The recruiting of the R.I.C. also increased greatly, and during September there was a general feeling that things were improving.[12]

The implementation of the Act in order to quell the growth in violence led to the arrests of large numbers of dissidents. In order to avoid these 'round-ups', many republican Volunteers went on the run.

> As the year wore on the pursuit became tougher and we were inclined to drift together, partly for company, but mainly because the 'safe areas' were now fewer and we usually met in them. The local Volunteers always posted men at night to warn of raids, and it was as easy to warn four as one and much easier to send a message to four widely separated men … We very quickly discovered that moving around in a group gave greater security and without any actual orders being issued other men 'on the run' drifted to us and our numbers grew.[13]

This was the inception of the flying column. The leadership of the IRA realised that under the ROIA and the launch of a British counteroffensive in early autumn an increased and more aggressive military campaign was called for if they were to succeed. As the number of men on the run increased, local units were under pressure to hide them and supply food, a dilemma that gave republican GHQ the idea to utilise this supply of manpower. A number of special organisers were sent to areas around the country in order to organise, train and equip resistance forces in the form of flying columns: small, mobile groups of men, numbering about 20 to 40. Their objectives were to inflict as much loss and damage as possible upon Crown forces while at the same time avoiding an all-out battle which could result in the column's defeat or capture. The strategy of guerrilla warfare incorporated a ceaseless and relentless offensive against British forces in Ireland. IRA units utilised the terrain, both in the country and in the city, to conceal their movements.

Many republican officers were veterans of the Great War and brought with them the basic military skills needed to train operatives in the use of weapons and explosives. These in turn developed the tactics of hit-and-run attacks that involved sabotage, ambush and assassination against the police and military. Many local IRA units used intimidation of the local populace as a weapon, as one County Inspector's Report from 1921 reads: 'On 10:9:21 Mrs. Parsons, wife of a barber at Thomastown, who was boycotted for working for the Auxiliaries, received a threatening letter warning her of danger if she did not pay £6:11:0, rent due to Mrs. Mullins, whose son, a member of the IRA, was killed in the Coolbawn ambush: The Parsons family have since left the country.'[14]

Women and children suffered at the hands of both the security forces and insurgents, with many living in abject terror, both day and night. Females accused of fraternisation were intimidated and threatened with violence, which was often followed by the humiliation of having their heads shaved. Night raids, by both the IRA and ADRIC, resulted in women and children, clad only in their night attire, being held outside in all weathers while their homes were ransacked.

While both sides in the conflict rejected allegations of physical assault and rape, a number of cases were documented by groups such as the American Commission and the British Labour Party Commission to Ireland.[15] Few women would have reported such assaults due to the stigma attached to such attacks. In relation to accusations of sexual assaults on the female population of Ireland by Crown forces, Sir Hamar Greenwood retorted:

> [It was the] most serious charge that can be laid at the door of any white man. We have over 60,000 armed men in Ireland, and there has never been one bit of evidence produced to show that there has been any outrage of this kind. The House will understand that

if there could be a case got up against the soldiers or policemen it would be gladly produced with all its loathsome details to harm the government and besmirch the name of these gallant men who are the representatives of this House in trying to out the greatest conspiracy this country has been faced with for many years.[16]

The lack of law and order enabled these crimes to be perpetrated on the vulnerable in Irish society. In the aftermath of the Irish War of Independence, those who had suffered at the hands of the belligerents were conveniently forgotten and written out of history by both sides.

As the Auxiliaries were deployed throughout the country, they not only had to deal with the insurgency but also with the republicans' elaborate use of propaganda. *The Irish Bulletin,* a weekly news-sheet, was printed and distributed by the IRA in Ireland and abroad. It detailed British 'atrocities' and portrayed the war as a moral and religious struggle, with no mention of republican 'outrages'. Two of the driving forces behind the paper were Erskine Childers and Frank Gallagher whose writing ability enabled them to win over foreign journalists. As the struggle ensued, newspapers such as *The Times, Daily News* and *The Guardian* reported on stories from Ireland but concentrated more on British atrocities than providing a balanced and informative viewpoint.

To counteract the IRA propaganda machine, British authorities established the Public Information Branch in Dublin Castle under the direction of Basil Clarke. The department's mandate was 'to give publicity to the facts of the Irish political situation and its incidents which at that time were seriously misrepresented to the public as a result of Sinn Féin and anti-British propaganda.'[17]

The Auxiliaries posed for a number of media photographs depicting the aftermath of an ambush, which they claimed had taken place in Tralee, County Kerry. No ambush actually took place but the resulting photos were to be used in the national press to show that the ADRIC were winning the war. The actual location of the photo shoot was Dalkey, County Dublin, and when this was discovered, republican propaganda disclosed the attempted deception publically through their papers. The new department had little success as republicans continued to capitalise on both the police and military's operational mistakes.

In June 1920, an RIC Inspector's report summed up the sentiment of the rank and file of the force:

> There is a feeling among the police which is becoming prevalent in places where murders of police have been committed that the only way to stop these murders is by way of reprisals or retaliation … It is becoming difficult to restrain men's passions aroused at the sight of their murdered comrades and when they have the means of executing vengeance it is likely that they will use them when driven to desperation.[18]

7

Extreme Prejudice
The Kilmichael Ambush, 28 November 1920

O n the morning of Sunday, 28 November 1920, No. 2 Platoon of 'C' Company of the ADRIC based in Macroom Castle in County Cork made ready to move out. The unit assembled, checked their weapons and prepared to mount their vehicles, two Crossley Tenders that had their engines ticking over in the castle courtyard. Since their arrival in the area in August 1920, the Auxiliaries had raided constantly and aggressively, appearing at any time, day or night. Their mission was to search for weapons caches and disrupt any enemy operations. They travelled fast, were well armed and were eliminating IRA resistance in the area by counter-insurgency.

The experienced group consisted of five former Royal Air Force officers and two former Artillery officers, the remainder being former Infantry officers.

Taking up his position in the passenger seat of vehicle number 1, Platoon Commander Francis William Crake MC ordered his men to mount up. The first vehicle was driven by Temporary Constable Arthur F. Poole. Those taking up position in the rear were T/Cadets James Gleave, Cecil Bayley, Leonard Bradshaw, Ernest Lucas, Benjamin

Webster, Philip Noel Graham and Christopher Wainwright. Vehicle number 2 was driven by T/Cadet Cecil Gutherie. Section Leader William Barnes, DFC, sat beside the driver. Those riding out were T/Cadets, Frank Taylor, H.F. Forde, Fredrick Hugo, William Pallester, Albert Jones, Stanley Hugh Jones and Horace Pearson.

The patrol was to take its usual route of Macroom to Dunmanway and then Bandon, across country, before returning to base. The roar of the vehicles' engines made conversation difficult among those seated in the box of the Tender. Routine patrols and raids had become rain-soaked, monotonous affairs and worse, predictable. One of the Auxiliaries based in Macroom wrote:

> Winter was now coming on and our patrols were no longer looked forward to, indeed they were becoming most unpleasant. We had only open cars and as it rained nearly all the time, as it knows how to in south-west Ireland, we finished each patrol soaked to the skin despite our mackintoshes. This discomfort I think may have been responsible for our disinclination to deviate from known roads. We would take patrols which we knew would only last so long, then we would be back to the dubious comfort of the castle. However it came about, it is certain that each section officer got into the habit of doing the same patrol each time he was on duty, on any particular day we knew where his patrol was going. All this was not lost on the other side. There was always careless talk in the town and it was easy for them to find out which section would be patrolling on any day some days ahead, and make any plans they thought fit.[1]

Commandant Tom Barry, commander of the 3rd West Cork Brigade flying column of the IRA, had noticed the platoon's complacency and prepared to ambush the patrol. The son of a policeman and an ex-soldier, Barry knew that a well-orchestrated ambush would leave no survivors.

The point chosen was on the patrol's return journey, 1½ miles south of Kilmichael. The road ran along a narrow S-bend through heavy bogland that sloped upwards for a couple of hundred yards to low rock and boulder-strewn hillocks. The land, mostly waterlogged, was

The Kilmichael ambush site in west Cork. (Joe Healy)

devoid of ditches and was barren except for a number of scattered rocky outcrops of varying sizes.

At 09:00 hours Commandant Barry relayed his orders to his unit and began moving his men into position. The disposition of his forces were as follows:

- The Command Post was situated at the extreme eastern end of the ambuscade (ambush site), and faced the oncoming lorries. It was a small narrow wall of bare stones, so loosely built that there were many transparent spaces. It jutted out on to the northern side of the road, a good enfilading position but affording little cover. Behind this little stone wall were also three picked fighters, John (Flyer) Nylan, Clonakilty; Jim (Spud) Murphy, Clonakilty; and Mick O'Herlihy of Union Hill. The attack was to be opened from here, and under no circumstances whatever was any man to allow himself to be seen until the Commander had started the attack.
- No. 1 Section of ten riflemen was placed on the back slope of a large heather-covered rock, ten feet high, about ten yards from the Command Post (CP). This rock was a few yards from the northern part of the road. By moving up on the crest of the rock as soon as the action commenced, the section would have a good field of fire.
- No. 2 Section of ten riflemen occupied a rocky eminence at the western entrance to the ambush position on the northern side of the road, and about 150 yards from No. 1 Section. Because of its actual position at the entrance, provision had to be made so that

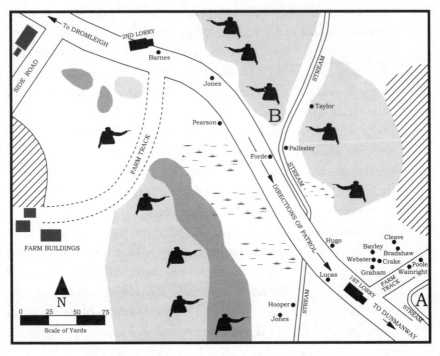

SITE OF AMBUSH IN KILMICHAEL AREA 28 NOVEMBER 1920.

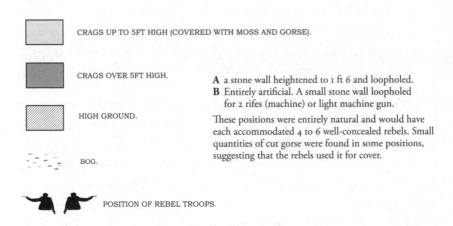

CRAGS UP TO 5FT HIGH (COVERED WITH MOSS AND GORSE).

CRAGS OVER 5FT HIGH.

HIGH GROUND.

BOG.

POSITION OF REBEL TROOPS.

A a stone wall heightened to 1 ft 6 and loopholed.
B Entirely artificial. A small stone wall loopholed for 2 rifes (machine) or light machine gun.

These positions were entirely natural and would have each accommodated 4 to 6 well-concealed rebels. Small quantities of cut gorse were found in some positions, suggesting that the rebels used it for cover.

some men of this section could fire on the second lorry, if it had not come around the bend when the first shots were fired at the leading lorry. Seven men were placed so that they could fire if the lorry had come round the bend and three if it had not yet reached it. Michael McCarthy was placed in charge of this section.

- No. 3 Section was divided. Stephen O'Neill, the section commander, and six riflemen occupied a chain of rocks about 50 yards south of the road. Their primary task was to prevent the Auxiliaries from obtaining fighting positions south of the road. If the Auxiliaries succeeded in doing this, it would be extremely difficult to dislodge them, but O'Neill and his men would prevent such a possibility. This section was warned of the great danger of their cross-fire hitting their comrades north of the road they were ordered to take the utmost care.

- The remaining six riflemen of No. 3 Section had to be used as an insurance group. There was no guarantee that the enemy would not include three, four or more lorries. Some riflemen, no matter how few, had to be ready to attack any lorries other than the first two. These men were placed 60 yards north of the ambush position, about 20 yards from the roadside. From here they could fire on the stretch of 250 yards of the approach road.

- Two unarmed scouts were posted 150 and 200 yards north of No. 2 Section from where they were in a position to signal the enemy approach nearly a mile away. A third unarmed scout was a few hundred yards south of the Command Post to prevent surprises from the Dunmanway direction.[2]

Commandant Barry planned to wear a tunic and Sam Browne belt to give the approaching Auxiliaries the impression that one of their own or a British army officer had become stranded. This action would force the leading vehicle to slow down in the kill zone before the attack commenced. Barry stated that no quarter was to be given and none was to be expected.

As dusk fell between 16:05 and 16:20 hours on 28 November, the first Crossley Tender, moving at high speed, came around the bend. The vehicles were travelling at 40 mph and were 50 yards apart.

Barry stepped out onto the road and raised his hand. The Tender began to slow down and when it was 35 yards from his CP a Mills bomb was lobbed into the open cab of the vehicle. The sound of the explosion was followed by the shrill blast on a whistle: the signal for his men to open fire. A barrage of rifle fire was unleashed on the lead vehicle, which slewed across the road and came to a halt a few yards from the small stone wall in front of Barry's CP. The patrol commander Crake and the vehicle's driver were both mortally injured by the grenade blast. As the remainder of the Auxiliaries debussed from the Tender, they were caught in a hail of gunfire.

Bullets sliced through the air as the officers ran for cover in a laneway and tried to make for high ground.

Commandant Barry realised the action the officers were taking. Leading his section, he moved forward, bayonets fixed, and a hand-to-hand fight ensued. Revolvers were fired at point-blank range and the officers were clubbed with rifle butts as they attempted to get out of the line of fire. Within minutes the nine Auxiliaries from the first vehicle lay strewn along the road and up the laneway, either dead or dying.

The second Crossley Tender was being engaged by No. 2 Section further back along the road. Barry pushed forward with his section, and noted small groups of Auxiliaries fighting desperately within a 25-yard range of No. 2 Section's position. The crack of rifle fire and puffs of smoke drifted through the air. The officers reloaded and returned fire. However, the onslaught was too much for the beleaguered T/Cadets and it is at this point that the controversy regarding 'a false surrender' originates.

In what some believed was an attempt to lure the IRA gunmen from their concealed positions, the Auxiliaries were heard to shout 'Surrender'. Volunteer Jack Hennessy later wrote:

> We heard three blasts of the O/C's [Barry's] whistle. I heard the three blasts and got up from my position, shouting 'hands up'. At the same time one of the Auxies about five yards from me drew his revolver. He had thrown down his rifle. I pulled on him and shot him dead. I got back to cover where I remained for a few minutes firing at living and dead Auxies on the road. The column O/C sounded his whistle again. Nearly all the Auxies had been wiped out.[3]

As members of No. 2 Section stood up to accept their plea, the Auxiliaries drew their revolvers and opened fire, killing Volunteers Michael McCarthy and Jim O'Sullivan and mortally wounding Pat Deasy. Commandant Barry arrived on the scene and ordered his men to keep firing until ordered to stop. This rapid fire against the remaining officers wiped out the remnants of the patrol. The 'Surrender call' may have been a ploy by the T/Cadets to lure their enemy from cover but it is possible that they may have intended to capitulate. However, on realising that the flying column had no intention of taking prisoners, the Auxiliaries, in a desperate act, may have attempted to shoot their way out. Commandant Barry was moving up the road towards No. 2 Section when the incident took place. As he blew his whistle to signal a ceasefire, he was not in the position to see all the remaining Auxiliaries. With the confusion of battle, the police officers, who did not know the insurgent signal to cease fire, may have mistaken the signal for a final assault on their position. In doing so they decided to open fire on their assailants and were in turn shot down. Whatever the case, the reasons behind this episode remain a mystery.

The bloody battle saw some close-quarters action and hand-to hand combat. The post-mortem results and subsequent court of inquiry revealed the extent of the injuries suffered by the sixteen officers. In his report, Doctor Jeremiah Kelleher noted 'a large gun-shot wound scorched over the heart inflicted after death' on one body; on another, he found 'extensive depressed fractures of the bones of the face and head caused by some heavy blunt instrument and inflicted after death'; a third had 'a large compound fracture of the skull through which the brains protruded, this wound being inflicted after death by an axe or some similar heavy weapon.[4]

The wounds inflicted may have been from rifle butts or the high velocity .303 rounds fired at close quarters, as the IRA advanced on their quarry.

Two Auxiliaries managed to survive the attack, Cecil Gutherie and H.F. Forde. Having been shot a number of times and at least once in the head, T/Cadet Henry Frederick Forde lay in the road until the following day when a column was dispatched to recover the bodies of the slain men. Forde was severely disabled from his wounds but managed to recover. He emigrated to Southern Rhodesia and died in 1941. Cecil Gutherie, the driver of the second Tender, managed to escape and travelled across country until he was intercepted by two IRA Volunteers. He was shot two days later and his body was buried secretly in Annahala bog. It was exhumed in 1926 and interred in the Church of Ireland cemetery at Inchigeela.

The day after the ambush, an Auxiliary officer, Lieutenant E. Fleming of 'C' Company, sketched a map of the battle scene, recording where each body was discovered and also some of the topography of the area. Another officer who went to retrieve the remains of those killed described the carnage as 'like nothing he had witnessed during the world war'.[5]

In the aftermath of the ambush, Barry's unit were in a state of shock, many of them never having been in combat before. They collected the weapons and remaining ammunition from the battle site, before conducting a Sensitive Site Exploitation (SSE) by searching the dead T/Cadets for paperwork and notebooks. The two vehicles were set on fire, the blaze lighting up the evening sky. Battle fatigue and the strain of the carnage on the road began to take their toll. In an attempt to jerk his men back to reality, Barry reprimanded his unit and began drilling them amongst the dead. For five minutes they were marched up and down the road, sloping and presenting arms. The flying column moved out and made their way to Granure, 11 miles from Kilmichael, where they rested.

The patrol's elimination was heralded as a great victory by the IRA who had overcome a group of men that had been considered invincible. The Auxiliaries, on the other hand, had suffered a huge defeat and learned that 'complacency kills'.

The incident at Kilmichael was to claim one more victim. Two years later, on 4 February 1922, the body of a man was found on Clapham Common, London. He had shot himself in the head with a service revolver. The man was a 46-year-old ex-army colonel, Barton Smith, who had been in command of the Auxiliaries in Macroom at the time of the ambush. He had resigned from his position a year after the attack.

8

Shadow Warriors
The Intelligence War

Sir Ormonde de l'Épée Winter, the Chief of British Army Intelligence in Ireland, inherited a broken and failed intelligence service that had been infiltrated by republican agents. The members of the DMP who had been employed on political work had been almost annihilated by republican death squads. Detectives were unable to walk the streets without the fear of being gunned down, leaving IRA operatives free to operate not only in Dublin but throughout the country. In the past, the British had paid informants and spies for their services but, with their intelligence network infiltrated, many of those who supplied information to the authorities were targeted and eliminated, a fact that discouraged others from such an undertaking. The British government, police and military had therefore to act and establish a network that would not only yield results but also enable them to take the fight to the IRA.

Having little experience of intelligence work, Winter initially depended on plain-clothes army officers who attempted to infiltrate the insurgent cells, and on the promise of rewards leading to the capture or death of republican operatives. A bounty of £10,000 was offered for Michael Collins, dead or alive. However, Collins continued to evade capture. In a report submitted to his superiors, Winter wrote:

Two things tend to make this rebellious movement remarkable; one is that it has, up to the present, produced no great man, and the other is that, for the first time in history, the Irishman has not succumbed to the temptation of gold.

The former is, possibly, due to the fact that, with one or two exceptions, the heads of the rebel organisation are recruited from a low and degenerate type, unequipped with intellectual education, and in the latter to the fact that a surfeit of terror has replaced an appetite for gain.[1]

There was a lack of coordination between the RIC, the army and the Directorate of Intelligence in London.[2] Winter was given the task of uniting the different organisations under the control of the police. In order to create a viable intelligence network, Winter would have to rebuild, bring in new blood and, above all, get results. However, this would take time and in the interim he would have to make do with the existing system. This would mean using the old police structure, which acted independently. General Sir Nevil Macready wanted Winter to bring together police and military intelligence, a task that could be easier said than done.

Winter had served on the Western Front during the Great War. He revelled in his new role as spymaster and looked the part, being described as 'conforming to the stock image of the spymaster'; he had greased-back hair, wore a monocle, permanently kept a cigarette dangling from the lips and surrounded himself with a dense cloak of secrecy – he preferred to be known by his codename 'O'.[3] Republican forces gave him the moniker of the 'Holy Terror' during his campaign against them.

British intelligence had been wound down after the war and was understaffed and under-equipped to deal with the escalating situation in Ireland. Military and police intelligence organisations failed to liaise and share information, a failure that often resulted in the deaths of Crown operatives. Because the RIC had been driven from their posts across Ireland and were virtually under siege in many of the towns, their intelligence network had broken down as the insurgents killed informers and their handlers.

Having been deployed to a number of regions where IRA cells were active, the Auxiliaries found themselves operating without a proper intelligence network. Tudor, the Police Adviser to Dublin Castle, realised that the existing intelligence network was flawed and, rather than having four separate independent organisations (the DMP, the RIC Crime Branch, and the Dublin military district and GHQ intelligence branches), he merged the first two under Winter. Using his codename 'O', Winter established a London Bureau where agents with an Irish background were recruited, hastily trained and dispatched to Ireland. It was into the morass of a failed intelligence system that an inadequately trained team would venture, to face a cunning enemy in a deadly covert war. One of them, Captain R.D. Jeune, wrote:

> A rather hastily improvised Intelligence Organisation was formed, of which I was a member, and after a short course of instruction at Hounslow, we were sent over to Dublin in the early summer of 1920.
>
> The first batch were instructed to pose, initially as RE [Royal Engineers] Officers but this rather futile procedure was soon dropped and the work consisted of getting to know the town thoroughly, tailing 'Shinners', and carrying out small raids, with a view to collecting all possible information which would lead us eventually to stamping out the revolt.[4]

Contrary to popular belief, many of the intelligence officers were, in fact, case officers rather than spies. They were tasked with recruiting and managing informants and creating a spy network. Some officers, however, did operate on the streets of Dublin and throughout the whole country at great risk.

Winter's agents intercepted and shot the leading republican operative Seán Treacy in Talbot Street in October 1920. However, the success of this operation was to be short-lived and would not be repeated as British intelligence in Ireland had once again been compromised.

Michael Collins and his counter-intelligence network immediately set about planning the demise of Winter and his spy network. Using two female clerks, one at British Army GHQ in Dublin, Lily

Merin, and the other, Josephine Marchmount, based at British 6ᵗʰ Division Headquarters in Cork, Collins was kept informed of all British clandestine operations and British intelligence operatives. IRA intelligence also had contacts within the police force.

> Another important agent we had was a McNamara of Dublin Castle. We also had several policemen amongst our agents, two of whom I remember were Constables John Kennedy and Terry O'Reilly, both of Fitzgibbon Street station. McNamara kept us informed of the movement and intentions, as far as he knew, of the Auxiliaries. Any instructions that were given to the Auxiliaries from their superiors were passed on to us.[5]

In Dublin city, Michael Collins received information that a number of British intelligence officers were actively seeking out his organisation. In order to counteract this threat, Collins ordered his men to compile dossiers on these enemy agents and planned a simultaneous attack on all of the addresses at which the men lodged. Some members of the IRA questioned the morality of such an operation. In reply to their concerns, Dick McKee, a prominent member of the IRA, answered, 'If we don't get them, they will get us.'[6]

On Sunday morning, 21 November 1920, Michael Collins ordered his Squad and members of the Dublin IRA to kill an estimated twenty British operatives at twelve different locations in Dublin city. Twelve British officers were shot dead, many of them in front of their wives, at hotels and lodging houses. Four officers were wounded. Two Auxiliaries, T/Cadets Frank Garniss and Cecil Morris, were also shot by an IRA unit providing overwatch for the assassination squads. Several of Winter's most efficient agents were killed and his other operatives were confined to safe houses or taken into Dublin Castle for safety.

In the aftermath of the attacks, Crown forces descended on Croke Park where a football match was in progress, in their hunt for the gunmen. There are conflicting reports as to what happened next but shooting erupted in the grounds resulting in the deaths of fourteen people in a day that was to become known in Ireland as 'Bloody Sunday'.

On Thursday 24 November there was a massive military presence in Dublin city as the bodies of eight officers and two Auxiliaries killed on Bloody Sunday were placed on ten gun carriages and transferred from King George V Hospital to the North Wall for transportation to England on the destroyer *Sea Wolf*. Also in the cortège were the remains of three Black and Tans killed in Clare and Cork that week. Thousands of troops, regular police and ADRIC took part in the funeral cortège while others lined the route. The public were in awe of this show of force on the city's streets with Union Jack flags being flown at half-mast and many businesses closing as a mark of respect. Those that chose to remain open were visited by the Auxiliaries and persuaded to join their business colleagues and close.

Frank Thornton, a principal officer in Collins' intelligence section, claimed that 'the British Secret Service was wiped out on 21st November 1920'.[7] British intelligence had been paralysed but not destroyed. Winter once again set about reorganising the unit and established a Central Raid Bureau (CRB). This section would provide a central and secure office where all information could be sent for collection, analysis and evaluation as well as being a specialist unit that would be able to interpret and provide that intelligence for those in most need. The work would involve:

- Material and Personnel Exploitation
- Covert Surveillance Duties
- Debriefing and Interrogation
- Imagery Analysis
- Close Operational Intelligence Support
- Counter-intelligence Operations.

The civilian staff for the CRB were security cleared by Scotland Yard, ensuring that information and operations were kept confidential.[8] Morale slowly began to improve. The RIC was augmented with new recruits, the Auxiliaries carried out widespread operations and Winter reported that, by the end of 1920, the RIC was once more asserting itself. There were regular patrols, the personnel were no longer confined

The funeral cortège of one of the victims of Michael Collins' Squad on its way to Glasnevin Cemetery, Dublin, 26 November 1920. T/Cadets form an escort while other police officers form a guard of honour. (Ernest McCall)

to barracks, and the ordinary channels of general police information were once again opened.[9]

The early months of 1921 were a busy time for those trying to build intelligence networks in Ireland. Good intelligence was critical to everything the British administration was trying to accomplish, but without it, the Auxiliaries, in particular, were impotent. However, Brigadier General Ormonde de L'Épée Winter was already rebuilding the system and it was up and running by early January 1921. The reorganisation of intelligence was as follows:

1. A large intelligence office controlling the R.I.C, D.M.P., Auxiliary Division and Secret Service, under the Chief of police who was responsible to the Irish government. This was situated in the Castle.
2. Martial law in the 6th Division area (i.e. the southern counties).
3. Military intelligence in the rest of Ireland where R.O.I.A. was in force.

4. In Dublin a special branch working under an officer on the staff of the Chief of Police, but attached, though not definitely or officially, to the military 'I' staff of the Dublin District for all practical purposes.[10]

Winter also realised the Auxiliary units had the potential to acquire information through raids and interrogations. He wrote:

There were Intelligence officers to Auxiliary Companies, R.I.C., but at first they had neither local knowledge nor an organised system. In some cases, however, where the officer commanding the company was an enthusiast, they achieved excellent results, and an intelligence course held for them at Divisional Headquarters in the martial law area, after the truce, proved of considerable value and showed that much might have been done by training a considerable proportion of this exceptional force in intelligence duties.[11]

Forty-eight T/Cadets served as intelligence officers with two, W.F. Hunt and H. Biggs, being killed on service and D. Wainwright committing suicide in 1939.[12]

Winter began utilising the unique skills of the Auxiliaries and in April 1921, 'Z' Company, an intelligence unit, was formed. Little is known about this Company: personnel were drafted in from other Auxiliary Companies and a requisition to RIC stores for 100 automatic pistols and 38 revolvers was submitted and acknowledged by the British War Office.[13]

The pace of the raids increased: intelligence gathered from one raid could lead to two or three others.

Within the Ops room at Dublin Castle, Auxiliary intelligence officers received information that Number 5, Blackhall Place, Dublin, was being used as an IRA training facility. Known locally as Columcille Hall, the five-storeyed house was under the guise of a Gaelic League Hall. A large room on the ground floor that at one time housed a miniature theatre was now being used as a drill hall for members of the 1st Battalion of the IRA.

Auxiliaries conducting a stop-and-search operation in Dublin, 1920. (Michael Curren)

On Friday night, 29 April 1921, two platoons of Auxiliaries mounted their Tenders, exited the gates of Dublin Castle and made their way at full speed towards Blackhall Place. As the convoy proceeded through the streets of Dublin, a number of vehicles left the group and took alternative routes in order to converge on the Hall from different directions. The O/C knew that speed and surprise were of the essence because as soon as the vehicles entered the street or the distinctive sounds of the Tenders' engines were heard in the vicinity, the republican sentries would warn the occupants of the hall that a patrol was in the area.

As the leading Tender turned onto the street, a sentry mounted his bicycle and pedalled furiously towards the hall. The driver of the Tender pressed down on the accelerator and hurtled towards the building, overtaking the sentinel. As the vehicle slewed to a halt, Auxiliaries baled out and ran towards the main door. Other vehicles converged on the building from every direction, disgorging their cargo of T/Cadets. The officers took up their positions, sealing off the street on both sides, and prepared to enter the building. Exits were covered, both front and rear.

While the cyclist had been apprehended and held, another sentry discharged his weapon into the air to warn those inside the building that a raid was commencing. A section of T/Cadets rushed up the steps of the building and unleashed a flurry of kicks and rifle butts against the front door, which splintered and burst open.

Amid screams, yells and thuds, men and women raced across the hall to try and escape through a door behind the stage. Finding this exit already covered by Auxiliaries, they fled back into the labyrinth of rooms rather than engage the T/Cadets. The Auxiliaries stormed the building from the various entrances and, using rifle and revolver butts, fists and boots, began to round up those within. Screams and shouts of abuse echoed through the building as those attempting to evade capture were caught and brought to the main hall. Those who resisted were dragged down to the makeshift assembly area.

Men and women were ordered to raise their hands and face the wall. Only a few men were captured in possession of weapons as others dumped their revolvers in a kitchen sink and disavowed any knowledge of republican activities. With the group under guard, a unit searched the house and discovered weapons, ammunition, important documents and papers, which were bagged and made ready for 'Z' Company at the Castle.

A number of women were found upstairs, members of Cumann na mBan conducting a class in first aid. Medical supplies were seized, including some splints marked with the distinctive Cumann na mBan motif. The prisoners were held in the main hall where a head count revealed that 53 insurgents had been captured, including an adjutant and a battalion quartermaster.

The prisoners were divided into smaller groups and taken outside where they were conveyed by Tender to Dublin Castle for processing. The information gleaned from the captured paperwork would, in time, lead to the discovery of further arms caches and arrests, which the IRA could ill afford.

The IRA recognised Winter as a serious threat to their operational capacity and, after sending him a number of threatening letters, made an assassination attempt on his life in April 1921. Though he survived the attack he was severely wounded in the hand.[14] However, Winter was undeterred and continued as Director of Intelligence.

With the newly formed unit utilising the Auxiliaries already based in Dublin Castle, both undercover and uniformed units began raiding IRA safe houses and taking republican suspects in for questioning. The information gleaned from these raids and the interrogation of prisoners enabled Winter's section to construct a more detailed intelligence portfolio. All of the interrogations were aimed at extracting information that would lead to the next raid, the next strike and the next capture or kill. Winter wrote:

> Of all sources of information, undoubtedly the most valuable was that derived from the examination of captured documents. After the first important capture which, to a great extent, was fortuitous, other searches were made from the addresses noted and names obtained, and the snowball process continued, leading to fresh searches, new arrests and the obtaining of a more intimate knowledge of the plans, resources and methods of the rebel organization, besides providing material for valuable propaganda. From August, 1920 to July, 1921, 6,311 raids and searches were carried out in the Dublin district alone.[15]

Uniformed military methods simply did not work in a restrictive, urban guerrilla-war environment.

Throughout the country, local centres were established, employing a group system. Working under cover, a member of the Dublin district intelligence network was sent to the local centre where he employed head agents who, in turn, recruited sub-agents. The head of the outside branch was the only person who corresponded with the Intelligence Officer of the local centre, making a secure line of contacts.

However, the Auxiliaries had informers within their own ranks. T/Cadet John Reynolds of 'F' Company stationed in Dublin Castle was passing on information to republican command for money.

> Through Reynolds, complete information was obtained of the movements and plans of Auxiliaries. He gave several photographs including one that was once published in the Capuchin Annual showing a group of Auxiliaries. He gave a key to this photo and thus all the prominent Auxiliaries became known as Mick Collins' squad. The information supplied by Reynolds led to many successful ambushes of the Auxiliaries and to the failure of many of their raids on Volunteers' houses.[16]

Volunteer Patrick Kennedy was assigned by IRA intelligence to handle informers and spies. He recalled:

> Some of the principal agents I was introduced to were Dave Neligan, Reynolds the Auxiliary and Ned Broy. Others of lesser importance were a waiter in the Gresham Hotel, a porter in the Shelbourne Hotel and a civilian working in the telephone exchange in Parkgate Street, headquarters of the Dublin Command.
>
> I cannot recall the type of information that Dave Neligan or Ned Broy passed out, but I do remember the nature of the information that we received from Reynolds. Reynolds reported the conversations of Auxiliaries describing how they carried out shootings, who carried them out and who the ringleaders were.
>
> Reynolds supplied us with group photographs and individual photographs of Auxiliaries in 'F' Company in the Castle. We also had photographs of Hardy and King. In group photographs the individuals that we were interested in were usually marked with an 'X', and our Intelligence officers were instructed to study them closely so that they would be in a position to identify them.[17]

Reynolds' superiors became suspicious of his activities and he was transferred to Corofin, County Clare.

A familiar exclamation by those carrying out a raid was, 'It's as if they knew we were coming.' Another raid on a republican safe house had resulted in no intelligence or prisoners being found. The comment that often followed was, 'They were here all right, just look at the food on the table and the beds are still warm. We must have just missed them.' By 1921, IRA operatives had become adept at keeping one step ahead of the authorities. Their intelligence network was widespread and Dublin Castle, the centre of the DMP's G Division (a cross between the CID and the Special Branch), had been infiltrated by Michael Collins' agents. Any planned military or police operations would be known to those working in the offices and in many cases operational orders were copied and sent directly to Collins' headquarters.

The republicans' greatest assets were a number of agents within the DMP. Eamon 'Ned' Broy worked as a clerk inside G Division where he copied many sensitive files and passed them on to republican intelligence. Broy also smuggled Collins into Great Brunswick Street (now Pearse Street) police station where Collins examined personnel files on members of the DMP. Later, some of these police officers would be executed by IRA operatives. David Neligan was assigned to G Division. He passed on sensitive information to Collins that resulted in the deaths of high-profile officials. In relation to the Auxiliaries, Neligan later described them as being a 'thoroughly dangerous mob, far more intelligent than the Tans'.[18] He also condemned the leadership of the Dublin Brigade of the IRA, saying, 'They failed miserably in fighting the Auxiliaries of "F" Company. Undoubtedly the Auxiliaries were a formable force and the Dublin IRA was very badly armed.'[19]

The Auxiliaries were inadvertently linked to the DMP and the RIC as the government considered them part of the policing force. However, with the respective departments infiltrated by spies and informers, the Auxiliaries were compromised from the beginning of their deployment, a factor that greatly hampered their security and operational capacity.

On the night of New Year's Eve 1920, Auxiliary forces raided the apartment of Miss Eileen McGrane at 21 Dawson Street, Dublin. A university lecturer at Earlsfort Terrace and a senior officer in Cumann na mBan, she was known to the authorities. They discovered a cache of documents belonging to Tom Cullen, a senior figure in Collins' network. Amongst the documents was a large number of copies of secret reports from the political section of the Detective Division. These documents had not been destroyed but had been kept in an unsecured manner. The Auxiliaries returned to their headquarters at Dublin Castle, having arrested McGrane as the occupier of the apartment in which the documentation had been found. The evidence discovered enabled the Auxiliaries to commence an investigation into how republicans had acquired them.

In early January 1921, a detective sergeant was able to link Broy with two of the reports discovered in Dawson Street. Broy managed to make excuses in relation to the copies and talked his way out of the situation. He admitted to typing the two reports. He said he had not made an extra copy but had simply used new copying-carbon sheets in each of the documents. Collins then got one of his secretaries to make copies of the carbon sheets on a portable typewriter, which wrote more characters to the inch than the police typewriters.

After a few days Broy was summoned to the Commissioner's office. He later recalled:

> The Commissioner handed me the sheaf of captured D.M.P. reports, which numbered about one hundred, and asked me for my comments. I stated that all closely resembled the Detective Office stationery and might have been typed in the Detective Office in Great Brunswick St. except in the two cases where the copies had been typed by a machine, of a model that did not exist in any of the police offices, and could not, therefore, have been made in a police office. I again admitted that I remembered typing reports which appeared to be, word for word, similar to the copies found.[20]

Realising that the leak of information had come from the station in Brunswick Street, all sensitive documents relating to political activity were transferred to Dublin Castle. The Auxiliaries and the police continued their investigation and during the third week of February Broy was once again summoned to the Commissioner's office in the Castle. While Broy was directed to remain in an ante-room, his superior, Superintendent Purcell, was instructed to enter and see the Commissioner. When Purcell emerged he informed Broy that he was to be arrested for giving out documents to the Sinn Féiners. Broy was searched and relieved of his service automatic pistol. He was taken to Arbour Hill Military prison in a DMP van under an escort of eight men and an inspector.

While Broy was detained, the British authorities realised that Collins' network of spies and informers was extensive. The Auxiliaries understood that their operations were being compromised by the weak communications structure they had inherited and decided to set up their own network. Their mission was to provide an efficient and effective communications and information network for the command, control and administration of the ADRIC.

Based in Dublin Castle, T/Cadets were seconded to 'S' Company from other units. During the war, advances in telecommunications had enabled widespread contact between headquarters and front-line units. Many Auxiliaries were efficient in Morse code and were able to encrypt and decipher messages through a telecommunications line. 'S' Company was also responsible for coordinating all communications, both radio and line, so that each Company within the ADRIC was connected. Dispatch riders were used to deliver communiqués to a higher command outside the ADRIC bases. To secure important lines of communication and to restrict the amount of intelligence falling into the hands of the IRA, Auxiliary patrols were increased. To thwart republican attacks on communication lines, the Auxiliaries deployed officers in plain clothes along a designated military route in a counter-ambush operation. T/Cadets only carried their distinctive tam-o'-shanter caps to distinguish them from IRA operatives. Regular firefights on city streets became commonplace.

British forces tapped phone lines in an attempt to intercept messages between IRA operatives and their respective commands. Republicans also tried to listen in on calls between the military, police and government departments but were unsuccessful. The time given to such operations by both sides and the meagre results obtained were considered counterproductive.

While the radios used in Auxiliary Forward Operational Bases (FOB) were large and cumbersome, they enabled isolated posts to receive daily reports. The negative side of having this type of device was that the batteries had to be taken by lorry to an army barracks to be recharged. This was a serious setback as the operation of recharging the batteries and conveying them to and from the FOBs ate up valuable manpower and transport. The convoy and their FOB were vulnerable to attack during these operations and regular police and army support was often called upon.

The establishment of 'S' Company greatly increased the operational effectiveness of the ADRIC through the provision of timely and accurate intelligence to the various district commanders located around Ireland. With efficient and secure lines of communications, raids began to yield results.

Head Constable Eugene Igoe, who headed up a specialist unit known as 'Tudor's Tigers' to counteract IRA activity in Ireland. (Kilmainham Gaol)

On Good Friday, 21 March 1921, Auxiliary Forces in Dublin conducted a number of search operations and discovered a substantial arms and weapons cache in stables located behind North Great George's Street.

The haul included revolvers, rifles, shotguns, hand grenades, over 15,000 rounds of small arms ammunition, bomb-making materials, artillery shells and a number of vehicles. At 100 Seville Place, Dublin 1, a number of insurgents were apprehended and a revolver and 90 rounds of ammunition were discovered.

Across Ireland, raids on IRA safe houses and republican headquarters yielded important documentation that revealed the extent of improved police operations. The capture of war materials by Crown forces and the arrest and imprisonment of experienced operatives was seriously hampering the planning and execution of IRA operations.[21]

Brigadier General Ormonde de L'Épée Winter knew the difficulty of infiltrating guerrilla groups and was dependent upon information derived from spies, captured insurgents or documentation. Intelligence gathering became the point of each Auxiliary strike, the documents and information being sent back to Dublin Castle for evaluation. Many Auxiliary Cadets seconded to 'Z' Company operated in plain clothes and worked with an intelligence cell called 'Tudor's Tigers'. This secret unit, organised by Winter, was under the command of Head Constable Eugene Igoe, a serving RIC officer; other Irish police officers were

Captain Jocelyn 'Hoppy' Hardy.
(O'Fallon Collection)

drafted in from the four provinces. His men collated information supplied by the RIC Crime Branch, the ADRIC and Military Intelligence. They also followed up leads supplied by the public. They patrolled the streets of the capital identifying suspects and in many cases eliminated IRA operatives. Suspects were also picked up and sent to the Castle for interrogation, as questioning prisoners was one of the viable means of intelligence gathering.[22]

Winter was already utilising Auxiliary Cadets for the collection of intelligence when he worked alongside Captain Jocelyn 'Hoppy' Hardy and Major William Lorraine 'Tiny' King, both T/Cadets of 'F' Company based in Dublin Castle.

During the Great War, Hardy had been commissioned into the Connaught Rangers and was captured and imprisoned in a succession of prisoner-of-war camps. He made numerous escape attempts and finally made it back to his own lines in January 1918. On his return to duty, he transferred to the 2nd Inniskilling Fusiliers and was severely wounded when he led a counter-attack near Dadizeele in Belgium in October 1918. In this action he lost a leg and was subsequently fitted with a prosthetic limb. He disguised the fact that he had an artificial leg by walking at a quick pace, an action that earned him the moniker 'Hoppy'.

Major King enlisted in the 1st Middlesex Royal Engineers as a sapper in 1901. He served in Africa where he later joined the South African Police. During the Great War he enlisted in the 2nd South African Infantry Regiment and served in North Africa. He later saw action on the Western Front during the Battle of Delvile Wood (a series of engagements in the Battle of the Somme) and then later at Vimy Ridge in April 1917. After the war he became a staff officer and instructor with the Gold Coast Police Force in Australia before joining the ADRIC in October 1920. IRA officer Ernie O'Malley described King as 'Huge in stature, a South African, who had made his way through the ranks. He was over six feet tall, well built, with an air of command and the lines on his forehead were drawn together when he spoke.'[23]

These two officers had a reputation for being very brutal in what they were prepared to do for the cause of national security. Though both officers were targeted by Collins' Squad on Bloody Sunday, they managed to evade their assassins. A British soldier stationed in Dublin Castle described suspects after being interrogated by Hardy and King as being 'more dead than alive'.[24]

Within Dublin Castle, prisoners were taken to a secure holding cell adjacent to the guardroom where they were seated in wooden chairs, their hands and legs bound to the armrests and chair legs. The room's only illumination came from a single electric light bulb suspended from a cord in the centre of the ceiling. Everything else had been cleared from the room but there was a drain in the middle of the floor and in one corner, a water pipe that ended in a spigot. A metal bucket filled with water sat next to the spigot, necessary for reviving the prisoner. Many republican prisoners showed signs of having been beaten by their captors. Interrogation techniques ranged from verbal abuse and threats to hitting prisoners with rifle butts. Fingernails were extracted with pliers and mock executions were often carried out. A prisoner could be subjected to a number of such interviews. Other methods included planting an Auxiliary in mufti in a cell with a suspect in the hope that the prisoner would confide valuable information to his cellmate. When all interviews were concluded, prisoners were transferred to Mountjoy Prison, Kilmainham Gaol or Arbour Hill detention centre, depending on their risk category. However, some did not make it that far.

In carrying out searches for known insurgents, Auxiliaries lacked the means of locating their target in the anonymous sprawl of a city or indeed a remote village. Intelligence officers began to improve and expand their registry and index-card system with the aim of establishing a database of Irish Republican Army personnel. Suspects were photographed for identification purposes, an operation that gave both the police and military units the ability to identify and apprehend known and unknown insurgents.

Major Lorraine 'Tiny' King was implicated in the murder of two suspects. After a raid in Talbot Street in February 1921, two men, Patrick Kennedy and James Murphy, were picked up and brought to Dublin Castle for interrogation. There they were repeatedly beaten and tortured for information. Major King, accompanied by two others, drove the suspects from the Castle to Clonturk Park in Drumcondra where both men were shot. However, James Murphy lived long enough to testify that King had taken them from the Castle, saying that they were 'Just going for a drive', before succumbing to his wounds. King along with T/Cadets Frederick Walsh and Herbert Hinchcliffe were arrested and charged with the murders of the two men and held in custody.

A field general court martial was convened at City Hall in April 1921 where, after a trial of three days, the three accused were acquitted as the testimony of the mortally wounded James Murphy was judged to be inadmissible.

T/Cadets checking identification papers at Amiens Street railway station in December 1920. (Michael Curran)

The Auxiliaries and Tudor's Tigers were an effective force against Collins' intelligence network and the IRA tried desperately to eliminate these threats. However, security had been greatly improved within the Castle and those suspected of being republican spies were moved out or given restricted access to sensitive materials. Republican squads failed to obtain information on these groups. Collins reported 'that things have been hard, in fact, too hard … the enemy brushed shoulders with me on Thursday and with my staff. They didn't get very much, but they got a few things that I would rather they had not got … They just walked into the office where they expected to find me working. The information was good.'[25]

Improved intelligence also enabled Crown forces to capture republican arms caches and key personnel, which weakened the organisation considerably. 'By the first week of May 1921, apart from those IRA men in prison serving time, the following were in internment camps throughout Ireland; 19 Brigade Commanders, 53 Brigade Staff officers, 77 Battalion officers, 182 Battalion Staff officers, 1407 company officers, and 1596 other ranks.'[26]

Republican forces began picking up suspected informers for questioning, believing that information was being gathered and sent to British intelligence operatives. Though no official record exists of these interrogations, it may be assumed that republican intelligence officers utilised similar methods to extract information as their British counterparts. Victims were held for a few days after their abduction and having admitted their guilt, often under duress, were then executed.

The net was slowly closing in on IRA units across the country and Michael Collins and his staff knew that, with no secure source of weapons and ammunition and with many of his experienced operatives in prison, it would be only a matter of time before they would be forced to the negotiating table or face annihilation.

9

Masters of Chaos
Errors & Retribution

'Revenge is a kind of wild justice; which the more Man's Nature runs to, the more ought Law to weed it out. For as for the first wrong, it doth but offend the Law, but the Revenge of that wrong putteth the law out of office.'[1]

On the evening of 20 September 1920, RIC Head Constable Peter Burke and his brother Michael were drinking at Mrs Smith's public house in Balbriggan, a village 20 miles north of Dublin, when IRA gunmen opened fire, killing Peter and seriously wounding his brother. Unofficial reports state that a gun battle took place between the two groups but this is unsubstantiated. Auxiliary Cadets and Black and Tans rushed to the scene from their camp in Gormanstown and, on arrival in the village, they broke into and looted a substantial amount of liquor from the first public house they came across. They surged through the village setting fire to buildings and firing wildly. The reprisal resulted in a large number of private houses, public houses and a factory being destroyed and in the deaths of two local men who were taken and executed by the police officers.

The ADRIC were frustrated if they could not identify a person as being a civilian or combatant, or whether a property belonged to a loyal citizen or a republican sympathiser. Was that same individual who took up arms during the day only to return home each night, a civilian or an insurgent?

The attacks by the T/Cadets caused outrage in Ireland, Britain and America. The liberal press questioned the government's policy in Ireland. If the police were there to protect the country's citizens, why were they systematically destroying their homes, possessions and livelihoods?

Though the Restoration of Order in Ireland Act (ROIA) was assisting the authorities, convictions for capital offences still eluded them. A military report stated:

> Even with the additional powers granted by the ROIA, it was extremely difficult, owing to intimidation, to obtain any evidence against the actual perpetrators of outrages. The result of this was that although a considerable number of rebels in whose houses arms or seditious literature were found during the searches had been sentenced to long terms of penal servitude, men who had committed murder and arson went free, and many prominent rebels in various areas lived unmolested in their houses.[2]

The incident at Balbriggan was to be the beginning of years of legal wrangling between Crozier and those who accused him of failing to control those under his command. This incident, however, was but the first of many.

Politicians and senior commanders in the British police and military were coming under increased pressure due to the deteriorating situation in Ireland.

> The violence seriously damaged the image of the Crown forces as upholders of the law. Although officially condemned by the government, it was, and was felt to be, supported by higher military and police officers. When IRA violence increased, such reprisals became common. Members of the Crown forces became less able to distinguish civilians with good intentions from Volunteers. As a result, they started to regard the entire population as hostile. In the worst affected areas, this turned most civilians against them.[3]

Instead of the situation dissipating, the press seized on the story. Questions arose as to why the Cadets were reinstated and why the military, police, civil administration at the Castle and Auxiliaries lacked coordination in dealing with such matters. Crozier was to be mired in controversy as many accused him of failing to control those under his command and believing that he was no better than those he commanded.

In the House of Commons debates Mr G. Jones asked the Chief Secretary 'Whether the police and auxiliary forces in Ireland are under the same disciplinary rules in regard to reprisals as the regular forces of the Crown in Ireland; if not, in what does the difference consist; and whether he will consider the advisability of assimilating the position of such police and auxiliary forces to that of the regular forces in this respect.' Sir Hamar Greenwood replied, 'The answer to the first part of the questions is in the affirmative. The remainder of the question, therefore, does not arise.'[4]

Those in government were increasingly being called upon to defend the actions of the police and military in Ireland and with the situation escalating and the death toll mounting, it would only be a short time before the international press began reporting in earnest on events.

Reprisals against towns and villages destroyed not only houses but local businesses such as granaries and creameries. Attacks such as these were seen as attacks on the local communities, and not a tactic of depriving the IRA of support.

Suspects were treated brutally, even if there was little or no evidence against them. At Killaloe Bridge three IRA members – Michael McMahon, Alfred Rodgers and Martin Gildea – along with innocent civilian Mike Egan, were interrogated by Auxiliaries, tied together and then executed. Their bodies were dumped into the River Shannon. In the aftermath of this killing, a retired civil servant from England, R.C. Grey, wrote:

> On the Monday afternoon I was walking across the bridge from Killaloe to Ballina ... All was quiet, but we saw a number of the Auxiliary police coming down from the Lakeside Hotel towards the village of Ballina. They carried rifles and other arms and

were led by their C.O. ... He carried a revolver and walked in a strikingly determined manner. Orders were suddenly shouted, the troops spread out through the village, and there was a general hold-up. The men within sight were ordered to stop and put up their hands. No notice was taken of me presumably because I wore rather better clothes than the others and looked, perhaps, even less offensive; but two men who had passed me on the bridge, both well known in Killaloe, were ordered back and compelled to stand facing the wall of this ill-omened bridge, with their hands up ... There was no shooting on that occasion, but if anybody but the police had been armed there might well have been. It did not strike one as an effective way of lifting the terror of the pistol, and looked rather as though on receipt of the news from Dublin these members of the police or perhaps their C.O. were seeing red.

That night there was a good deal of shooting in Killaloe, and though nobody was hurt the inhabitants were given a realistic object lesson of what was liable to take place in certain circumstances; of what did habitually take place elsewhere. On the following night machine-guns were brought out and a demonstration made which continued for many hours ...

The Colonel of these Auxiliary police himself went through the town on the Monday night, pushing his revolver against men whom he met, threatening to shoot, and insisting that all shops should be closed by seven o clock. He gave out that if a shot was fired in Killaloe he would have the whole place burned down ... Danger to the lives of the inhabitants, however, still continues. A friend of mine, walking down the street to his house after dark some days ago, had four revolver shots fired in front of him. This was done by some Black and Tans, but ... these men go through the town at night singing Irish songs and jeering, shouting 'God save Ireland,' and doing all they can to excite the people to retaliation, there is no response. The Irish are wonderfully patient and I fear their spirit is being broken. The odds are too great.[5]

In the aftermath of an ambush at Rineen near Milltown Malbay, County Clare, on 22 September 1920 six people were executed by police, including two elderly men and a teenage girl, Norah Fox. Only one of those killed, Patrick Lehane, was an active member of the IRA.

On 15 December 1920, a platoon of Auxiliaries travelling in two Crossley Tenders left Dunmanway, County Cork, to travel to Cork city to attend the removal of Temporary Cadet S.R. Chapman who had been killed in an ambush at Dillon's Cross four days previously. As they travelled along the road the unit came upon three men attempting to restart a motor vehicle. The three, Canon Magner, parish priest of Dunmanway, Timothy Crowley, a local farmer's son, and one P. Brady, the resident Magistrate from Rosebank, Skibbereen, watched as the lorries passed by. Canon Magner had come across Brady and his stricken vehicle while out walking and, with the assistance of 24-year-old Crowley, they were attempting to push the car in order to restart the vehicle. The Tenders continued a further 100 yards before screeching to a halt, then reversing back towards the group at the side of the road.

Section Leader Hart dismounted from the Tender, walked over to Crowley and asked him for a permit. Before Crowley could answer, Hart unholstered his Webley revolver and shot Crowley dead. The T/Cadet then turned to Canon Magner and began talking to the priest. Two of Hart's colleagues moved forward but Hart turned around and waved his revolver in a threatening manner, forcing the two T/Cadets to withdraw back towards the vehicles. Section Leader Hart seized the hat from the priest's head and tossed it to the ground. The priest was forced to kneel down and Hart opened fire, wounding Magner. He then fired again, the second shot killing the canon. Brady, witness to the two killings, was also threatened but he managed to take cover and escape.

Section Leader Hart was later arrested, disarmed and court-martialled. At his trial, evidence was given that he was a good friend of T/Cadet Chapman who had been killed four days previously at Dillon's Cross. Hart had been drinking heavily since hearing of Chapman's death and medical evidence produced at the trial stated that Hart was insane at the time of the murders and the verdict of the court martial concluded that the T/Cadet 'was guilty of the offences with which he was charged, but was insane at the time of their commission'.[6] He was discharged from the ADRIC in early January 1921 and sentenced to be detained at his Majesty's pleasure in a criminal lunatic asylum.[7]

The killings were raised in the House of Commons when Joseph Kenworthy MP, Liberal member of Hull, addressed Sir Hamar Greenwood where he asked the Chief Secretary:

> Was he aware that Mr. Brady, resident Magistrate, present at the murder of Crowley and Canon Magner, stated that the other Cadets in the lorry made no attempt to interfere, that Mr. Brady's house was subsequently raided; whether Mr. Brady was called as a witness at the special investigation; whether these other Cadets were punished in any way, and whether any of them are now employed in Ireland.[8]

Greenwood replied that, 'A written statement by Mr. Brady, setting out the full circumstances of the murder, was fully considered in the course of the official investigation into the conduct of the Cadets who were witnesses of the occurrence. As a result of this investigation it was decided that these Cadets were in no way responsible for the crime, and that no action was called for in their case.'[9]

Section Leader Hart was later released from incarceration and moved to South Africa, where he resided until his death in 1937.[10]

An Auxiliary unit based at Drumharsna Castle near Ardrahan in south Galway took Patrick Loughnane and his brother Harry in for questioning from their home on Friday, 26 November 1920. This action was in response to an ambush at Castledaly on 30 October 1920 where RIC Constable Timothy Horan had been killed. The suspects were members of Sinn Féin and were well known in the area. (Patrick Loughnane had been a member of Beagh Company IRA. He was involved in a raid for arms at the house of a former RIC Constable, John Carr of Tierneevan, Gort, County Galway. Though the raiders wore masks, it is believed that those held up recognised Patrick due to his weak voice, in comparison to his large stature.[11])

ADRIC Platoon Commander Lieutenant John Francis Ulic Burke DSO of 'D' Company was in command of the police sortie on the day. A native of Hamilton, near Glasgow in Scotland, he escorted the prisoners to the Gort Bridewell before they were transferred to ADRIC headquarters at Drumharsna Castle, where Section Leader C.W. Owen was the officer in charge.[12] He processed the prisoners and was responsible for them while in custody. Both men were severely beaten while in custody before they disappeared. Official reports stated the brothers had escaped along with other prisoners. However, eyewitnesses state they saw two bloody men stretched behind a lorry. On investigation, it was discovered that the two men had been taken from their cells, at 22:00 hours, their hands tied and then tethered to the rear of a lorry. They were then made to run behind the lorry until they dropped and were then dragged along the roads for miles before being executed in Moyville Woods.

To cover up this crime, the bodies were partially burned and then dumped in a pond at Owenbristy near Ardrahan. The bodies remained hidden under 3 feet of water for a number of days before they were discovered. A post-mortem examination carried out by Dr James Sandys on the bodies of the two men detailed the horrific wounds they received before death, including broken bones, lacerations and evidence of torture. Both bodies were naked when retrieved from the water. The letters 'IV' were cut into the charred flesh in several places, two of Harry's fingers were missing and his right arm, which was broken completely across the shoulder, was hanging off. Nothing remained of his face except his chin and lips and the skull was entirely blown away.[13] Both of Patrick's legs and wrists were broken and his face had been removed, rendering him unrecognisable. His skull had also been fractured in a number of places. The doctor thought it possible that explosives were used, i.e. hand grenades may have been placed in the mouths of their victims and then detonated. The subsequent military inquiry was inconclusive and no person or persons were ever charged with their killing.

As the conflict continued, the killings intensified.

On Sunday 21 November 1920, an estimated 100 IRA gunmen, including members of the Squad augmented by the Dublin Brigade Active Service Unit, assembled in Dublin city and were sent to various addresses where they shot and killed a number of suspected intelligence officers. While some were the intended targets, others included military officers, Auxiliaries, civilians and one member of the RIC.

As these events were unfolding in the city, two of Collins' highest-ranking officers, Dick McKee and Peadar Clancy, Commandant and Vice Commandant respectively of the Dublin Brigade, had been arrested during a raid and taken to Dublin Castle for interrogation. An official statement released states that the two men along with another man, Conor Clune, were shot dead while trying to escape. This version of events was not and is still not believed.

IRA Intelligence Officer Patrick Kennedy received information from an Auxiliary named Reynolds on the incident. Kennedy later wrote: 'He [Reynolds] told us that these three men were kicked and beaten first in order to extract information from them. The authorities did not succeed in getting anything from the three men, and as a result they were shot in the Castle. I believe that Captain Hardy and Captain King were two of the British gang implicated in the murders.'[14]

The incidents in Dublin were raised in Westminster. While many condemned those from both sides who took part in the attacks, others sought to support the forces in Ireland. Lieutenant Colonel J. Ward stated:

> I beg to move to … add instead the words: 'and thanks the military and police and the other servants of the Crown for the courage and devotion with which they are fulfilling their duty in Ireland in circumstances of unexampled difficulty; and expresses its approval of the steps which are being taken by His Majesty's Government to restore peace in Ireland.' One would gather from the speeches generally delivered today that the debate has been overshadowed by the occurrence last Sunday in Dublin. One would have thought that the atmosphere created by that terrible tragedy would have suggested to those who had been officers in His Majesty's service the necessity of speaking respectfully, at least, of the dead who tried to do their duty. It is strange, however, during the whole of the debates relating to Ireland, excepting in one case, that the

most vindictive speeches with regard to the honour and chivalry of our soldiers have been made by an hon. and gallant Member who was himself an officer … but it does certainly seem strange to me, coming back again to our British public life, to find the worst said of men who are trying to perform their duty – perhaps not always understanding what the policy of this House may be, but trying to the best of their ability to give expression to that policy, and to carry out the orders that are given to them … The suggestion for instance, in the last remarks of the hon. and gallant Member that our troops and our auxiliaries who recently were troops in the Great War were carrying on a war against women and children is so utterly at variance with the known character of the British officers and soldiers that it is impossible to conceive that there can be the slightest truth in it.[15]

Major General Douglas Wimberley recorded that the Auxiliaries 'were totally undisciplined, by our regimental standards, and members of this curious force undoubtedly committed many atrocities, and, in retaliation, dreadful atrocities were, in turn, committed on them by the Sinn Féin bands roaming the countryside.'[16]

Unofficial and violent reprisals continued throughout the country, isolating the British government in Ireland, which, under pressure from police and military commands, sanctioned official reprisals that took the form of mass punishments of towns or villages. The first of these took place on 29 December in Midleton, County Cork, when six houses were destroyed after a republican ambush that resulted in the deaths of three police officers. In the months that followed it is estimated that 107 of these official reprisals were sanctioned and carried out.[17]

Fairs, markets and creameries were closed by force, which had a detrimental effect on local communities. Other government actions included the destruction by explosives of the houses of wanted Volunteers or the residences of those who lived in the vicinity of an ambush site. The lack of intelligence meant that the Crown forces were unable to act against the perpetrators but took out their revenge attacks, in many cases, against innocent civilians.

In the House of Commons, Sir Hamar Greenwood was called upon to explain the violent and bloody reprisals that were being conducted with Crown approval.

> My submission is that I can accept in substance the resolution of the right hon. Gentleman, namely, that reprisals should not be carried out except on purely military grounds. I go further, and say that they are not carried out in any form except in the martial-law area, and in that area never carried out except on military grounds. I think I have shown that orders have been issued in reference to reprisals, and have been successful ... One must do the best one can having regard to the political remedy of this House which is applied to Ireland in the face of rebellion in a considerable part of the country. We are faced with that rebellion. The military have been criticized, I think very unfairly. The police of the Auxiliary Division come in very often for a very great deal of criticism again I think unfairly. What are the facts? Within a few miles of this House there is a sinister and highly paid rebellion going on, carried out with the object of separating for ever Ireland from the United Kingdom. That object is being carried out by the Irish Republican Army, as it is called. It consists of men who wear no uniform and no distinctive mark; they generally carry concealed weapons as civilians one minute, and they are murderers the next, contrary to all the laws of civilized warfare. The object of this Irish Republican Army – which is a negligible minority of the Irish people, who would be grateful to the Government if they could rid the country of this terror – is to intimidate this House and the British people into a surrender to Irish independence. I shall never consent to that.[18]

As the conflict developed, many journalists from abroad descended on the country to cover the increasing number of incidents. The war in Ireland made little impact on the British public until September 1920, when a series of high-profile reprisals by government forces received extensive coverage in the British press.[19] Reprisals conducted by Black and Tans, Auxiliaries and certain army units captured the attention of the press in Ireland, England and overseas, especially in the United States. The British government was accused of conniving in these reprisals against the populace of Ireland.[20] International pressure, especially from the United States, criticised British actions, urging restraint and calling for an immediate cessation to retaliatory measures. In England, the public were outraged at such actions being taken. In his concluding paragraphs in a letter to *The Times,* Sir John Simon wrote:

> … the policy of reprisals is both politically disastrous and morally wrong. Instead of restoring peace it is intensifying war. Instead of vindicating British prestige it is exposing us to the scorn of the world. It is adding day by day to the store of bitter memories which keep Britain and Ireland apart. It is turning Mr. Lloyd George's heroics about the rights of small nations into nauseating cant. It is undermining the character and self control of hundreds of young Englishmen by permitting them to indulge in deplorable excesses of every kind. It is directing the energies of hundreds of young Irishmen into the horrible channels of assassination and outrage, when their inextinguishable devotion to their own land ought to be working out a better and happier future for Ireland.
>
> Surely it has become plain that the policy and method of reprisals must be entirely abandoned and these new forces must be wholly withdrawn and disbanded, and that a truce must be offered in which a new solution may be sought by mutual conciliation and understanding.[21]

Republican reprisals were also common: houses belonging to Loyalists were put to the torch in retaliation for the burning or destruction of properties of suspected republican sympathisers. The IRA were also conducting a war of terror in many of the areas where they operated, and spies, informers and loyalist sympathisers were arrested, interrogated and sometimes executed for assisting Crown forces. Others who fraternised with police or military personnel were ordered to leave the country or face the consequences.

Attacks on the police and military in the province of Munster were escalating at a considerable rate. With security forces making little or

A photographer being arrested outside Elverys & Co. sports shop on Sackville Street, Dublin. (Michael Curran)

no headway in the area where the population were openly hostile, a number of police officers decided to take the law into their own hands. After Cork city Lord Mayor, republican Terence MacSwiney, died on hunger strike in Brixton prison, his successor Tomás Mac Curtain was shot and killed in his home by masked men, not only as a reprisal killing but to send a message to nationalists that no one was beyond the reach of the Crown. These deaths had a far-reaching effect on the morale of the IRA. Military patrols discovered abandoned ammunition and caches of weapons discarded by republican units that no longer wanted to run the risk of engaging the police or army. [22]

Many years later, IRA Brigade commander Florrie O'Donoghue was recorded as stating that:

> There was a semi-secret organization within the R.I.C., led by foreign elements now gaining influence in that body, which carried out a number of murders, including that of Tomás MacCurtain, then Brigade O/C and Lord Mayor of Cork. Not much was known

of the intelligence activities of this body, but there was evidence that their actions were based on detailed information which they had, in part at least, acquired through their own efforts.[23]

An attack on an Auxiliary patrol at Dillon's Cross on Saturday, 11 December 1920 in County Cork killed one Auxiliary Cadet and wounded several. That night, Auxiliaries supported by Black and Tans entered Cork city and in an orgy of revenge, set fire to large tracts of the city and destroyed residential, commercial and administrative buildings.[24] Those who attempted to intervene were shot or beaten. As the fires engulfed the city, a death squad made their way to the home of two brothers, Con and Jerh Delany. Both men were shot dead and their uncle William Dunlea was wounded.

The war in Ireland had descended into one of tit-for-tat killings, where Crown forces and republican insurgents waged a war of terror on each other and also on the population, both Catholic and Protestant. As the killings escalated, Ireland's 'Dirty War' began to make headlines, not only at home but also abroad.

The Bishop of Chelmsford wrote a letter to the press criticising the British security policy in Ireland. In reply, British Prime Minister Lloyd George wrote:

> Why was the Auxiliary Division constituted? Authority for the formation of the Auxiliary Division, which is comprised of ex-officers of the Navy, Army and Air Force, was given on 10th July 1920, after 56 policemen, 4 soldiers and 17 civilians had been brutally assassinated, and it did not come into really effective operation until over 100 policemen had been murdered in cold blood. For all these murders no murderer was executed, for no witnesses to enable conviction were forthcoming, largely because of intimidation, although many of these murders were committed in the open street, in the presence of non-participating passers-by.
>
> Can it be contended that, when a rebel organization which is based on the repudiation of constitutional action in favour of violence, sets to work to achieve its end by the deliberate and calculated murder of members of the police force, 99 per cent of

St Patrick's Street in Cork lies in ruins following the destruction wrought by the ADRIC and Black and Tans on 11 December 1920. (National Library of Ireland)

whom are Irish and 82 per cent of whom are Roman Catholic, which has always held an extraordinary high reputation for tolerance and goodwill to the population it served, that the Government should stand idly by? It seems to me that all liberal-minded and law respecting citizens must recognize that any and every Government must take prompt and decisive steps to protect the police, and to bring to justice those who invoke the weapons of assassination. Hence the creation of the Auxiliary Division …

As some evidence of what the Chief Secretary and his colleagues are doing, I may state that during the last three months 28 members of the R.I.C. and 15 members of the ADRIC have been removed from the force as a result of prosecutions, while 208 members of the R.I.C. and 59 members of the Auxiliary Division have been dismissed on the grounds of being unsuitable as members of the police force. In addition, 24 members of the R.I.C. and Auxiliary Division have been sentenced by court-martial.

There is no question that, despite all difficulties, discipline is improving, the force is consolidating, and the acts of indiscipline – despite ambushes, assassinations and outrages, often designed to provoke retaliation for the purpose of propaganda – are becoming increasingly infrequent. I venture to believe that when the history of the past nine months in Ireland comes to be written, and that the authentic acts of misconduct can be disentangled from vastly greater mass of reckless and lying accusations, the general record of patience and forbearance displayed by the sorely tried police, by the Auxiliaries, as well as the ordinary constabulary, will commend not the condemnation but the admiration of posterity.[25]

Across the Atlantic, organisations in America were also taking note of the government's reaction to events in Ireland. The American Committee for Relief in Ireland was established in 1920 through the initiative of Dr William J. Maloney with the intention of giving financial aid to civilians in Ireland who had been injured or suffered severe financial hardship due to the ongoing conflict. A number of other similar commissions not only raised financial aid but also attempted to influence American foreign policy in a manner sympathetic to the goal of Irish secession from Britain.

In January 1921, the Labour Commission to Ireland published a report that was highly critical of the government's security policy. Describing the army as being raw and ill trained, the commission's military adviser, C.B. Thompson, also stated that its officers were ignorant of their basic duties.[26] Thompson kept his most damning criticism for the Auxiliaries, whom he described as being the most powerful and most ruthless of the Crown forces. He questioned as to whom the unit was answerable as they did not seem to recognise any commander or the authority of Dublin Castle. His report concluded that the government had 'liberated forces which it is not at present able to dominate'.[27]

On 20 February 1921, an IRA flying column, resting in an isolated farmhouse at Clonmult, County Cork, was surrounded by British troops. A fierce gun battle erupted between the two groups, with the British commanding officer sending for reinforcements. Two Tenders of Auxiliary Cadets arrived and fanned out, covering the western side of the farmhouse. The besieged IRA Volunteers were called on to surrender but, knowing that they might be summarily executed, continued to fight on, until the building was set on fire. Forced to abandon their position, the Volunteers reluctantly surrendered. However, as the group exited from the farmhouse they were lined up by the Auxiliaries and seven men were shot, one by one. A British army officer intervened and stopped the executions. Twelve IRA men had been killed, eight wounded and one had evaded capture in what was to be the greatest single loss of IRA Volunteers during the period.[28]

The British government had unleashed a force in Ireland that it was unable to control. However, many politicians knew that, though the police were now being condemned internationally for their actions in Ireland, they were slowly beginning to get results.

Within the corridors of Parliament, those who created the Auxiliaries believed they were a necessary evil, an evil that would have a lasting legacy in Ireland.

10

Requital
Dillon's Cross & The Burning of Cork, December 1920

The burning of Cork city was, without doubt, one of the worst orgies of violence and destruction witnessed on the island. The events that preceded this episode began on the evening of 11 December 1920 in the quiet working-class suburb of Dillon's Cross.

A Mills hand grenade hurtled through the air, landing on the bed of the Crossley Tender with a metallic clank. 'Grenade!' T/Cadet Fitzgerald shouted instinctively, as he ducked low, curling himself into the wall of the vehicle to shield himself from the blast. As the bomb detonated, the bodies of the men in the rear of the truck convulsed in the force of the blast. The lorry slewed to a halt and other explosions could be heard coming from the second Tender travelling a few feet behind. The men baled out over the side, many bleeding profusely from shrapnel wounds. Inhaling a lungful of smoke, T/Cadet Fitzgerald scrambled to his feet and quickly levelled his rifle at the place he believed the bomb had been thrown from. Through the smoke he could see the rebel, leaning over the wall to look at the effect of the grenade attack. Held tightly in the man's hand was a revolver, his finger on the trigger.

Within seconds, there was a series of loud bangs as the insurgent and his colleagues opened fire into the ranks of the Auxiliaries. The T/Cadets could hear the bullets whizzing over their heads, some ricocheting off the vehicles that were now at a standstill, smoke rising in black plumes from the beds of the lorries. Throats raw from the acrid smoke, the dazed and confused T/Cadets sought cover while some returned fire on their attackers. As the barrage of gunfire subsided, the ambushers disappeared into the night, leaving the Auxiliaries to care for their casualties: one killed, eleven wounded. The attack was over, but this action at Dillon's Cross in Cork would set in motion a series of tragic events that would shock the world.

The topographical features of Cork city made it very difficult for the Irish Republican Army's 1st Battalion Active Service Unit (north city) to operate. On its approach to the city, the River Lee divides in two, into the north and south channels, which enclose the centre of the city. After an attack on Crown forces, the routes of withdrawal lay over one of the river's many bridges at which many RIC barracks were located. At the sound of gunfire or explosions, these bridges were quickly sealed off by the police who conducted searches of those attempting to pass. Victoria Barracks in the city was headquarters to the 6th Division, consisting of three brigades under the command of Major General Sir Peter Strickland, KCB, KBE, CMG, DSO, the General O/C of British forces in Munster. Companies of Auxiliaries were billeted in Victoria Barracks and also at the Imperial Hotel. There were an estimated 5,000 military personnel holding Cork city. Recent police activity within the city had not only hampered IRA operations but had discommoded locals who resented the police's heavy-handed approach when patrolling and searching for suspects. A plan was devised by the IRA to launch an attack on 'K' Company Auxiliaries who were stationed at Victoria Barracks.

Intelligence reports revealed that a mobile Auxiliary patrol consisting of two Tenders usually left the barracks at 19:00 hours each night and travelled towards the city centre via the Old Youghal Road and Dillon's Cross. A year previously, Volunteer James O'Mahony had carried out a detailed reconnaissance of the area, detailing potential ambush sites and routes of escape.

The site chosen was an old stone wall that ran for 43 yards between Balmoral Terrace and the shop and houses located at Dillon's Cross. The route of escape after the attack was an open area, known locally as O'Callaghan's Field, which led down into the Glen, an area covered by trees which provided cover for the attackers to withdraw.

The plan of attack was audacious as the ambush was to take place only 300 yards from the main gate of Victoria Barracks. Within minutes of the attack and the noise of explosions and gunfire, British forces would be able to deploy thousands of men into the area. The ambush would have to be short and sharp, inflicting maximum damage and enemy casualties while leaving enough time to escape. A hit-and-run attack was devised that would involve slowing down or stopping the ADRIC vehicles and attacking them from concealed positions with grenades and small-arms fire.

The operation was planned for 8 December. Fifteen men under the command of Captain Seán O'Donoghue, armed with revolvers and hand grenades, took up position behind the stone wall. A scout was stationed near the barracks to alert the unit that the patrol was on its way. Seán Healy took up position and waited. He later recalled:

> We heard numerous lorries of military passing to and fro, but the Auxiliaries made no appearance that night. They probably went in the opposite direction, as the city could also be reached by another route. After what appeared to be an interminable hour of waiting and watching, we had to disperse, in order to reach home before curfew hour, which was 10.00 p.m. At least 1,000 soldiers would pour out of Victoria Barracks at this hour and take over complete control of the city.[1]

The group withdrew but took up position again the following night. However, once more, the Auxiliaries did not show and the operation was postponed. While the unit brought their guns with them, the grenades were given to Anne Barry of Cumann na mBan for safekeeping. On the nights that followed, the area in the vicinity of the barracks was inundated with police and army patrols, leading the IRA to believe that their plan of action had either been leaked or that the large loyalist population in the area had noticed their infiltration and had reported it to the authorities.

On Saturday 11 December at 16:00 hours, Captain Seán O'Donoghue received information that the police patrol would be heading out that night. The officer decided to launch an attack but with such short notice he could not muster his complete unit. The available men, Seán Healy, Michael Baylor, James O'Mahony, Micheal Kenny and Augustine O'Leary, once again loaded their weapons, primed their grenades and took up position.

In order to get the Crossley Tenders to slow down, O'Donoghue would signal the lorry to prepare to stop. He wore a Macintosh overcoat, scarf and cap, giving the impression to an oncoming motorist that he was a British officer. He would raise his hand and when the Tender had entered the kill zone, he would give two blasts on a whistle to signal the beginning of the attack.

The gates of Victoria Barracks swung open and two Crossley Tenders exited at full throttle and came into view. As the vehicles approached Harrington Square, O'Donoghue raised his hand and the leading truck began to slow down. The ruse had worked. Two blasts on a whistle were sounded and the attack commenced.

Michael Baylor and Augustine O'Leary lobbed two grenades into the first Tender while O'Donoghue and Seán Healy targeted the second vehicle. They all then opened fire, emptying the contents of their revolvers into the occupants of the trucks. The vehicles screeched to a halt, smoke pouring from the rear of the lorries. Wounded T/Cadets fell from the Tenders while others that had been blown out of the vehicles lay motionless on the ground. T/Cadet Leslie Emanuel later recalled that the first grenade had landed in his lap and, though he managed to throw it out of the vehicle, the second bomb detonated, blowing him and his colleagues out of the lorry. Many of the T/Cadets were showered with shrapnel and the vehicle and road were smeared with blood.

As the last round was fired, the insurgents made their getaway via the designated escape route. The ambush had been short, sharp and brutal, leaving twelve T/Cadets wounded. Cadet Chapman would later succumb to his wounds.

On hearing the tumult, thousands of soldiers and police officers rushed from their barracks and flooded the city, conducting house-to-house searches. Armoured cars and searchlights were dispatched to the area to try and locate the assailants, but to no avail. Tracking units with bloodhounds made their way through O'Callaghan's Field but failed to locate a scent and pick up the insurgents' tracks.

The attackers had split up, each man managing to evade capture. Seán Healy recalled:

> It was now a case of every man for himself to try and make a safe getaway. Under cover of darkness, and hugging the walls, we ran towards Goulding Glen and reached it in safety. A large stream ran through the Glen. This was swollen by the winter rains. We crossed the bridge over the stream and got away into the open country near Blackpool. I stayed at the house of Lieut. D. Duggan's father on that eventful night.[2]

Captain O'Donoghue made his way to a nearby farm owned by republican sympathisers, the Delany family. Here he deposited the remainder of the grenades and continued on his way.

The Auxiliaries were incensed at the attack and in the immediate aftermath of the ambush barged their way into a local public house, threatening the locals and demanding they lend medical assistance to the wounded. Many in the locality pleaded with the T/Cadets that they were loyal ex-servicemen but this resulted in even more aggressive behaviour as the officers, referring to the former soldier Tom Barry, shouted, 'It was an ex-serviceman who killed all our men at Kilmichael.'[3] As the wounded were conveyed to hospital, word reached 'K' Company that the attackers had escaped. With one colleague dead and eleven others seriously wounded, 'K' Company was not willing to let this one go.

At 21:30 hours, lorries filled with Auxiliaries and armed British soldiers left Victoria Barracks and drove with haste towards Dillon's Cross. On reaching the cross, the police and military began raiding the houses, forcing the occupants at gunpoint out onto the street. Furniture was piled high on the ground floors of the houses and set alight. Several houses were set on fire, the military standing guard, making sure that no one intervened. Anyone who objected or tried to save their meagre possessions was beaten, punched and kicked. One resident described the scene:

> While in the act of saving my own home from the encroaching flames, two members of the Crown forces, dressed in khaki uniforms, tam-o-shanter caps and carrying revolvers in hand, jumped on me, roaring and demanding to know what I was doing. I replied, 'saving our furniture'. They asked, 'were you in the war?' I said, 'No' and immediately I was dealt a severe blow on the face by one of them causing my teeth to come through my upper lip. I was then dragged into a neighbour's backyard, placed up against a wall there by the taller of them. What happened there I can't remember, but one of my sisters pleaded for my life, and the answer she got was that his heart was as hard as the wall and that it was no use speaking.
>
> From here I was taken to Dillon's Cross, and while here I was surrounded by Crown forces dressed in khaki and tasselled caps. They carried revolvers and made use of terrible language. They were accompanied by a civilian of low stature; fresh, fair features, wearing a light overcoat and black tweed hat. His language was more frightful than his companions. He spoke with a foreign accent and asked me to point out the houses of Sinn Féiners. This I said I could not do. I was also asked questions about the ambush by another of them, but told him that I knew nothing about it. Then, when I was preparing for the worst, on account of their threatening demeanour, a soldier, a private in the Hants. Regiment, rushed on me. He saved my life and managed to get me near my own house. Here I was again met by one of the Crown forces, who questioned me and asked me to sing 'God Save the King' but the good soldier stood by me and managed to get me safe in home.
>
> An Auxiliary, who was standing by the door, followed us into the kitchen. He was a fine big man, dressed in R.I.C. frieze overcoat, soldier's ordinary military cap, and khaki trousers. He

was a walking arsenal, his pockets bulging out with bombs. These he showed us and offered to make us a present of them. He said he was an Auxiliary, and they, the Auxiliaries, were going to blow up the city. He said he was due to go at 1 a.m. He left shortly after midnight ... While I was at Dillon's Cross under the threat of being shot, I saw an ordinary 'Tommy' bring a small bath full of paraffin or petrol, probably the former, from some house, nearby and throw the contents into Brian Dillon's house which was burning rapidly. Auxiliaries were looking on at this. A Red Cross ambulance, military, was stationed nearby on my left.

While indoors with my father, brothers, and sisters, we went through a terrible time. The house next door was by this time fiercely burning and the fire was gradually encroaching on ours, but we dared not move to save either. The Crown forces kept guard over the burning houses, and anybody trying to save even their own property was fired on.[4]

The Auxiliaries and the military, many of them drunk, mounted their vehicles and drove towards the centre of the city. From his vantage point on the second floor of the Shamrock Hotel on Grand Parade, one Michael O'Donoghue watched as the most notorious reprisal in the Irish War of Independence commenced.

About 9.30 p.m., desultory rifle fire was heard in the direction of Patrick's Bridge. The shooting came nearer. Then some minutes later, about 20 or so tall figures in 'civvies' (trench coats and headgear, caps, hats or glengarries) appeared suddenly from Patrick St. direction. All were heavily armed. They crowded around 'Sean Jennings' Furniture Store, at Tuckey Street – Parade Corner, opposite the R.I.C. barracks, about 8 yards distant. They pounded on the shutters with their rifle butts. Then a small bar or bayonet was used to wrench the shutters free and make a large gaping entrance to the front window. Bang! A terrific report and the windows at our heads rattle. Instinctively we duck. Bang! Bang! Bang! More explosions. Peeping out cautiously I see the tall figures crouched down on the opposite pavement at Jennings. They are throwing bomb after bomb into the furniture display rooms. With each explosion comes the noise of breaking glass and fallings and smashing wood. A pause. The men stand up, crowd round and look at their handiwork.[5]

Destruction continued throughout the city with shops and public houses being looted and then set alight. The fire brigade was called and arrived on the scene but the firemen intimidated and threatened at gunpoint. One recalled, 'We were useless. They were cutting the hoses and they were firing all around them.'[6]

The flames spread rapidly and soon the city was an inferno. People caught out were searched, beaten and threatened to be executed. Five people were wounded by gunfire. The author Alan Ellis walked down the city quay and witnessed the city fire brigade pinned down under heavy fire from a party of Black and Tans who had entered City Hall. A fireman reported seeing '"men in uniform" carrying cans of petrol into the Hall from the very barracks on Union Quay that I had just been released from. Around four o'clock there was a tremendous explosion. The Tans had not only placed petrol in the building but also detonated high explosives. The City Hall and adjoining Carnegie Library, with its hundreds of priceless volumes, was suddenly a sea of flames.'[7]

As the fires raged in the city and the fire brigade was prevented from attending the scene by Auxies who brandished their guns in a threatening manner, a group of armed men made their way to a farm belonging to a well-known republican family named Delany at Dublin Hill on the north side of the city. Mr Delany said:

About 2.00 a.m. a number of men came to my door and demanded admission in a loud voice, and beat the door harshly. I opened the door, and they called me out. The man who seemed to be in command asked if I was a Sinn Féiner. I answered, 'I don't understand you'. He then said, 'Are you interested in politics?' I answered, 'I am an old man and not interested in anything'. He then asked 'Who is inside?' I said, 'Nobody but my family.' 'Can I see them? said he. 'Certainly,' I said. 'They are in bed'. He asked me to show them up. Then at least eight men entered the house and went upstairs. A large number remained outside, as I could hear them moving and see them in the yard. The men who went upstairs entered my sons' bedroom, and said in a harsh voice, 'Get up out of that'. I was in the room with them. My sons got up and stood by the bedside. They asked them if their name was Delany. My sons answered, 'yes'. At that moment I heard distinctively two or more shots and my boys fell immediately. My brother-in-law, William Dunlea, who was sleeping in the same room in another bed was fired on by the same party and wounded in two places. My brother-in-law is over sixty years of age. As far as I could see, they wore long overcoats, and spoke with a strong English accent.[8]

It is believed that a hat found at the scene of the ambush at Dillon's Cross had led Crown forces using bloodhounds to pick the scent of O'Donoghue who had hidden the unused grenades at Delany's farm.

The following day, Sunday, the havoc wreaked on the city could clearly be seen. Florrie O'Donoghue, a member of the IRA, wrote, 'Many familiar landmarks were gone forever – where whole buildings had collapsed, here and there a solitary wall leaned at some crazy angle from its foundation. The streets ran with sooty water, the footpaths were strewn with broken glass and debris, ruins smoked and smouldered and over everything was the pervasive smell of burning.'[9]

Over 40 business premises, 300 residential properties, City Hall and the Carnegie Library had been destroyed, at an estimated value of £3 million.

After their drunken night of mayhem and destruction, 'K' Company of the Auxiliaries, the Black and Tans and British soldiers who had taken part returned to barracks. The following day, 'K' Company were removed from the city and sent to new billets at the Workhouse in Dunmanway.

A letter written by an Auxiliary Cadet of 'K' Company in the aftermath of the burning was intercepted by IRA intelligence. Its contents reveal the extent of the mayhem the Division unleashed on Cork city and its inhabitants.

16.12.20

Dunmanway, Co. Cork.

My Darling Mother,

I have just received your letter of the 10th enclosed with one from Dorothy of the 12th. We came here from Cork and are billeted in a workhouse – filthy, dirty half of us are down with bronchitis. I am at present in bed, my camp bed, which I fortunately brought with me recovering from a severe chill contracted on Saturday night last during the burning and looting of Cork in all of which I took perforce a reluctant part. We did it all night never mind how much the well intentioned Hamar Greenwood would excuse us. In all my life and in all the tales of fiction I have read, I have never experienced such orgies of murder, arson and looting as I have witnessed during the past 16 days with the R.I.C. Auxiliaries. It baffles description and we are supposed to be officers and gentlemen. There are quite a number of decent fellows and likewise a number of ruffians.

On our arrival here from Cork one of our heroes held up a car with a priest and a civilian in it and shot them both through the head without cause or provocation. We were kindly received by the people but the consequences of this cold-blooded murder is that no one will come within a mile of us and all shops are closed.

The brute who did it had been sodden with drink for some time and has been sent to Cork under arrest for examination by reporting lunacy. If certified sane he will be court-martialled and shot. The poor old priest was 65 and everybody's friend.

The burning and sacking of Cork followed immediately on the ambush of our men. I, as orderly Sergeant had to collect 20 men for a raid and they left the barracks in two motor cars. I did not go as I was feeling sickly. The party had not gone 100 yards from barracks when bombs were thrown at them from over a wall. One dropped in a car and wounded 8 men one of whom has since died.

Very naturally the rest of the coy. were enraged. The houses in the vicinity of the ambush were set alight and from there the various parties set out on their mission of destruction. Many who witnessed similar scenes in France and Flanders say that nothing they had experienced was comparable to the punishment meted out to Cork.

Reprisals are necessary and loyal Irishmen agree to that but there is a lot which should not be done, of course it is frequently unavoidable that the innocent suffer with the guilty. The sooner the Irish extremists recognize that they will not gain their point by the methods they deploy the better it will be for this unfortunate and misguided country ...

We had a lot of guard duty to do about four nights each week, 24 hours on duty at a time, and no sleep at all for the sergeant of the guard who has to post the sentries every two hours – that's me – I maintain we would not be overpaid at £5 *per diem*. It is the hardest life I have ever stuck but we get used to everything in time. A general Higgenson arrived this morning to have a 'straight talk' to us about discipline etc., as he put it. I am afraid we struck terror into him for the 'straight talk' never materialized. He was most amiable. I could tell you much more but sufficient for the day etc.

The weather has been bitterly cold but the frost gave this morning. I wish this play was set in the Cameroon's [*sic*] or somewhere near the equator, then I would not mind it so much. The country round here is quite poorly and very hilly. Our friends the gunmen are in their holes and we are here to round them up. They may or may not remain to face the ordeal.

It is well that you know everything. I have named Monica as my next-of- kin. Ireland has to pay very substantially for every R.I.C. casualty. A mere flesh wound is paid and so on up to £5000 to a man's widow. The widow of a young fellow who was shot in a raid in which I took part in Dublin received the latter amount.

Please send me the papers about Dorothy's concert and give me all the gossip about it. With much love my darling mother,
Charlie.[10]

The reaction of some senior officers to the incident in Cork once again contributed to the marginalisation of the population of the country. General Crozier wrote:

I received a telegram in code from Downing Street 'ordering' me to suspend a Company Commander on account of the burning of Cork which enabled Lloyd George to get up in the House during the Cork Debate to say a Company Commander had been suspended and several individuals had been punished for their share in the destruction. Nothing much happened to the Company Commander after the fuss had blown over.[11]

Major General Sir Peter Strickland, General Officer Commanding the 6th Division in Ireland, submitted a report in relation to the burning of Cork city and the murders of the Delany brothers. General Macready wrote of the report:

An inquiry was immediately held, as a result of which there was no doubt that the fires and subsequent looting were the work of a company of the Auxiliary Division of the police who had recently arrived in Cork, and who had been exasperated by a rebel ambush at a place called Dillon's Cross. No lives were lost though some shooting took place between the Auxiliaries and rebels in the streets.[12]

'K' Company was disbanded a few months later with their commanding officers and T/Cadets being redeployed to other Auxiliary Companies. The Castle authorities chose to suppress the findings of Strickland's report and to this day it has never been made public.

11

The Force of the Crown
Waging War in Ireland 1919–21

The asymmetric warfare waged by the republicans across Ireland was having the desired effect on the military. A British army report stated that:

There was no objective for operations; there was no defined theatre of war, since non-combatants and loyal persons were intermingled with rebels in every district; there was no 'Front Line' or 'No Man's Land', and the only secure base for any body of troops was inside its own barracks walls. The troops were, in fact living inside the enemy's lines, where their every movement was known as soon begun, and was in many cases betrayed even before that. No means of communication was safe except by armoured cars; telegraphs, post offices and railways were almost entirely staffed by men and women who were either confessed rebels or else intimidated into aiding and abetting them. The rebels, on the other hand, had almost everything in their favour. They were indistinguishable from harmless civilians until they had fired, and consequently they had little difficulty in carrying out ruses upon sentries and small bodies of troops …

Neither did the more ambitious projects of the IRA, such as attacks on small detachments of troops or police, require any great skill in the operation, or courage in the execution. The principle [*sic*] military difficulty in beating an enemy in detail is the successful and secret concentration of superior forces at the given time and place. To the rebels, having no uniform and being able to move into a locality without molestation in twos or threes, there was no difficulty in assembling in force in house adjoining their objective or in positions of ambush near a road.[1]

The British military issued the following warning to its men:

It is to be remembered that every person in this country in mufti, man or woman, is a potential enemy, but while insisting on all ranks behaving with the ordinary courtesy due to their profession, we must insist on everything being done to prevent men getting on too friendly or intimate terms with civilians, as this is a source by which the enemy gain information, though done in such a way that the giver of information does not realise it.[2]

Following the end of the war in Europe, Lord French expected reinforcements to bolster his force but due to demobilisation he received inexperienced conscripts, unsuitable for the task in hand. Many of the troops were young recruits with little training. Under the incessant guard duties, patrolling in urban environments, living with the threat of ambush and with little sleep and recreation time, the morale of the men slowly deteriorated. Vehicles and equipment, the remnants of the Great War, were often obsolete and unsuitable for the campaign in Ireland.

Initially, infantry were often used to give fire support in counter-insurgency operations led by the RIC and Auxiliaries. Later, however, especially in areas where martial law had been declared, the military mounted their own operations against the IRA. Notes issued by the military at guerrilla-warfare classes held at the Curragh camp stated that:

The tactics employed by the rebels are those of ambush. These ambushes are dependent on secrecy, which is easily obtainable owing to the fact that they are dressed as civilians and move amongst the population of sympathisers similarly attired. These ambushes are dependent for their success on surprise and fire effect at close range, and do not aim at further offensive action, the rebels having small stomach for fighting at close quarters or suffering heavy casualties.

Individuals cutting peat in a bog may not be as harmless as they appear.[3]

Sir Nevil Macready, writing about the Auxiliaries to Sir John Anderson in February 1921, stated that 'They treat the Martial Law areas as a special game preserve for their amusement.'[4]

Being ex-military, the ADRIC were unsuited to police duties and having spent four years fighting a conventional war, they were focused on total annihilation of the IRA. This mindset, often termed the 'kill-capture' approach, was seen by many as the only way to achieve victory by either eliminating the enemy or forcing them to capitulate. On being designated a particular county in Ireland, an ADRIC Company would carry out a reconnaissance in the area in order to locate a secure Forward Operating Base, often one of the big houses of the landed gentry. Usually loyalist sympathisers who were out of the country due to the troubles, they permitted the ADRIC to occupy their property. Soon after arriving, platoons would carry out familiarisation patrols in the area. Liaising with the local RIC they would then begin to conduct counter-insurgency operations.

In relation to the deployment of the Auxiliaries, Lieutenant General A.E. Percival, Intelligence Officer and Commanding Officer of the 1st Essex Regiment in Cork, stated:

They [the Auxiliaries] consisted entirely of ex-officers and worked by companies, each company being allotted a district where the rebels' organization appeared to be strongest. They entirely came under the military area commandant for tactical purposes, and were of assistance in taking over responsibilities for parts of the military areas, but their independent status did not always make for smooth working, and the old difficulty arose of a force being under one commander for tactical purposes and another for administration.[5]

In Dublin city, there were 400 Auxiliaries stationed between a number of Companies with 10,084 British troops and 1,600 regular police officers against 2,000 men of the Dublin Brigade IRA, of which fewer than 100 were in the Active Service Unit (ASU).[6]

From the outset, the Auxiliaries fell between two stools, that of the police for administration purposes and the army for operational reasons, a problem that would continue to escalate and burden the unit so much that it would later affect its operational capacity.

Operating without eyes or ears in a hostile environment, the ADRIC realised that in order to take the war to the IRA they would have to improvise, and provide their own intelligence officers until reliable intelligence was received from Dublin Castle. Those who volunteered for the role of Company intelligence officers may have thought the task easier than patrolling and raiding. However, on deployment, the dangers of the job were soon realised.

> Our intelligence officer (I.O.), who, although doing his best had not been helpful at first, was now learning his job and one or two raids on outlying districts had almost brought results, only being thwarted by good look-out men. On several occasions we found traces of very recent meetings, indeed so recent in some cases we found cigarette-ends still burning.
>
> One evening our I.O. went out on an expedition and never returned. We were not unduly perturbed for the first day as he had taken to going farther a-field for his information, but after three days we had to conclude that we had seen the last of him and that he was now lying at the bottom of a bog. We never really got to know what his fate was.
>
> Another I.O. was appointed but before the week had elapsed he also disappeared. Now we began to be uneasy and to think perhaps our luck was running out. Our next I.O. was sent from H.Q. in

Dublin and was a man of experience who managed to remain alive but got very little information.[7]

With a large number of flying columns now in action across Ireland, casualties amongst Crown forces began to rise. Given the conditions, the odds favoured the insurgents. Firmly entrenched behind cover, they maintained a definitive three-to-one numerical advantage when conducting an ambush, knew the terrain, held the element of surprise and had pre-planned their disengagement routes. In the aftermath of an ambush, the insurgents, by stashing their weapons in hidden caches, were able to transform from combatant to non-combatant.

In response to the attacks on their supply convoys, patrols and personnel, the military issued the following notice:

> Whereas recent outrages have been committed against the forces of the Crown and other persons travelling in motor cars by the discharge of firearms and the throwing of bombs and other explosives: now, I Colonel Commandant R.D.F. Oldman CMG, DSO, commanding the Dublin District, the Competent Military Authority, hereby give notice that should such outrages continue, known rebels will be carried as hostages for the safe conduct of the occupants in all motor vehicles the property of the armed forces of the Crown. This notice applies to the city of Dublin and the Counties of Meath and Dublin.[8]

The hostages were usually Sinn Féin councillors or suspected republican sympathisers and were displayed prominently on ADRIC vehicles in order to dissuade any attacks on their convoys or patrols. A former officer in the Connaught Rangers, Colonel Maurice Moore, penned a letter to the *Irish Independent* on 5 January 1921 condemning the use of hostages by the military and ADRIC. Colonel Moore was known to the authorities as a nationalist sympathiser and an officer who had exposed human rights abuses by British forces during the Boer War. Because of this, his residence at Seaview Terrace in Donnybrook was raided where a copy of the *Irish Bulletin* was discovered. He was arrested and held overnight by the military before being used as a hostage in a

Prisoners being brought in to Tralee barracks by Auxiliaries after an ambush. (Capuchin Archives)[10]

series of patrols through the streets of Dublin. He was later released. His experience at the hands of the ADRIC was raised in the House of Commons on 21 February in relation to the deteriorating Irish situation.[9]

This modus operandi was to be extended to many counties throughout Ireland and, though considered by some to be inhumane, it reduced attacks and saved the lives of those tasked with convoy and escort duties.

The police supported by the military slowly began to adapt to this new type of warfare. Insurgent tactics were studied and countermeasures were devised to kill or capture those waging war against the Crown.

> Offensive action should always be taken against the flanks and rear of ambushers. It must be remembered that the rebels are not highly disciplined troops and that a threat to their line of retreat usually makes them bolt. This tendency must always be borne in mind when efforts are made to round them up. The rebels use a considerable amount of cunning both in their raids and ambushes and have a well-organised system of intelligence which works easily owing to the fact that the population are sympathetic.

Raids, patrols, and escorts by troops in order to be successful must employ every ruse and camouflage that can be thought of, such as starting in the wrong direction and using a detour to reach the objective – sending out men hidden in a lorry to be dropped and hidden in the country while the lorry returns apparently full to where it came from – sending out bicycles hidden in a lorry and dropping a bicycle party for the purpose of carrying out the raid.

It may also be useful for a party to march by night across country, bog or mountain and lie up by day.

In short the one essential condition for success in raids, searches and drives is *surprise* and every ruse by which surprise can be obtained should be studied and practised. Without the element of surprise the most perfectly organised operation will be ineffective.[11]

Auxiliaries increased the number of raids they were carrying out and by using stealth and surprise, slowly began to get results. Volunteer Mícheál Ó Súilleabháin wrote: 'A tough crowd. I knew them well. I had seen them jump walls with their rifles in their hands, hampered by their revolvers and other equipment. They travelled by night and day on byroads, and came from totally unexpected directions. I had plenty of experience of their physical fitness when I had to run from them on several occasions, and when, were it not for the darkness, they would have had me.'[12]

On the deployment of Auxiliaries in County Cork IRA Commandant Tom Barry later wrote, 'The Auxiliaries were killers without mercy … the alternative now was to kill or be killed; see to it that those terrorists die and are broken'.[13]

Violent raids became an everyday occurrence in towns and cities throughout the country. The playwright Seán O'Casey recalled one such nightly visit on the tenement where he lived:

A raid! … Which were they – the Tommies or the Tans?

Tans, thought Sean, for the Tommies would not shout so soullessly, nor smash the glass panels so suddenly; they would hammer on the door with a rifle-butt, and wait for it to be opened. No, these were the Tans …

A great crash shook the whole house and shook the heart of Seán ... A mad rush of heavy feet went past his door, to spread over the stilly house; for no one had come from a room to risk sudden death in the dark and draughty hallway ... Yet Seán knew that the house must be alive with crawling men, slinking up and down the stairs, hovering outside this door or that one, each with a gun tensed to the last hair, with a ready finger touching the trigger. He guessed that a part of them were Auxies, the classic members of sibilant and sinister raiders. The Tans alone would make more noise, slamming themselves into a room, shouting to shake off the fear that slashed many of their faces. The Auxies were too proud to show a sign of it. The Tommies would be warm, always hesitant at knocking at a woman's room, they would even be jocular in their funny English way, encouraging the women and even the children to grumble at being taken away from their proper sleep.[14]

In the days that followed Bloody Sunday, the ADRIC increased the number of raids they were carrying out, targeting a number of known and suspected Sinn Féin members and their meeting places. On Wednesday 24 November, Liberty Hall, the head office of the ITGWU, was targeted. Crossley Tenders pulled up outside with T/Cadets rushing the building. The union's General Treasurer Alderman William O'Brien, General President Tom Foran and Secretary of the Labour Party and Irish Trades Union Congress Thomas Johnson were all detained. A five-hour search uncovered a revolver, bombs, and assorted ammunition and gun components. The interior was systematically taken apart as the T/Cadets moved from floor to floor, smashing the fixtures and fittings. It was estimated that £5,000 of damage was done to the building, making it uninhabitable. The union had to move to temporary business premises in Parnell Square. The Auxiliaries removed union flags, banners and publications to Beresford Place where they set them alight. Anything of value was removed back to their centre of operations.

Hated by the people and condemned by the press, the Auxiliaries continued their campaign but slowly began to change their tactics. Utilising speed and mobility, the force began to inflict shock and dread.

Improved intelligence and their ability to adapt to a new type of warfare began to worry senior republican commanders in the field. Regular RIC and Auxiliary units supported by the military began large-scale operations to lock down areas and search for insurgent operatives and arms caches. The implementation of martial law in certain areas in the latter part of 1920 improved morale and gave the military and police some respite. Judicial procedures were radically changed as battalion-level courts martial were established for minor offences and a central board was raised for capital cases, including arms violations and attacks against military personnel. Further laws enabled the military to detain civilians without trial, declare curfews, restrict the use of vehicles and prohibit or curtail public gatherings at fairs or markets.

While the IRA was forced to scale down its campaign in rural areas, attacks were still carried out in towns and cities against the police, with the perpetrators often evading capture in the urban sprawl. The failure to capture or kill insurgents before, during or after these attacks caused much frustration amongst the Auxiliaries. Restricted by their police superiors and by rules of engagement, the T/Cadets watched as their colleagues' deaths went unavenged and the perpetrators were not apprehended. It was only a short matter of time before the situation reached a tipping point. The violent revenge attacks of some ADRIC were to have far-reaching consequences for the force.

12

Internal Affairs
Discipline in the Ranks

P rime Minister Lloyd George insisted that the 'Irish job' was 'a policeman's job'. The military should support the police, not the other way round – 'if it becomes a military job only, it will fail.' The Prime Minister supported Churchill's assertion that 'on balance Tudor and his men were … getting to the root of the matter quicker than the military'.[1] Politicians were more worried about Britain's reputation on the world stage than initiating a military response to deal with the escalating violence.

The deployment of the ADRIC and their tactics of kicking in doors, verbally abusing civilians and destroying the property of the local populace may have demonstrated the government's determination to tackle the escalating crisis but they failed to completely understand those whom they faced. Their actions radicalised many, sending them into the hands of the IRA and creating an endless supply of young Volunteers. Continuous patrolling, sudden firefights and long periods of waiting for something to happen resulted in the breakdown of order in some ADRIC Companies.

Discipline amongst the various units became a major problem for Brigadier General Crozier. Every draft that arrived in Ireland was lectured on the dangers of drink and a qualified RIC officer addressed the men in relation to the treatment of the local population. However, in many cases these lessons were not taken on board. When the Companies moved out to their areas of operations, Crozier had no control over how they behaved. He depended on individual company commanders to enforce discipline but he soon discovered that some of those appointed to senior posts within the Auxiliaries were not up to the job. Crozier later wrote:

> It was found that the R.I.C. code was not suitable, in so far as punishment was concerned, and a scale of fines was drawn up by me and approved by the Police Adviser [Tudor]; this scale has since been increased and was in operation before I left the division. A company commander could fine a man five days' pay 'off his own bat' (£5. 5s); the commandant could fine a man seven days' pay (£7. 7s).
>
> The question of dismissals was carefully dealt with. At one time the commandant had the power of dismissal; in October [1920] the power was, by the Police Adviser's (P.A.) orders, reserved for the PA alone and the following rules became operative: – (a) the commandant could call upon a man to resign; if he refused he could dispense with his service as being 'unsuitable for service with the Auxiliary Division,' the man having the right to appeal to the Police Adviser; (b) the commandant could dispense with services as above; (c) the commandant could recommend dismissal.[2]

A number of T/Cadets were fined or dismissed for a variety of offences that included drunkenness, improper accounting and looting while others managed to continue within the ranks of the Division, having been transferred from one Company to another.

However, problems continued. Lloyd George wrote to Sir Hamar Greenwood, Chief Secretary of Ireland:

> I am not at all satisfied of the state of discipline in the Royal Irish Constabulary and its auxiliary force. Accounts reach me from too many and too authoritative quarters to leave any doubt in my mind that the charges of drunkenness, looting and other acts of

indiscipline are in too many cases substantially true … [this is] causing grave uneasiness in the public mind … it is vital that the violence and indiscipline which undoubtedly characterizes certain units in the Royal Irish Constabulary should be terminated in the most prompt and drastic manner. It is weakening seriously the hands of the executive … Public opinion, which is already unhappy, will swing round and withdraw its support from the policy which is now being pursued by the Government in Ireland. There is no doubt that through indiscipline, looting and drunkenness the Royal Irish Constabulary is alienating great numbers of well-disposed people in Ireland and throwing them into the arms of Sinn Fein.[3]

Addressing the Chief Secretary in the Houses of Parliament, London, Captain Elliot asked, 'How many of the Auxiliary Division, Royal Irish Constabulary, have been dismissed from the force; and of how many have the services been dispensed with since the formation of the division?'

The reply was that 'Forty-eight members of the Auxiliary Division have been dismissed, and 12 have been permitted to resign since the formation of the division.'[4]

In an attempt to appeal for discipline amongst the ranks of the T/Cadets, Viceroy Lord French addressed 'F' Company, saying:

You have all served as officers in that magnificent Army, which saved the Empire from destruction in the most critical and dangerous years of its history, and I am personally proud to know that I can claim many of you as comrades in the field during the earlier period of the war.

Arduous and perilous as that splendid service was, you have once more offered yourselves for service which is not free from either hardship or peril. You have taken up the duty of assisting and supporting the Royal Irish Constabulary in putting down rebellion and re-establishing law and order throughout Ireland.

To strengthen and support such a magnificent Force as the Royal Irish Constabulary is a task worthy of soldiers who have proved their prowess and metal on many a blood-stained field of battle …

You have all shown yourselves to be possessed of courage, energy, skill and discipline in a very high degree; but in the performance of the duties which lie before you tact, judgement and self restraint are also required, and I feel sure you will in this respect as in all others act up to the glorious record you have established in the field.

You may rest assured that in carrying out that work you will have the good will, sympathy and hearty support of every loyal subject of the King in Ireland or elsewhere.

I am proud indeed to see in these grounds to-day men who have fought and bled for their country. Your watchword on those glorious fields where you so much distinguished yourselves was the salvation of the Empire and the upholding of the flag. In the work that lies before you, you cannot have better mental guides than these.

In carrying out your work you have my earnest and heartfelt good wishes.[5]

Animosity arose between the regular RIC and the Auxiliaries in relation to pay and conditions. In an edition of the constabulary's publication *The Weekly Summary*, the paper stated that the ADRIC had been created to 'combat murder' and that the regular police force was not there to compete with it, but to cooperate with the new unit.[6]

An incident in Trim, County Meath, was to have a long and lasting effect on the force.

Trim was a known hotbed of insurgency. During the summer and autumn months of 1920, attacks on police and military patrols were regular occurrences. Within the civilian population there were cells of passive support for the insurgents. Many local businesses, whether through fear or support for the IRA, refused to serve or supply Crown forces in the area. In many cases, Auxiliary units were forced to forage for food to complement their meagre supplies while in other districts food supplies had to be transported under armed escort from Dublin to the area of operations. This often resulted in an unsatisfactory diet that rarely altered and considerably affected morale.

A section leader, 'F' Company, in Dublin Castle. (Ernest McCall)

On 9 February 1921, 'N' Company ADRIC, based at the Industrial School, prepared to conduct a search mission for arms and ammunition in Trim. Their target was a locally owned shop and pub. The operation would be conducted at platoon strength and, for their mission that day, the Auxiliaries would be utilising surprise, speed and violence of action. They would get as close to the target building as possible using their vehicles and then act with overwhelming force to secure the building and its environs. This type of action would ensure that any insurgents on the premises would be apprehended and that any arms caches could not be dumped or destroyed. They would be supported by regular RIC and the military.

The Auxiliary platoon arrived at the premises of Richard and Frances Chandler at 13:00 hours. The building was surrounded. Two squads of T/Cadets secured the perimeter and began searching the outhouses while others entered the building and began searching through the shop, pub and private residence of the couple. Both Mr and Mrs Chandler were held at gunpoint. They protested at the intrusion, strongly objecting to the search and that they as Unionists and loyal to the King of England should be subjected to such an abomination. A small quantity of ammunition was discovered and Mr Chandler was taken in for questioning. As he was being placed in a Tender, Auxiliaries began loading the other vehicles with food, drink and linen. The operation had taken an hour and a half to conduct. Chandler was released later without charge but the couple made an official complaint to the RIC, submitting a claim for goods that had been taken during the raid. They stated that goods to the value of £355, including brandy, bacon, sugar and other foodstuffs, jewellery and other valuables, had been taken. They also averred that Mrs Chandler had been treated roughly by the T/Cadets during the operation.

Brigadier General Francis P. Crozier investigated the incident and on 13 February he dismissed 21 T/Cadets and placed five men, all holding the rank of platoon commander or section leader, under arrest. They were immediately disarmed, transferred to Beggars Bush Barracks and then sent to England to await court martial. The group of T/Cadets objected strongly to being dismissed from the force and went to the Irish Office in London where they sought an audience with the RIC Inspector General Henry Hugh Tudor. The Chief of Police listened to the grievances of the group and conceded that Crozier had acted precipitately in dismissing the men without giving them the chance to defend themselves against the allegations. Tudor ordered that the men be reinstated subject to further investigations.

In a letter dated 14 February Tudor wrote,

> Dear Crozier,
> I think it will be best for you to keep these twenty-one T/C (Temporary Cadets) till I come back. I want to discuss it with the Chief Secretary. He gets all the bother. My main point is that it is an unfortunate time to do anything and looks panicky. I

think also these T/Cs will have a distinct grievance if the platoon commanders and section leaders are acquitted. Tell these twenty-one they are suspended pending my return, or if you prefer, keep them on by not completing their accounts till I come back.
Yours Sincerely
H.H. Tudor.[7]

Crozier, however, having already dismissed the T/Cadets, was incensed at their reinstatement and was angered by his superior's actions.

Bad press also contributed to the Trim affair. A letter in *The Times* of 12 February called for the dissolution of the ADRIC. On 22 February in the same paper, a letter appeared written under the moniker 'Patria' defending the Division. The author believed unfair criticism had been levelled against the force, citing the incident in Trim, and declaring that Crozier had investigated the affair, brought the troublemakers to book, but had been overruled by a senior officer who had little or no knowledge of what had actually taken place.

'Britannicus' is wrong when he says that the Auxiliary Cadets are an armed force without discipline, but he is right when he asserts that it [ADRIC] has been put in an impossible position by the Government. The force was hastily conceived and brought into being before any organization whatever had been provided for it. It still, six months after its foundation, has no disciplinary code on which to work. The responsibility for any lack of discipline in the Division lies not with the Division itself, but with the politicians who cannot or will not realize that a state of discipline can only be maintained by the officers of the Division, wholeheartedly supported by and not interfered with in the discharge of their duties by their political superiors.[8]

On hearing of Tudor's actions, Crozier was livid and, believing that his authority had been undermined, he tendered his resignation.

Crozier was replaced by Commandant E.A. Wood. The T/Cadets that had partaken in the raid were tried by court martial in City

Hall, Dublin. All were acquitted though four were held in custody to face other charges along with five other T/Cadets. The incident on 9 February became known as the Looting of Trim. The *Times* reported on the case:

At Trim Sessions, yesterday before county Court Judge Fleming, there was a sequel to the Trim lootings, which led to the resignation of General Crozier. Mrs. Frances Chandler of Robinstown claimed £355 which Mr. Reilly said was for compensation for brandy, bacon, sugar, money, jewellery, bedclothes, household requisites, knives and forks and for damages to premises. The articles, he said, were taken away by uniformed men on February 9th. About 1 o'clock on that day a number of military, police and Auxiliary forces visited Mrs Chandler's place at Robinstown, three miles from Trim. It was alleged they discovered some ammunition and they immediately took into custody Mr. Richard Chandler. They remained an hour, went away, and later on returned, rearrested Mr. Chandler, who had been released, and demolished the shop.

Answering the Judge, Head Constable Roberts of Trim said there was no appearance on behalf of the police.

Mrs. Chandler, an elderly woman, said in evidence that some of the men had tin hats and others had little round hats. About forty of them were all over the shop.

The Judge – Did they seem to be under command of an officer? – They all seemed to be officers.

Mrs. Chandler continuing said the men were those with the round caps and a little tassel in the centre; they were auxiliaries. They all had revolvers. They stayed from 1.30 to 2.30. They removed two bags of candles, a quantity of soap, boxes of condensed milk, bacon and five sovereigns. They had eleven lorries and threw the bedclothes out of the window into the lorries.

About 10.30, twenty-eight or thirty of the same men came back. A tall man with a black coat and scarf around his neck knocked at the door and four or five auxiliaries caught him by the collar. They said, 'You are the fellow who shot six of our fellows yesterday,' and called on the others to take him out to the lorry and shoot him.

The men then went from one room to another looting, taking four pairs of sheets, a white counterpane quilt and blankets. They came downstairs and took four rings, two field glasses, two gold watches, a silver watch, two gold bracelets, two silver flasks, ten silver forks, a gold brooch, a box of four penny pieces and breast pins. The men also took from her shop all the drink – whiskey, new milk, rum, port, wine, stout, ale, twenty-three bottles of brandy and champagne – and two CWT of sugar. They swept everything into the lorries. They broke the bottles, made a mess of the whole place, took nineteen fowls, put four bullets into the water barrel, and damaged the pony and trap. One silver chalice was returned. On the following Sunday an officer called on her, and she got the cheque produced for £30. He said it was not his party who did the whole thing.

Answering the Judge, Mrs. Chandler said the R.I.C. did nothing of which she was complaining.

The Judge – It is only in fairness to the R.I.C. to say that they had neither hand, act nor party in the affair. Mrs. Chandler – No. The R.I.C. and I are always friends.

Mr. Reilly – Not only that, but we received considerable courtesy from the local constabulary with reference to Mr. Chandler's own trouble.

The Judge adjourned the case.[9]

A regular RIC police constable, Eugene Bratton, who had been present during the raid, later stated that there was more to the raid than just simple looting:

When Chandler's of Robinstown was looted by the Auxies I was the only policeman to stand his ground and watch what was going on. The other police went in through the fields by the way they were looking for dumps of arms. Incidentally this raid was responsible for the resignation of General Crozier. I had to attend the subsequent identification parade of these Auxies and gave evidence to their court martial in Dublin. I could only identify two of them. Five of the other Auxies also identified the ones who did the looting. I believe some of them, including their commanding officer, were found guilty, he getting 18 months imprisonment. They smashed up Chandler's house and business premises and looted it.

Constable Martin's wife and Chandler's wife were on bad terms. Martin planted ammunition in Chandler's house for the Auxies to find. This drove the Auxies frantic. I knew the ammunition when I saw it. I had seen it with Constable Martin previously. They arrested Mr. Chandler and brought him to Trim with them. County Inspector Egan subsequently got Chandler out of prison. Mr. Chandler who was a Protestant and, I understand, a loyalist, did not take any open part, at least, in politics. He would probably be a supporter of the British regime.[10]

Crozier later publicly stated that a blackmailer who had been dismissed from the force by him was in regular payment from the state to keep his mouth shut about an incident at Killaloe Bridge where two men had been murdered. Another T/Cadet, who Crozier claimed was sentenced to ten years' imprisonment in England for conspiring to sell British secrets to Russia, was the one who induced the T/Cadets dismissed for the actions in Trim to claim redress and seek immediate reinstatement. This would be the price for keeping their mouths shut over events in Ireland, especially actions that took place in Cork city. They were all returned to duty.

On 19 April 1921, Captain D.I. Wood organised a platoon of Auxiliaries for a raid on the Shannon Hotel, Castleconnell, 6 miles from Limerick. Information received stated that three suspicious men were holding a meeting in the bar of the premises. The plan was for two officers and three squads dressed in civilian attire to move into the hotel and locate the targets. The remainder of the unit, with two Lewis machine guns, were detailed to erect a cordon around the building. As the group arrived at the hotel, they noticed a number of men running across the fields. The Auxiliaries debussed from their vehicles and instead of entering the hotel covertly, they rushed the building shouting, 'Hands up'. Three off-duty RIC officers, sitting at the bar, took the abrupt entrance of the group of men in civilian dress, brandishing revolvers, as being IRA gunmen. Weapons were drawn and a shootout erupted between the two groups. When the smoke cleared, one T/Cadet, one RIC officer and the hotelier lay dead.

The 'blue on blue' (accidentally opening fire on your own side) incident was raised in Parliament with the heavy-handedness of the Auxiliaries being debated. The inquiry that followed covered up the incident; eyewitness accounts submitted by those patronising the bar on the date were disregarded. However, the military were not impressed with the subsequent report, with both General Macready and the Deputy Adjutant General being in no doubt as to what had actually happened. The Deputy Adjutant General, Brigadier General John Bartholomew Wroughton, wrote: 'They all had the wind up, blood up, and did what they used to do in the trenches in France. In the circumstances you cannot hold them criminally responsible, but they are not fit to be policemen – but are any Auxiliaries?'[11]

While the deaths were regrettable, the cover-up by the British government repulsed the RIC and military commanders who condemned Tudor's undisciplined force.

The frustration of fighting a war of counter-insurgency resulted in further breaches of discipline within the ranks of the Auxiliaries throughout Ireland. During their deployment in Ireland 64 T/Cadets were convicted of criminal offences, including three murders. The majority of offences were for fraud with those convicted serving a few months in prison or being granted probation.[12]

By June 1921, Tudor and his senior officers had dismissed over 50 Auxiliaries and ordered their platoon commanders to quash indiscipline and report all crimes so that the appropriate action could be taken.[13] However, in many cases, a blind eye was turned not only to looting but also to murder. For the ordinary citizen in Ireland, law and order, it seemed, would no longer protect them and the escalating situation would only bring new terrors and more death and destruction.

There were also problems with the Auxiliaries' relationship with the military. Army commanders believed that if they had the resources allocated to the Auxiliaries they would be able to conduct viable counter-insurgency operations. The military stated that 'if they had a regular company with five good officers, and provided with transport on the same scale as the Auxiliary Company, would do as well.'[14] The army was under-strength and under-equipped after the Great War and there was a delay in providing adequate armoured transport to commands in Ireland. Many of the new recruits were poorly trained for their deployment and the military had no overall strategy devised to combat the IRA campaign. The Auxiliaries were seen as a unit that brought the fight to the republicans and used similar tactics to those of their adversaries, with their overall strategy being one of annihilating the enemy by every means possible.

An article published in the *London Magazine* in 1921 attempted to show in a good light the often-strained relationship between the military and the ADRIC and the operational pressures experienced by both units while serving in Ireland. In it, Lieutenant Colonel Cavendish, CMG, DSO, commanding the 9th Lancers at Longford, remarked that:

> In 23 years of service, he had never worked with 'finer fellows or better pals than the Cadets of M Coy., Auxiliary Division R.I.C.'
>
> At Longford, a county town midway between Dublin and Sligo, one is reminded very forcibly of wartime scenes behind the lines. Irish 'grocery' bars take the place of the cafes of France and the estaminets of Belgium. In their dimly lit interiors the sergeants of the 9th Lancers spend their leisure moments with the Cadets of M Coy., Auxiliary Division.
>
> There they tell over again their stories of the Aisne, of Ypres, Festubert and of the Somme. 'Well I'm blest,' says a stalwart warrant officer to a Cadet who wears the ribbons of a military cross and 1914 star, 'd'you mean to tell me you were wounded on the 23rd March at Bapaume? – so was I!'
>
> 'Were you really,' exclaims the Cadet delightedly. 'Perhaps we shared the same shell', then after a silence … 'I was commanding a company in those early days.' 'Well, to tell the truth, so was I,' answers the warrant officer with a sly wink – 'You see I was a company sergeant major in the infantry!'

Sometimes their talk is of their more recent experiences among the 'Shinners', whilst as if in silent challenge to the British Empire, sits behind the bar a girl in a knitted jumper of emerald green whose brother perhaps is 'on the run'. She may be herself an active Sinn Féiner, or just an innocent onlooker who finds it difficult to associate these pleasant fellows with the murderous instincts attributed to them by Sinn Féin leaflets.

In their book the same friendly spirit is apparent. They have taken part in countless drives together, the Lancers surrounding a district and the Cadets searching the enclosed area for arms, ammunition and wanted men of the Irish Republican Army, they have done much to relieve Longford of the Sinn Féin terror. The promoters of a recent Hunt Ball were warned that the ball must not take place. This proved unfortunate, since both the Auxiliaries and the officers of the 9th Lancers had been invited.

Together they assumed responsibility for carrying out arrangements according to plan, and in spite of a threatening letter received by many of the guests, everyone was able to attend. Ladies in smart ball dresses and men in evening kit were taken to and from the ball in armoured Lancias of the Auxiliary Division.

There have been some bad ambushes in County Longford, but of late the IRA appears unwilling to take the offensive, and the Crown forces meet with nothing more formidable than occasional sniping at Auxiliary cyclist patrols, entrenched roads, felled trees and destroyed bridges.

In areas where the forces of the Crown prove too strong for them, it is customary for the IRA to direct their efforts mainly against the civilian population – to shoot ex-soldiers, burn the houses of loyalists, steal bicycles, telephone equipment etc. At one time, so great was the terror inspired by Sinn Fein gunmen, that a person suffering from injury from these methods, although he might know the offenders quite well, would not divulge his knowledge to the authorities.

Encouraged by the effective methods used by the military and auxiliary forces, however, people in the Longford area are often willing to impart information. Thus the rebels are now up against a new difficulty; one that the Crown forces in their turn have overcome. They find it difficult to discriminate between friends and enemies.[15]

Depending on where the military were stationed, opinions differed greatly, as Bugler Todman of the South Wales Borderers, stationed in Dunshaughlin, County Meath, recalled: 'Played football with them [ADRIC] on a number of occasions and they were a pretty tough crowd of men … showed itself in violence on the football field … Whenever they came to play they would mount 20 Lewis guns around the whole area to show their presence … The stories I heard from the troops and things, they certainly were not liked.'[16]

One Major General Douglas Wimberley, who served with the Cameron Highlanders in Cork during the War of Independence, wrote:

> So undisciplined were some of these auxiliary policemen, who had been recruited to reinforce the remnants of the Royal Irish Constabulary, most of whom by this time had been killed, that whenever some of them accompanied me, on any search, patrol or foray, in which I was in command, my first action was always to detail two or three of my Jocks simply to watch over them, and see that they did not commit any atrocities such as unlawfully looting or burning houses, when they were acting under my command, or even shooting prisoners, on the grounds that they were attempting to escape.[17]

While many serving British army officers disapproved of the Auxiliaries and their methods, some did agree that the new force was tackling the problem and getting results. Major General Hawes, Royal Garrison Artillery, stated 'that the additional police met the rebels on level terms and beat them at their own game'.[18]

In many cases, British army and regular RIC officers intervened and stopped Auxiliary Cadets from shooting suspected IRA Volunteers. Some military officers insisted that prisoners were handed over to them to be escorted back to base as some prisoners in the custody of the

ADRIC never made it back for interrogation. Volunteer Patrick Duffy wrote: 'In raids and in barracks, the British military were, as a rule, well behaved. The "Tommies" treated prisoners as well as the regulations permitted.'[19]

The only exception was that of the Essex Regiment based in County Cork.

> The British had been executing men found in possession of arms or taken prisoner in the course of engagements since February 1921. These men were being tried by court martial, which would seem to indicate that they were prisoners of war, but, despite this fact, a number had been executed. So far no man from Cork III Brigade had been dealt with in this manner – it appeared to be the policy of the military [Essex regiment] and Auxiliaries operating in our area to shoot anybody found engaged in military activities out of hand.[20]

Major A.E. Percival, Intelligence Officer of the Essex Regiment, was stationed in west Cork and was noted for his harsh treatment of prisoners. Having worked closely with the ADRIC, he believed that they were 'generally a very fine lot of men, and would have done well under other conditions'.[21]

In his memoirs, General Sir Nevil Macready, in relation to the Auxiliaries, wrote: 'Those Companies that had the good fortune to have good commanders, generally ex-Regular officers, who could control their men, performed useful work, but the exploits of other Companies under weak or ineffective commanders went a long way to discredit the whole force.'[22] However, like many at that time, he realised their potential but too late in the conflict. 'Some became first class fighting units, but many succumbed to drunkenness and gained a reputation as perpetrators of the most calculated and destructive reprisals'.[23]

Caroline Woodcock, the wife of a serving British officer, witnessed at first hand the security forces' operations on the streets. She wrote:

> Soldiers picqueted every corner, a house-to-house search was made and usually numerous streets effected. Throughout tanks waddled

slowly up and down the street ... During these raids, ever the most awe-inspiring sight for me was the car loads of Auxiliaries: eight or ten splendid-looking men in a Crossley Tender, armed to the teeth ... I know little of what the Auxiliaries have done or left undone but I do know that they have put the fear of God into the Irish rebels. When criticizing them, it should never be forgotten that these men are the survivors of the glorious company of those who fought and died for England.[24]

Depending on their experiences, opinions on the ADRIC and their actions varied. British soldiers were being killed, on and off duty, while others, taken as hostages, were executed by their captors, often as retaliation. Major Bernard Law Montgomery, a career officer stationed in Cork, later wrote: 'It never bothered me how many houses were burned. I regarded all civilians as "Shinners" and I never had any dealings with them.'[25]

The 6th Division's official history refers to the population of Cork as being evil as well as being actively or passively hostile.[26] The Irish Command described the inhabitants of Cork city as 'being mainly of the lower orders and ... on the whole bitterly opposed to the Crown Forces, the proportion of loyal persons being very small'. General Sir Nevil Macready, in an interview with American newspaper correspondent Carl W. Ackerman, said: 'What we are trying to do is stop the campaign of assassination and arson, initiated and carried on by Sinn Féin, with as little disturbance as possible to people who are and who wish to be law abiding.'[27]

However, the counter-insurgency campaign was failing to win the hearts and minds of the populace, and the reprisals carried out against the people by the Auxies were marginalising the police and the military. The situation was rapidly deteriorating as death and chaos reigned.

13

A Chance in Hell
The Arrest of Ernie O'Malley, December 1920

On entering the room in O'Hanrahan's house, Section Leader A.C. Stopher knew that something was amiss. He trained his Webley revolver at the man seated by the table. Another man stood nearby, reading *The Kilkenny People*. The tension in the room was rising by the second. T/Cadet Godfrey, his rifle slung over his shoulder, was on the far side of the room, searching through the drawers of the kitchen dresser. The man standing in the corner folded the paper he was reading and looked towards the door. He seemed agitated while the seated man, though reading a book, was taking in the events that were unfolding in the small room. He casually turned a page, revealing the cover of the book as *Mr. Britling Sees it Through*.

'What's your name?' Section Leader A.C. Stopher demanded.

'Stewart,' the seated man replied.

'Your Christian name?'

'Bernard.'

'What are you doing here?'

'Visiting my Aunt.'[1]

The Auxiliary at the back of the room had stopped his search and when Stopher asked if he had searched the men, the T/Cadet replied in the negative. Suddenly, the man jumped up from the table, sending the chair careering backwards. He bounded for the back door, reaching into his pocket at the same time. Section Leader Stopher rushed forward and pinned the man to the wall. T/Cadet Godfrey searched the man and discovered a loaded automatic pistol in his pocket. The gun had become entangled in the lining of the pocket, hampering the weapon's quick release. A number of Mills bombs were also discovered during the search.

'I'm sorry I didn't shoot, you dirty swine,' Stopher said through gritted teeth. 'Take him out, blindfold him, and stick him up against a wall.' The other man was searched and also taken outside at gunpoint. Papers, maps and a notebook that were on the table were collected and bagged.

E.M. Drane arrived on the scene and ordered the blindfold to be removed from the suspected insurgent. 'Who are you?' the officer demanded harshly.

'I am a member of the Irish Republican Army,' the man replied.

'What rank?'

'Volunteer.'

'What is your company?' There was no reply.

'Who is your captain?' Once again there was no reply.

'So you are not going to talk, you bastard,' Drane said. As the officer turned and walked away he said, 'Well, we'll make you.' With that, a revolver was cocked and pointed at the prisoner while another Auxiliary blindfolded and handcuffed the man before kicking him down the lane towards a waiting car in which he was taken to 'A' Company's HQ.[2]

In September 1920, 'A' Company of the ADRIC under the leadership of Captain C.W.V. Webb occupied Woodstock House, Inistioge, County Kilkenny. In the months leading up to 9 December 1920 and the arrest of the men at O'Hanrahan's house, the Company had increased patrols and raids in the area, tactics that were aimed at defeating insurgent operations and establishing control of the region. In certain parts of the country, these types of tactics, involving sheer weight of numbers and firepower, helped the British regain the initiative and build some momentum.

The maps found in the house detailed military and police dispositions and strengths of stations in the area. The notebook contained the names and addresses of local insurgent leaders and the strengths of IRA units in the vicinity. The force was listed as having eight battalions in four brigades with armaments consisting of 103 rifles and 4,900 rounds of ammunition, 471 shotguns with 2,010 refilled cartridges and 1,480 ordinary cartridges.

At Woodstock House, the prisoners taken at O'Hanrahan's were interrogated and threatened with execution. The Auxiliaries realised that the man calling himself Bernard Stewart was using a pseudonym and that he was not an O/R (other ranks) Volunteer but was in fact an important target. Not only was he apprehended carrying papers and an automatic pistol but he was also wearing military attire in the form of a military-issue cardigan under his jacket. Some officers believed he might have been involved in an attack at Macroom in County Cork while others believed he was a significant player in the republican command. Unable to break the individual within the designated time frame, both prisoners were handed over to the local RIC who were entrusted to transport the men to Dublin Castle for further questioning. O'Hanrahan's house was burnt for harbouring rebels, the plumes of black smoke rising into the sky as the prisoners mounted their transport for the barracks in Kilkenny.

Unknown to 'A' Company of the ADRIC, the man they had just captured was Ernie O'Malley.

Given the task of organising and reorganising the IRA into companies, battalions, brigades and flying columns, O'Malley reported the countrywide situation directly back to Michael Collins and Richard Mulcahy. Also unknown to the Auxiliaries was that O'Malley was in the area to plan and carry out an attack on their base at Inistioge.

A large mansion situated in the centre of a large wooded demesne, Woodstock House had been vacated by its owners, the Tighe family, who moved to England during the summer of 1920 leaving the house and grounds in the care of their servants. The demesne was bounded on the east by the River Nore and on the remaining sides by a high stone wall. IRA Brigade Headquarters had been preparing plans for an attack on the base when O'Malley arrived in the area to take charge of the intended attack. With O'Malley now incarcerated in Dublin Castle and the ranks of the Kilkenny IRA either imprisoned or on the run, the attack on the Auxiliary base was shelved.[3]

The raid produced an abundance of valuable information that set the insurgency in the area back months. O'Malley's extreme carelessness in keeping intelligence notes in his pocket led to the identification and subsequent capture of almost all the active IRA members in the region.

On 21 February 1921, O'Malley along with two other prisoners, Frank Teeling and Simon Donnelly, made a daring escape from Kilmainham Gaol. During his incarceration, O'Malley's real identity was never discovered by the authorities.

One month later, on Saturday 26 March 1921, three Crossley Tenders came to a halt approximately 500 yards from Inistioge Bridge over the River Nore. The T/Cadets from 'A' Company debussed from their vehicles and, watchful that they might be about to walk into an ambush, the men spread out and began a slow and deliberate search. Intelligence reports stated that an IED had been placed under the bridge. Roads and bridges throughout the country were being laced with mines, exposing convoys to insurgent ambushes.

Platoon Commander A.M. Gordon assigned his men positions where they could provide security. A T/Cadet in the lead vehicle pulled the cocking handle back on his Lewis machine gun and began scanning the surrounding landscape for gunmen or lookouts. Having discovered the location of the bomb on one of the bridge's piers, a 360-degree perimeter was established. T/Cadets trained their rifles on the treeline a dozen yards away, tense and ready for action.

With no dedicated Explosive Ordnance Disposal technicians, the job fell on the Auxiliaries to defuse and make the device safe. They were able to draw on their experiences of dealing ad hoc with unexploded shells on the Western Front.

A squad under Section Leader W. May crept towards the bridge. The bomb affixed to the central pier would have to be removed and examined. Two T/Cadets remained on the bridge, providing cover, as the other three descended the bank and made their way along the arches towards the device. On reaching the device, they noticed the command wire looped out of the box, leading off towards the far bank. The trigger mechanism was an electrical type, possibly connected to a battery. Using pliers, the wire was cut and the device disassembled. Taking the bomb with them, the T/Cadets moved back onto the bridge. The pieces were loaded into the Tender to be examined back at base. A possible fingerprint or a telltale knot could lead to the apprehension of the bomb makers. The device contained several hundredweight of ammonal (an explosive compound of ammonium nitrate and aluminium powder) and a fuse. The bomb was not only designed to damage or make the bridge impassable but was set for the destruction of an Auxiliary patrol. A quick sweep for any secondary devices proved negative; the patrol remounted and with the roar of engines headed back towards Woodstock House.

The detection of the IED had stopped 'A' Company's Commander R.H.L. Conlan's worst nightmare, a mass casualty situation. A carefully positioned IRA ambush unit would have wreaked havoc on the remnants of the patrol and also the first responders. It is unknown if this attempted attack was planned by local insurgents or if Ernie O'Malley, having escaped from prison, deployed a group from Dublin to carry out the attack on 'A' Company.

14

A Toss of the Coin
Counter-insurgency Warfare

Counter-insurgency (COIN) has been defined as 'comprehensive civilian and military efforts taken to simultaneously defeat and contain insurgency and address its root causes'. Insurgency is the organised use of subversion and violence to seize, nullify or challenge political control of a region. As such, it is primarily a political struggle, in which both sides use armed force to create space for their political, economic and influential activities to be effective.[1]

The modern study of unconventional warfare has identified differences between terrorism and insurgency which enable governments and military forces to deal with these threats.

> There are stark differences between terrorism and insurgency frameworks. The terrorism framework sees terrorists as unrepresentative and abnormal outliers in society. Insurgency is the manifestation of deeper, widespread issues in society. Terrorism isolates terrorists from negotiation or constructive engagement. Insurgency is premised on winning hearts and minds. Terrorists' methods and objectives are condemned. Insurgents' methods are condemned but their objectives might be reasonable if pursued

through political means. Terrorists are seen as psychologically defective – seeking violence for its own sake. Insurgents see violence as part of a broader political-military strategy. Terrorism is seen as either a law enforcement or military problem, rooting out a few bad apples. Insurgency is a social problem, requiring mobilization of all elements of government power. Counterterrorism is tactical, focusing on catching particular terrorists. Counterinsurgency is strategic, seeking to undermine the insurgent's strategy and envisioning capture as secondary. In essence, terrorism is subordinate to insurgency. Terrorism is a particular tactic. Insurgency is the rejection of a political order.[2]

The ADRIC found themselves operating in a very hostile environment with little or no help from the local populace. Their counter-insurgency operations did sometimes yield results, however, as proved by the experience of 'B' Company (stationed at Upperchurch, County Tipperary) on 22 May 1921.

Raising his binoculars to his eyes, RIC District Inspector Thomas Naughton watched intently as the group of figures under his observation moved across the street and entered O'Dwyer's shop. He adjusted the focus and scanned the building from back to front. He moved his field of vision to the church gate where three men stood waiting for the others to return. Within seconds, the roar of engines cut through the still evening air and a number of lorries, laden with military and Black and Tans, appeared at Pendy's Cross and turned off the main Thurles–Newport road. They careered towards the village, the sound of the engines growing louder as the speed of the vehicles gradually increased. 'I have you now, you bastards,' exclaimed Naughton.

This carefully planned operation had been months in the organising. Every attempt to intercept the IRA unit in this area had been foiled. They had managed to evade capture by using a pre-planned escape route out of the rear of O'Dwyer's shop, up a hill towards a byroad leading to Templederry. However, this time, unknown to the insurgents, DI Naughton had positioned a unit of Auxiliaries to intercept the fleeing men. The T/Cadets had travelled unseen along the Moher Road from the Borrisoleigh direction and had debussed from their vehicles 150

Members of 'F' Company, Dublin Castle. This photo shows the arsenal of weapons carried by the ADRIC while on patrol. (National Library)

yards from the junction with the Gurtnaskeha Road.[3] They immediately took up concealed positions and, like DI Naughton, could look down upon the village where they watched the rear exit of the shop.

Having heard the approaching vehicles, the men at the church gate ran to the shop and shouted a warning, alerting those inside that a raid was commencing. Those outside made a dash back towards the church but Naughton had them all cornered.

At the rear of the shop, four men – Con Gleeson, John Ryan, Thomas Stapleton and Tom Stapleton – appeared at the doorway and ran out, guns at the ready. The Auxiliaries opened fire, the crack of small-arms fire echoing throughout the valley. The men bounded forward, running the gauntlet of rifle fire directed at them. Taking cover behind hedgerows and broken stone walls, Con Gleeson opened fire in an attempt to cover his comrades who sprinted forwards, low and fast, in an attempt to gain cover. These actions were repeated every dozen yards or so as they tried to put distance between themselves and the Auxiliaries who were beginning to advance down the hill. Incoming rounds ricocheted off the walls and thudded into the trees around the four men. They knew they were surrounded and the only way to evade capture was to shoot their way out.

Gleeson aimed his automatic pistol at the Auxies' position on the hilltop and squeezed the trigger. Finally the weapon's slide locked back, the magazine spent, a thin wisp of smoke rising from the barrel. He quickly inserted another magazine and opened fire once again. The Auxiliaries moved down the hill to positions that had complete control of the space, hemming in the Volunteers. Having the advantage in firepower with their .303 Lee Enfield rifles, the Auxiliaries were able to use fire and manoeuvre to advance towards their targets. T/Cadets zigzagged down the hill, many in a low crouch, taking turns to run and cover.

A barrage of fire erupted from the T/Cadet positions and a moment later Con Gleeson's lifeless body slumped to the ground. As John Ryan broke cover he received a severe wound to his hand. The T/Cadets advanced rapidly, closing the distance between them and their quarry. 'Drop your weapons, and put your hands up' was shouted continually by the advancing officers. Ryan clutched his shattered hand while Thomas Stapleton raised his hands in surrender. However, Stapleton had managed to dump his weapon and Ryan's revolver before they were captured. As they walked towards their captors, both men looked at Gleeson's lifeless body, his eyes gazing vacantly at the sky.

Tom Stapleton managed to evade capture by crawling out through a drainage ditch and into nearby low-lying wetlands. He hid amongst the rushes, the bogland providing enough cover that the pursuing T/Cadets gave up the search and returned to the village.

Having watched the events unfold, DI Naughton notified the military that some of the insurgents had been seen entering the grounds of the church. The T/Cadets, supported by the military, entered the church and found a dozen terrified old men, women and children cowering in the dimly lit interior. They searched the building but failed to discover the men. Volunteer Paddy Kinnane later wrote:

> After alerting the four boys at O'Dwyer's, Jim Stapleton, Fahy and myself returned to the church, and, by a secret passage known only to a few, we entered a secret hiding place or dump which was situated under the floor of the church at the back of the altar. The British forces entered and searched the church, and took out and maltreated people who were praying there. Our hiding place was not discovered, and we remained there until the sacristan came with the news of what had happened, and gave us the all-clear signal.[4]

Another local man, John Bourke, was wounded as he tried to get clear of the gun battle. The police rounded up a number of men in the village and loaded them on to the lorries along with the prisoners taken in the gun battle. Together with Gleeson's body, they were conveyed to Templemore Barracks. The wounded Volunteer, John Ryan, was taken under escort to the military hospital in Tipperary where he had three of his fingers amputated.

The operation had been a success: three insurgents captured and one dead. The police also recovered an estimated 80 rounds of ammunition, field glasses, wire cutters and seditious literature.

DI Naughton's counter-insurgency operation had depended on overwhelming force and repression in order to succeed.[5] He was commended for his actions and was later promoted to District Inspector First Class.

15

Making the Rounds
Patrols & Raids

At the beginning of 1921, the British administration in Ireland, supported by the police and the military, had launched a concerted attempt to retake the country. Initially the IRA picked up the gauntlet and the towns, cities and countryside were soon scenes of intense daily firefights in which the British forces with their armoured cars and Tenders were pitted against gunmen, IEDs and ambushes.

Police and military commanders had come up with a bold plan to wrest control back from the insurgents. Increased patrols, raids and searches, conducted by thousands of personnel, resulted in the lockdown of areas across the country, a tactic that made it difficult for republicans to operate.

'R' Company ADRIC became operational at the end of April 1921 and was initially based in Dublin. Other Dublin-based Companies, such as 'F' and 'Q', were preoccupied with securing the docklands and inner city while 'I' Company had been moved to the north side of the city. Police units often amalgamated for large operations and there is a good possibility that the raid on Blackrock College was conducted by 'R' Company with the support of other Dublin units.

On the morning of Tuesday, 31 May 1921, Auxiliary forces, supported by military personnel, acting on intelligence received, conducted a search operation at Blackrock College, Dublin. Founded by the Holy Ghost Fathers in 1860, the Catholic Boys' School covered an estimated 60 acres of buildings and parkland. At 03:00 hours a force of 100 T/Cadets breached an entry into the college campus through the front gates. Lorries filled with British soldiers followed the police into the complex where the military immediately began to place a cordon around the college grounds. Armoured cars took up strategic positions, training their guns on the buildings while powerful searchlights, positioned on the beds of lorries, scanned the buildings and grounds. Police and military storming parties prepared to enter the buildings. This type of operation was intelligence driven, targeting high-value individuals (HVIs), cache sites and bed-down locations. The initial advance through the grounds of the college was rapid, with all target buildings identified.

Police and troops entered the college buildings and the school hostel. This kind of operation involved lockdowns, door kicking and the thorough searching of individuals as well as the buildings. Students were awakened and questioned as every area was cleared and secured.

The Auxiliaries had been briefed that every raid must produce intelligence and police raids had begun to yield results. Realising that the correct breach point into a building was critical for speed and surprise, the Auxiliaries were tasked with entering 'Clareville', a building that was separated from the main complex. The Auxiliaries scaled the walls with ladders and entered the house through the skylights on the roof. This building was occupied by aged and retired priests who were awakened by the police. Reports state that the priests were shown every consideration and courtesy as a thorough search was conducted. Nothing was found and the operation was concluded when the grounds were thoroughly searched. The police and military had breakfast in one of the playing fields before returning to base.

At 14:00 hours on Thursday, 9 June 1921, a column numbering 43 men of 'G' Company, ADRIC, was returning from Kilmihill in south-west Clare to their operating base at the Lakeside Hotel at Killaloe.

Information received through local RIC sources reported that a number of flying columns were active in the area. The mission plan for 'G' Company ADRIC was a 'Find, Fix and Finish' operation against insurgents in the area but they had failed to make contact. The terrain in and around Kilmihill consisted of bogland and gorse, which was difficult to navigate and was suitable for the hit-and-run tactics of the insurgents. In order to infiltrate the area, the Auxiliaries used bicycles and packhorses as the operation required stealth and speed and the use of motorised Crossley Tenders would only alert the insurgents that the police were in the area.

A scouting party moved ahead of the main column, which was spread out over a mile. As the leading section came into Darragh and was adjacent to the local post office, a barrage of rifle fire was unleashed on the advance party. Shouts of 'take cover!' were passed down the line. The T/Cadets jumped into the drainage ditch by the side of the road, weapons at the ready, scanning the terrain for targets.

Gunfire was emanating from the high ground south-east of their position. As the Auxiliaries prepared to engage their attackers, additional rifle fire was directed at the officers on the road from concealed positions in the high ground to the north-west. Bullets sliced through the air as the Auxiliaries tried to identify the Volunteers' firing positions.

Platoon Commander A. Brigdens scanned the hillside ahead for any sign of movement. With his Lee Enfield rifle he could not lay down a hail of fire to force the insurgents' heads down, but only pinpoint those enemy fighters coming out from cover and then try to shoot them before they had a chance to take a shot.

Two Lewis machine guns were brought into action, the suppressive fire enabling the officers to move along the road and engage the enemy from better positions.

The West Clare Brigade flying column under the command of Joseph Barrett had been bivouacked in the area when news reached them of the returning Auxiliary column. Barrett planned to ambush the column in a shoot-and-scoot action. His main position, just 500 yards from the Kilrush–Ennis road, was held by fifteen men. Approximately half a mile away on his right flank, three men were posted on a byroad. His left flank was secured by two men at a distance of 350 yards from the main section. As the column came into the kill zone, Barrett signalled his men to open fire. After the opening volley, the shooting became desultory.

On coming under fire, the Auxiliaries immediately began to assess the situation: how many insurgents were in the attacking group and where were the positions? Having identified their exact locations, they deployed the attack.

Using the ditches and low stone walls as cover, the police column broke into sections, the main body attacking the insurgents and the advance guard making a flanking manoeuvre from a line running north. The gunfight increased in intensity as the officers moved out from cover. Rounds chipped off the stone walls and whistled past them as they advanced towards the Volunteers' main position. The noise of the firefight was physical, a thundering staccato of violence. Noticing there was little resistance coming from Barrett's right flank, the Auxiliaries began to exploit this weakness. However, rapid fire from the insurgents' main post forced the Auxiliaries to seek cover. Bullets cut through the heather and gorse as each side tried to outmanoeuvre the other. T/Cadet Walsh fell flat as a weapon cracked, a bullet soughing past his ear.

A Lewis gun was brought up the line and enfilading fire was directed against Barrett's main force, pinning them down. Barrett's brother Bernard was tasked with securing the left flank. Realising the main force was pinned down and in danger of being overrun, he took careful aim and fired at the Lewis gunner, hitting him in the shoulder. T/Cadet W.D. Clarke was thrown backwards with the force of the impact. A .303 round had plunged into his shoulder and burst out through his back, spurting blood. T/Cadet Shiner came to his aid, tore open his tunic and applied a shell dressing. The intense gunfire quickly halted the flanking movement. With the machine gun disabled, it bought vital time for the flying column to plan their next move. While this was taking place, Joseph Barrett continued to move back and forth between the open field and his unit's defensive position, alternating between his sections in order to engage the enemy. He also continued to provide his unit with tactical instructions and direct their fire, as the tempo of the fighting increased. Noticing that the ADRIC were gaining ground, Barrett ordered a section of seven men to occupy an old fort, 400 yards to their rear. He later recalled, 'This fort was on an eminence which commanded the ground over which the enemy was trying to advance, and, from it, the section which had retired were able to pin him down while I and the remainder of the main party were retreating to the fort.'

Covering fire was laid down, and the main force managed to reach the relative safety of the fort without casualties. Each Volunteer section managed to fall back and regroup at the fort.

The Auxiliaries pressed forward, crouching and hugging the ground for cover. Bullets whined and cracked through the air and the rattle of the Lewis guns added to the crescendo of battlefield chaos.

A section of Volunteers fought a rearguard action, allowing the main force of insurgents to fall back and cross the Rathkerry River near where it touches the Ennis–Kilmaley Road.

At this point the ADRIC were forced to break off their pursuit and return to the main road. Truckloads of British troops arrived in the area and began combing the countryside, but the insurgents, knowing the area and making use of the difficult terrain, escaped the net.

The action had lasted two hours with no fatalities on either side.

Increased patrols and raiding parties continued throughout the country. On 30 June 1921, as their reconnaissance patrol in Derrynoose was drawing to a close, 'I' Company ADRIC stationed at Hope Castle, in Castleblaney, County Monaghan, received a tipoff that republican insurgents were preparing an ambush. Their target, a bread van from Belfast escorted by a number of armed police, was travelling through the townland of Carrickduff, Carnagh, County Armagh. The Auxiliary platoon, travelling in two Tenders, decided to investigate the report and set off towards Crossnenagh on their way to Carrickduff.

The IRA unit, under the command of Captain Peter Woods and comprising twenty men, was well equipped with rifles, shotguns and grenades. For a number of weeks previously, Bernard Hughes's bread vans had been engaged in supplying Belfast bread to some local shops. One of these vans had been destroyed but a replacement van, which was now under a police escort, had returned to the district. On 30

June 1921, a scout was sent into Keady and ordered to keep the bread van under observation and to report to the ambush command post with information regarding the number of guards protecting the van. Captain Woods' unit occupied positions along the railway line at Carrickduff, which ran parallel to the Keady–Castleblaney road. From these positions, the insurgents would be able to maintain an effective fire on their target. Within 100 yards on the Castleblaney side of their position, a minor road branched off the Keady–Castleblaney road and ran across a bridge that spanned the railway line, overlooking the insurgents' ambush position. At 11:00 hours the scout returned and reported that the van was coming with an escort of five RIC constables. Captain Woods ordered his men to make ready and not to fire until the target was identified and within the kill zone. The ambush party took up position, lying with their rifles at the ready. As the vehicle came into range, a Volunteer shouted, 'Jesus, look at the bridge, the Tans are on the railway bridge.' The two Tenders of Auxiliaries had split up, with one turning onto the crossroads and continuing to the bridge spanning the railway line while the other vehicle proceeded down the main road opposite the republican positions to lend support to the van.

As the insurgents turned towards the bridge, they watched as a section of Auxiliaries alighted from their Tender and mounted a machine gun on the bridge with its muzzle pointing in their direction. The T/Cadets had not only the advantage of surprise but also that of elevation.

Realising that his operation had been compromised, Captain Woods ordered one section to fire at the Auxiliaries on the bridge and another section to engage the RIC on the road. However, Woods' men scattered in an attempt to evade being surrounded. While the majority of insurgents ran across the railway line northwards towards Annyalla, four men ran in the opposite direction towards the Carnagh, which fronted their position. Two short bursts of Lewis machine-gun fire were directed at this group as they ran. Bullets cut through the air as other Auxiliaries opened fire with their rifles. Volunteer Thomas Carragher had been caught in the blast of machine-gun fire and seriously wounded. Two cousins, Thomas and Michael McEnnaney, had been killed with the first burst of machine-gun fire. Carragher crawled past the bodies and lay on the ground, conscious but bleeding profusely from a number of bullet wounds. He later recalled:

> I proceeded on for a short distance where I heard footsteps and looking around I saw a member of the Auxiliary force had me covered with his rifle. He was only about 1½ yards from me and he fired point blank at my head. The bullet entered my right jaw and my tongue and made an exit on my left jaw, shattering all my teeth on both sides. I fell and feigned that I was dead. The Auxiliary stood over me for a while and then an officer in charge of the Auxiliaries came along and told the man that he was not authorized to shoot wounded men. The Auxiliary replied that the wounded man might have shot him had he got the chance. The man who was in charge of the machine gun then came along and stated that his gun had jammed and only for that he would have got most of us.[2]

The other Volunteers retreated down the railway embankment before they managed to get into the cover of the fields. There were several minor casualties in this scramble for cover who had to be helped by their colleagues. The group had to cross 150 yards of open space in order to avoid encirclement. It was only then that they returned fire on the Auxiliaries. However, their fire was ineffective. Though the breastwork of the bridge was grooved and pitted by republican rounds, the stone parapet of the bridge afforded the T/Cadets more than adequate cover.

The sound of the battle receded as the Volunteers disengaged and fell back west towards Clontibret. The Auxiliaries broke contact and began a search of the battleground, which revealed twelve loaded rifles, extra charged magazines and two tins of petrol, evidently for the destruction of the bread van.

The bodies of the two dead Volunteers were collected and placed in the rear of a Tender along with the wounded man, Thomas Carragher, and were taken back to Auxiliary H.Q. at Lord Hope's Castle in Castleblaney.

A thorough search of the district was conducted later that day but no further arrests were made. Volunteer Eugene Sherry later stated that 'This affair has all the appearance that our position for this ambush was given away to the British authorities. The Auxiliaries must have got minute details of the position we were to occupy as they proceeded without hesitation to the best points of attack and it is most unlikely that they could have seen us before they opened fire on our position.'[3]

Volunteer Thomas Carragher was treated for his wounds and taken to Louth County Infirmary, later transferred to King George V Hospital in Dublin and then moved to Dundalk military barracks. A truce between British Crown forces and the Irish Republican Army came into effect on 11 July 1921. A treaty was signed in December of that year. Carragher was released from custody in February 1922 under the truce agreement.

Soon after the gun battle, the bodies of the two dead Volunteers were returned to their relatives for burial. They were interred in the graveyard of Annyalla Chapel with full military honours.

16

Harbingers of Death
The Coolavokig Ambush, 18 January 1921

From their base at Lennaboye House in County Galway, Platoon Commander T. Simmonds DSO, DCM, MC, was to take his section and travel to Headford on 18 January 1921. As it was fair day, the Auxiliaries were to provide security by closing off all avenues of ingress and egress to the town square, allowing plain-clothes detectives and regular RIC to conduct a general search for subversives.

As the eleven men made ready, each checked his kit; magazines were charged for their primary weapons, .303 Lee Enfield rifles and revolvers or automatic pistols. The T/Cadets had worn their handguns or secondary weapon low slung in leg holsters, but now, due to the increased attacks, the fashion had changed to open-topped, waist-high holster rigs that enabled quick release of the weapon. Others cradled pump-action shotguns and the squad automatic weapon, the Lewis machine gun, was loaded into the rear of the Crossley Tender.

The group exited the grounds of Lennaboye House and drove towards Headford. The journey, like so many before, took the unit through the winding roads of the Irish countryside. At 09:40 hours the vehicle was 4 miles from Headford on the Corrundulla side of Kilroe when the driver was forced to slow down due to an oncoming horse and cart. At a sharp bend in the road the two vehicles came abreast. Those in the rear of the Crossley caught sight of a hand grenade looping through the air towards them, a Mills bomb, its fuse burning down towards detonation. The bomb missed its target and exploded with a flat crack on the road.

The horse bolted amid the smoke and debris from the explosion. 'Ambush,' was shouted by those in the vehicle as a barrage of gunfire erupted from the trees on both sides of the road. Bullets punctured the radiator of the vehicle, rendering it useless. The T/Cadets baled out of the Crossley, taking cover under its chassis. A number of men were hit as they scrambled for cover. Section Leader Simmonds knew that his section was up against a sizeable enemy force and that the only way out was to repulse the attack.

For the ambush, the IRA had drafted in men from four different Companies. Thomas 'Baby' Duggan had 40 men under his command and had placed them 5 to 10 yards apart on either side of the road. Scouts had watched the approach roads, waiting for the Auxiliaries to enter the kill zone. Duggan's men were armed with a variety of weapons: rifles, shotguns, grenades and revolvers. However, their supply of ammunition was limited and Duggan knew that he had to gain the upper hand in the early stage of the assault.[1]

The initial hand grenade was the signal to open fire on the vehicle. However, his men had hesitated so as not to hit the driver of the horse and cart, an error that gave the Auxiliaries vital seconds to debuss and take cover.

Simmonds' unit fought back with skill and determination. Having taken the Lewis machine gun from the vehicle, T/Cadet Craig dropped prone and fired a couple of short bursts in an attempt to keep the insurgents' heads down. Further explosions and rifle fire ripped through the air along the roadway. The T/Cadets directed their fire at the puffs of smoke that revealed the positions of the insurgent fighters. Four Auxiliaries were suffering from serious wounds while another six had received superficial injuries. Bullets ricocheted off the vehicle's bodywork as intense fire was directed onto the road. Simmonds directed his men to keep firing and halt any advance on their precarious position. T/Cadet Harold Dawkins, realising that they could be overrun at any moment, decided to get help. Though wounded in the face, he made a dash from under the vehicle, across the road and into a nearby field. Bullets kicked up dirt around him as he ran the gauntlet of fire. Dawkins commandeered a horse and rode away from the ambush site to get help.

The insurgents' ammunition was soon exhausted and Simmonds, realising this, ordered his machine-gunner to lay down suppressive fire against the attackers. IRA Commander Duggan ordered his men to disengage and pull out. One of his men had received a serious wound to his hand and he was led away, suffering from a loss of blood.

As the firing from the line of trees became sporadic, Simmonds ordered his men to withdraw to a more secure position by the side of the road. Taking their wounded with them, the unit fell back to a berm, or raised bank. From here they could cover both sides of the road and would be in a better position to repulse an all-out attack.

Though the gunfight had lasted 30 minutes, casualties had been light on both sides. T/Cadet Dawkins had managed to summon assistance and a relief column soon arrived to assist the wounded Auxiliaries on the road. In many cases, republican attacks were fought off because T/Cadets knew that if they were captured they would face almost certain death. Routine operations were as hazardous as patrols.

The Commander of the Auxiliary detachment, Section Leader Lieutenant T. Simmonds, was awarded the Constabulary medal for bravery during the ambush. The citation reads: 'Although suffering from very painful wounds in the back, he organized his defence splendidly, drove off the attackers and then withdrew with all the wounded clear of the wood to a place of vantage, where a defence position was taken up until the arrival of reinforcements.'[2]

In response to this ambush at Kilroe, the Archbishop of Tuam, Dr Thomas P. Gilmartin, issued a letter to be read at all Masses, which read: 'The misguided criminals who fired a few shots from behind a wall … have broken the truce of God, they have incurred the guilt of murder … and then having fired their cowardly shots, they beat a hasty retreat, leaving the unprotected and innocent people at the mercy of uniformed forces.'³ The Church condemned the actions of both sides as the number of violent incidences increased. More innocent civilians were being caught between the warring factions, prompting the clergy to begin a campaign of condemnation of IRA actions and also berating the British military in their failure to control the insurgency.

Lieutenant Colonel Guard, the Commander of 'D' Company ADRIC, was tasked with apprehending the attackers. With the assistance of the army and regular RIC, Guard began tracking the wounded Volunteer, Charles Quinn. He was traced to a number of safe houses and a nursing home but managed to evade capture. During the searches a man named Thomas Collins was arrested and handed over to the regular RIC. While in police custody, he was shot trying to escape. The medical report, carried out by a member of the Royal Army Medical Corps, reported ten bullet wounds to the body.

On 25 February 1921, Major James Seafield Grant, MC, O/C 'J' Company ADRIC, ordered his driver to slow down. A decorated veteran of the Great War, Grant knew that the enemy was lying in wait, ahead of his column. From his touring car, Major Grant raised a pair of binoculars to his eyes and adjusted the focus. He scanned the roadway ahead, moving to the stony hillocks and high masses of boulders that overlooked the road. The position, he thought, was ideal for an ambush.

'J' Company operated from two bases, Macroom Castle and the Eccles Hotel in Glengarriff, County Cork. The Cadets patrolled and raided aggressively in and around Ballyvourney and had become a serious threat to republican activity in the area. Word had reached Grant that an IRA flying column was lying in wait for his patrol but its exact position and strength was unknown. The officer ordered his men to keep their eyes skinned as the column slowly trundled along the road at Coolavokig, on the road between Macroom and Ballyvourney. Grant's command consisted of 50 T/Cadets, one sergeant and six regular RIC. For insurance, the Auxiliaries carried four hostages, either captured IRA officers or local Sinn Féin sympathisers. As they advanced in to what many believed was a deathtrap, they hoped that this tactic would help deter any attack on the column.

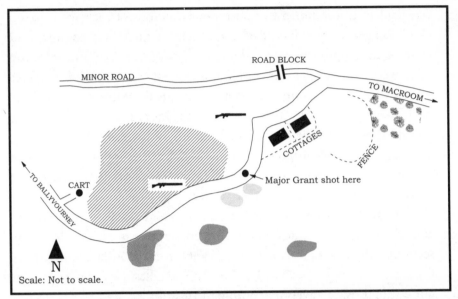

COOLAVOKIG AMBUSH 25 FEBRUARY 1921.

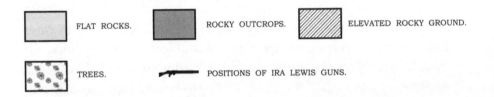

Seán O'Hegarty, O/C, Irish Republican Army 1ˢᵗ Brigade, County Cork, had spent weeks planning the attack on Major Grant's patrol. The aim of the operation was to surprise and overwhelm the Auxiliary convoy, securing their arms and, more importantly, gaining a vital supply of ammunition.

Republican intelligence agents and local sympathisers reported that the patrol never left Macroom before 09:00 hours, and travelled via Coolavokig to their destination, Ballyvourney, at 09:30 hours. Using the knowledge of local Volunteers, O'Hegarty carefully chose Coolavokig as his ambush position.

Located on the main Macroom–Killarney road, about 7 miles from Macroom and 2 miles from Ballymakera, this section of winding road was flanked to the north by continuous outcrops of rock 10 to 15 feet high. Rugged terrain was ideal for concealment with a commanding view of the approach roads. From the various rocky vantage points there were wide fields of fire in all directions that overlooked hundreds of yards of barren ground adjacent to the road. A low stone wall ran parallel to the road, broken in places, the stones scattered along the ground. The landscape to the north, south and west provided enough cover to ensure safe routes of withdrawal for the ambush party. Two cottages, both vacant, stood at the eastern end of the ambush site, slightly obscured by a small grove of trees.

O'Hegarty's handpicked unit of 60 men was taken from the 1st, 7th and 8th Battalions of the 1st Cork Brigade, and was divided into four sections. These men included local Volunteers as well as men from Cork city. Weapons consisted of Lee Enfield rifles, two Lewis machine guns, shotguns, revolvers and automatic pistols.

The IRA attack force went into carefully planned positions north of the road.

No. 1 Section was detailed the main attack force and took up positions overlooking the road. The first Lewis machine gun was set up to cover this area with fields of fire covering the cottages extending along the road. Dan Corkery positioned the men, ordering them to hold their fire until the signal to attack was given. O'Hegarty established his command post within a natural redoubt of stone that gave a clear view of the site.

No. 2 Section was detailed to occupy positions that commanded the road in front and to the east of the kill zone. Ned Neville was tasked with commanding this area. The second Lewis gun was set up here though its field of fire was somewhat restricted by large rocky outcrops. However, the men stationed here had an excellent command of the low ground to the south.

No. 3 Section took up position to the west where they covered the flanks. Michael O'Sullivan ordered his unit to camouflage their positions so that they were not visible from the road. They were also responsible for enabling the roadblock of a horse and cart that was to be pulled across the road, preventing the convoy from driving through the ambush and out the other side.

No. 4 Section was concealed behind the isolated rock formations to the south with a field of fire that extended from the cottages to the roadblock.[4]

The men armed with shotguns were posted in support of the riflemen and also to cover the flanks. An observation post was established on Rahoonagh Hill, a mile from the site. This position gave the scouts a clear view of the approach roads that covered 4 miles to the east and 2 miles to the west. Reports were to be sent to O'Hegarty's CP by means of semaphore.

A secondary road was trenched to channel the convoy towards the ambush site and to block any attempt by British forces to bypass the kill zone. O'Hegarty detached a section to cover this obstruction in case there was any attempt to backfill the trench and escape the attack.

For six days, the Volunteers moved into positions and waited for the convoy but it never materialised. The men sat for hours and waited patiently but to no avail. Morale deteriorated as O'Hegarty's men suffered from exposure. The weather was bitterly cold with sleet, hail and heavy rain showers. Each evening, under the cover of darkness, the sections withdrew from their ambush positions and moved back to their billets and rested up. The column was housed by some local sympathisers but food and supplies were sparse. Morale was also damaged by the fear that their plan had become known to the authorities. Informers had in recent weeks reported a number of republican operations to Crown forces, resulting in arrests.

Eventually, just after 08:00 hours on 25 February 1921, the scouts warned O'Hegarty that a convoy was approaching. The officer ordered his men to make ready.

The first vehicle to come into view was a touring car closely followed by six lorries. Another car brought up the rear of the column. The Auxiliaries in the lorries were standing up, rifles at the ready, scanning their arcs, watching the stony outcrops above them.

With years of fighting experience on the Western Front, Major Grant instinctively knew that this was it and signalled the column to halt. The lorries came to a stop, the tailgates slamming down with a clang as T/Cadets debussed rapidly from the vehicles. The ambushers watched as the vehicles suddenly halted and T/Cadets began dismounting from their vehicles, spreading out and moving forward under the cover of the hostages. IRA marksmen from No. 1 Section, overlooking the road, began snapping back the bolts of their rifles, chambering rounds. A number of single shots were fired off in quick succession, the marksmen hitting the advancing T/Cadets, enabling the hostages to gain cover by jumping a fence and disappearing from the fight. Major Grant shouted, 'Take cover.' The Battle of Coolavokig had commenced. Casualties were sustained from the opening seconds of the battle and they mounted rapidly.

Tucking the stock of his machine gun into his shoulder, Volunteer Hugh O'Sullivan took careful aim and squeezed the trigger. The short, staccato bursts of fire forced the advancing T/Cadets to dive for cover. However, the first machine gun had jammed and the other was out of range as the column had stopped short of the kill zone.

A relentless stream of bullets from the riflemen chiselled smoking lines along the stone walls and those taking cover were showered with chips of stone. Rounds were ricocheting off the vehicles as a number of T/Cadets set up their machine gun and returned fire against their attackers. Within minutes both gunner and spotter were hit and the gun knocked out of action. Fierce gun battles between T/Cadets and Volunteer riflemen were taking place up and down the road. The suppressive fire from the insurgent machine guns had hemmed in the column while the rifle fire picked off T/Cadets who failed to get into cover. RIC Constable Arthur Cane, driving the lead vehicle, was struck by enemy fire and mortally wounded.

The Volunteer Lewis gun, manned by Patrick 'Cruxy' O'Connor, an ex-British soldier, had jammed, enabling the car at the rear of the convoy to reverse out of the ambush. The driver gunned the engine as he accelerated away from the gunfire and headed back towards Macroom. The machine gun was to remain out of action for the rest of the battle. The gunfight continued along the road with the Auxiliaries returning fire at their hidden attackers and some T/Cadets attempting to rush the positions occupied by No. 1 Section. This attack was repulsed, the Auxiliaries being forced back onto the road.

Major Grant had alighted from his car and was providing his men with tactical instructions and directing their fire when he was shot through the head. Flesh and brains exited from the back of his skull, his body propelled backwards, crashing to the ground.

The intense and sustained gunfire forced the Auxiliaries to fall back towards the cottages. The T/Cadets zigzagged along the road at a low crouch, taking turns to run and cover. Taking shelter in some small fields east of the cottages, the T/Cadets were prevented from retreating further as an IRA section closed in, pinning them down. The T/Cadets that had reached the sanctuary of the cottages began boring loopholes in the walls and returned fire on their attackers. Wounded officers lay on the road and in the fields, many of them crawling to the cottage doors and begging to be taken in. The firefight increased in intensity as O'Hegarty ordered his men to concentrate their fire on the cottages. A barrage of rifle fire from No. 1 Section was unleashed on the two buildings, enabling No. 2 and No. 3 Sections to advance nearer the road. Within the cottages, spent cartridge cases littered the ground. Bullets tore into the stone walls and ricocheted through the rooms. T/Cadet Cleve Soady suffered a serious stomach wound that would later prove fatal.

The republicans planned to rush the western cottage, outflanking the T/Cadets to the east and encircling their position. At this critical stage in the fight, firing from the cottages became sporadic. O'Hegarty believed that the beleaguered police officers were about to capitulate.

The IRA closed in and, as they were preparing to bomb the cottages, large numbers of RIC and military reinforcements approached from the Macroom Road and began encircling the area. The second touring car that had managed to drive out of the ambush had reached Macroom and had raised the alarm. However, the advancing reinforcements were delayed due to the roadblocks.

O'Hegarty had no option but to break off his attack and, with the blast of his whistle, signalled for his men to fall back. They withdrew in order, section by section, with No. 4 Section fighting a rearguard action as hundreds of British troops attempted to encircle the republican forces. The withdrawal was successfully carried out and the republicans managed to evade capture and escape the net, withdrawing to the north-west of the ambush site.

Thirty-four lorries of reinforcements from Cork, Ballincollig, Bandon, Clonakilty, Millstreet and Macroom descended on the area. Others came from Killarney, Bantry, Skibbereen and Dunmanway, bringing an estimated 600 soldiers to cordon off the district. A plane circled overhead but failed to spot the IRA flying column as it withdrew from the battle.

Nearby, at Coomachloy, members of the flying column took refuge in a local farmhouse and prepared to billet there for the night. However, as they were about to sit down for a meal they heard the distinctive sound of a Crossley Tender approaching. Grabbing their weapons, they exited the house, took up defensive positions and fought a running battle with British soldiers. No. 4 Section arrived on the scene and also engaged the soldiers, who were forced to retreat.

It transpired that the large force of British soldiers were part of an encircling operation over the Muskerry area tasked with eliminating the flying column, and that the Auxiliaries were tasked with pinning down the republicans but had failed to realise the strength or disposition of the force.

In the days that followed, search-and-destroy missions were launched by Crown forces, resulting in the destruction of many local houses and farmsteads suspected of harbouring republican forces involved in the attack.

The battle had lasted four hours. Casualty figures are to this day debated by both sides. British figures state that there were three fatalities while republican forces state that there were between fourteen and sixteen British soldiers and Auxiliaries killed. There were no casualties reported by the IRA.

Major James Seafield Grant's body was repatriated to England and buried at St Peter and St Paul's Parish Church, Aldeburgh, Suffolk. T/Cadet Cleve Soady was buried in Macroom, one of only two Auxiliary officers interred in Ireland.

A British 6th Divisional Area report stated that 'the Collavokig operation was a case where an excellent opportunity of defeating the enemy was missed, owing to bad tactics, and failure to work out a proper plan of operations based on information received'.[5]

British forces had been engaged by a well-trained and well-equipped insurgent group and had failed to kill or capture their attackers. After the ambush and the military's subsequent search operation, British forces ceased raiding and patrolling in the area west of Macroom, effectively handing the area over to IRA control.

The IRA believed that, though Major Grant did not know of the exact location of the ambush, he had been forewarned of the attack. In recent weeks, many republican operations had been compromised and their commanders suspected that there was an informer in their midst. Four weeks earlier, members of the 6th Battalion were surprised by British forces while waiting to ambush a military convoy near Dripsey, about 13 miles west of Cork city, resulting in the capture of five Volunteers who were subsequently executed.

After the Coolavokig ambush, suspicion fell on Patrick 'Cruxy' O'Connor, a decorated former British soldier, who had manned the Lewis gun that had jammed as the battle commenced. Senior officers in the Irish Republican Army believed that, rather than it being an equipment failure, O'Connor had purposely not fired on the Auxiliaries. An after action report by the IRA revealed the failings of the ambush and the witness evidence from the day strongly implicated Cruxy as having informed on the operation. His disappearance from the locality also confirmed his involvement with Crown forces. Republican intelligence agents reported that O'Connor was living in New York and working at Altman's department store. An ASU consisting of Pa Murray, Martin Donovan and Danny Healy was ordered to travel to New York and eliminate O'Connor. On arrival in New York they were assisted by a republican sympathiser named Mullins, who reported O'Connor's routines and the fact that O'Connor may have realised that his life was in danger. On 22 April 1922, the hit squad confronted O'Connor. In an article entitled 'An Irish Vendetta', *The Times* reported:

> Patrick O'Connor, a former soldier of the Irish Republican Army was shot four times last night in a crowded New York Street by an unknown assailant, whom the police believe to a Sinn Féin agent.
>
> Connor [*sic*] was walking down Central Park West last night when a man climbed over the park wall and fired a pistol at him

with the exclamation, 'Now I've got you!' Though hit, O'Connor ran round an electric tramcar filled with passengers in search of shelter. His assailant following in pursuit, firing a second shot which brought the young Irish man to the ground.

As he lay there, the man fired two more shots into his body, then placing the pistol in his pocket fled in the direction of Broadway. A crowd of over 100 people took up the chase but the criminal out distanced them. It is believed that a motor car with confederates was waiting for him at a corner and that he made his escape in this. O'Connor, wounded in the stomach, jaw, right side and back, was carried to hospital where he still lingered today though his life is despaired of.

He is 26 years old, came here a year ago and was employed in one of the leading department stores of Fifth Avenue. His brother stated he had been shadowed for several weeks.[6]

With the death of O'Connor, the final chapter of the Coolavokig Ambush had been closed.

17

Fighting for Your Life
The Clonfin Ambush, 2 February 1921

The blinding flash was followed by a tremendous explosion as the IED detonated under the engine of the lead vehicle. The explosion sucked the oxygen from the air and showered those in the vehicle with grit and stone. The Tender careered out of control across the middle of the road, as smoke and debris ascended into the sky. The driver of the second vehicle hit the brakes and swerved to avoid the crater the bomb had made, and a torrent of gunfire was unleashed from either side of the road. The effect of the withering storm of bullets was immediate and decisive. The two trucks slewed and lurched, finally rolling to a stop as the men on board baled out, seeking what cover they could, either under the vehicle chassis or in some depression along the road. The ADRIC Cadets were engulfed in a hail of small-arms fire that whizzed over their heads, ripped into the dirt and sliced through the vegetation along the hedge line. A desperate gun battle commenced as the muzzle flashes from the IRA's weapons drew return fire. The Auxiliaries took stock of their situation: they had driven into a predetermined kill zone, where the terrain provided little or no cover. Each officer realised they were fighting for their lives.

Formed on 6 August 1920, 'M' Company ADRIC was billeted at the County Infirmary, County Longford. They regularly patrolled and raided in the area and were returning to Longford from Granard on the afternoon of 2 February 1921 when they were attacked. The sixteen T/Cadets were under the command of District Inspector Francis Worthington Craven, a former Lieutenant Commander in the Royal Navy. Craven had been awarded the Distinguished Service Order and American Navy Cross for his seamanship and gallantry during the war when he rescued almost 350 American troops when their ship, HMS *Toronto*, collided in rough seas with one of its escorts.

The patrol was divided between two trucks with the lead vehicle carrying the squad automatic weapon, the Lewis machine gun. The men were armed with Lee Enfield rifles and .45 long-barrelled Webley revolvers. The officers also carried .38 Webley revolvers, hidden inside their tunics. T/Cadet Thomas Jocelyn Wilford, seated in the leading Tender, was later to write: 'We had our fair share of the "crather" [i.e. alcohol] in Granard and this may have accounted for our hilarious rendering of "Swanee" which was cut short in the middle of the second stanza by an explosion.'[1]

That explosion was the signal for the Longford flying column to begin their attack.

Acting on the intelligence that a police patrol travelled daily from Granard, republican Commandant Seán MacEoin had selected the ambush position, midway between Granard and Ballinalee, at a place called Clonfin. His plan was to detonate a mine under the lead vehicle while one of his sections concentrated their firepower on the second truck. His unit took up position at 05:00 hours. He divided his force into four sections, each concealed and tactically positioned alongside the road, providing them with superior fields of fire.

No. 1 Section under the command of Captain M.F. Reynolds was ordered to cover the right flank, from the Granard direction. This unit was to hold up any reinforcements that may come from the direction of Granard. A command post was established by No. 2 Section in an old fort overlooking the road. Captain Seán Duffy and Commandant Seán MacEoin took up position here. This position had a commanding field of fire onto the road and also a view of all the approach roads. Captain Hugh Hourican with No. 3 Section took up position on the opposite side of the road and was in command of the mining party that had laid the explosive device in the road.

Volunteer Paddy Callaghan had constructed the mine that would be detonated via an electrical circuit. The device was placed in a hole sunk in the road and a small trench was cut from the bomb to the firing point in order to conceal the electrical wires. The barrel of a shotgun was procured and buried in the trench with the wiring running through, so that the wires would not get damaged from other vehicular traffic.

As the Volunteers waited in their designated positions, locals supplied them with provisions. By early afternoon, no military or police patrols had driven into the trap. Commandant MacEoin instructed Miss Mulligan, a member of the local Cumann na mBan, to cycle to Granard and get any information about the movement of British forces in or out of the town that day. She returned a short time later and reported that no patrols had moved out from their barracks. The flying column settled back in to wait.

At 14:00 hours, the sound of engines straining with speed reached their ears; two vehicles came down the road and into the kill zone. Commandant Seán MacEoin signalled to his men to prepare for action.

As the two-vehicle convoy passed over a small bridge at the bottom of a slight incline, Volunteer Callaghan pressed the detonation switch, completing the circuit. The mine exploded under the engine of the leading lorry, shattering it and wounding the driver. The senior officer, DI Craven, seated beside the driver, escaped injury. The T/Cadets debussed rapidly from the two trucks, taking up firing positions, using the chassis of the vehicles for concealment.

Every Irish Volunteer facing the road opened fire on the second vehicle in the convoy. There was very little cover and it became obvious to the T/Cadets that the area had been cleared in advance to give an unhindered field of fire. They knew from the sheer volume of fire striking their position that the attackers were numerous and well armed. The machine gunner in the lead vehicle had managed to alight from the truck with the weapon. Lying beside the Crossley Tender, he brought the Lewis gun to bear on MacEoin's position and opened fire. He managed a few short bursts before he was hit. Temporary Cadet C.H. Maddox rushed forward and took control of the weapon. He continued to fire towards the republican command post. The gun soon ran out of ammunition, the extra magazines for the weapon still inside the first vehicle. The concentration of insurgent fire was so great that it was impossible for anyone to retrieve the magazines. The IRA continued their relentless assault, their surprise attack giving them fire superiority over those on the road.

DI Craven stood in the open road, controlling the fire of his men and brandishing two revolvers shouting, 'Where are the bastards?' He was shot in the leg and fell to the ground. As the officer sat up to apply a shell dressing to his wound, he received a fatal gunshot to the neck.

Under intense fire, T/Cadet Wase moved out from cover to treat the wounded. Many T/Cadets fell back towards the bridge, moving through a drainage ditch and then into the River Camlin, which came up to breast level. They fired over the bank, the *zip, zip* of incoming rounds hitting the water around them. T/Cadet Richardson took refuge in the river and, wading under the bridge, decided to make a run for it in order to get help. As he made a break for it, he was hit in the leg but managed to cut across the open country, avoiding further injury and capture. DI Taylor, who was on the road, trying to get to the safety of the ditch, collapsed as he was shot in the chest and stomach. With their ammunition spent, the remaining Auxiliaries decided to surrender.

Commandant MacEoin signalled the ceasefire, and moved down with his section onto the road. He instructed the T/Cadets to lay down their weapons, which they did, ordering his own men to attend to the wounded and collect the surrendered arms and ammunition. Casualties consisted of three T/Cadets killed in action, ten wounded and only two uninjured. Their senior officer would later succumb to his wounds. Republican forces suffered no casualties in the ambush. Captain Seán Duffy was directed to search the T/Cadets, and discovered that each officer carried a concealed revolver. This was a distinct breach of the surrender terms. They tried to explain that they had forgotten about the weapons, but MacEoin ordered further searches of the dead and wounded and found more concealed weapons. The Volunteers were incensed at being deceived and contemplated taking action against their prisoners. MacEoin recalled:

> At this point, one of the Auxiliaries came up, and asked for the officer in charge of our men, stating that his commanding officer wished to speak to him. I asked where he was, and instructed the Auxiliary to take me to him. On the roadside, I found this officer, a man of good physique, bleeding profusely from several wounds. I attempted to staunch some of them, without success. He told me not to trouble as he felt he was gone past medical aid. He then asked me was I the O/C of his attackers to which I replied 'Yes'. He then said, 'I am not worried about myself, but I am anxious about my boys, and want to know what you are going to do with them'. I then explained quickly about the concealed arms, and asked him, if our positions were reversed, what would be the result. He replied, 'is it as bad as that?' I told him 'No, it is not. You have surrendered and are now disarmed. I will treat you as best I can, by attending to your wounded and giving you one lorry to take them to hospital. The unwounded men I will decide about later.[2]

The two commanding officers continued their conversation, exchanging names and previous military experience. The wounded former Royal Navy commander said that MacEoin was a murderer, to which the Irish officer replied:

> Had they remained in the Navy or in England, I would not have had any occasion to shoot them down, that this was our country, that we were the army of the Irish people, acting under proper authority, and that our mission was purely to fight our nation's battle for the independence which was our right. I further stated that, so long as they, an alien force, remained in the country, we would continue to shoot them down, that we were fighting for freedom to govern ourselves only, that the killing by them of any of our people was murder, as they had no right here. To this Craven replied, 'I believe you are right. I wish you success. Be kind

to my fellows and remember your promise.' These were his last words before he expired.[3]

As MacEoin took his leave of the dead officer, a shout came from Captain Seán Duffy who pointed towards the Ballinalee–Longford direction: a truck carrying British reinforcements was coming at high speed towards their position. T/Cadet Richardson, who had managed to escape, had commandeered a motorcar and travelled to Ballinalee where he had raised the alarm.

Commandant MacEoin ordered a squad to engage the truck, forcing the reinforcements to dismount and advance to contact. At the ambush site, the vehicle damaged by the IED explosion was set on fire and the wounded T/Cadets were lifted into the rear of the undamaged Tender. As that vehicle pulled away, the T/Cadets glanced back along the road at the bloodied bodies of their colleagues lying prostrate on the ground. Through the smoke, they could see the pathetic sight of the smoking Tender, pockmarked with bullet holes and heavily spattered in blood.

The remainder of the Irish attacking force was ordered to fall back, and take up position on a hill, slightly north of their original position. As the Volunteers made their way across the fields, a large force of Auxiliaries and Black and Tans attempted to outflank MacEoin's retreating force.

A brief firefight ensued as the Irish engaged the advancing British force. However, with the light failing, Crown forces were forced to call off their attack. MacEoin suffered one non-fatal casualty in this brief skirmish. The flying column regrouped in a nearby wood and took stock of the situation before splitting into smaller groups, which took refuge in a number of local houses where they rested for the night.

Later that month, having given a brief account of the ambush at Clonfin in Parliament, Sir Hamar Greenwood, Chief Secretary of Ireland, retorted to an attack on the Crown's performance, in particular the actions of the Auxiliaries in Ireland.

This is the type of man who won the war for this country, and he is winning the war now in Ireland, and yet the right. hon Member for Paisley made this reference in a speech given to the Liberals at

Cambridge on 7th January: 'After an interlude of barbarism which recalls the worst achievements of both ancient and the modern Hun.' Who are these rivals of the ancient and modern Hun? They are the forces of the Crown in Ireland. There is no question about it.[4]

The Auxiliaries suffered four fatalities during the ambush, DI Francis Worthington Craven, and T/Cadets George Bush, Harold Clayton and John A. Houghton. The wounded – six stretcher cases – were evacuated by special train from Longford to Dublin where they received medical attention at Steevens' Hospital.

Known as the Blacksmith of Ballinalee, MacEoin's exploits had made him a prominent target for Crown forces. In March 1921 he was wounded and captured at Mullingar railway station. The prisoner was escorted to Dublin and held in Mountjoy Prison. A trial by military court was scheduled where the accused would without a doubt face the death sentence. Michael Collins made it a priority that MacEoin was to be got out by any and every means possible. This would lead to one of the most audacious plans ever undertaken by the IRA during the period.

On 14 May 1921, a Peerless armoured car came to a halt outside the gates of Mountjoy Prison in Dublin. 'C'mon, c'mon, for God's sake open the gate.' The driver of the vehicle was impatient. Through the driver's slit, he watched as the wooden gates slowly opened. He gunned the engine and drove forward through the gates into the small, confined space that was sealed ahead by an iron railed gate. The wooden gate closed behind the vehicle before the gate in front creaked open. The armoured car proceeded into this section and waited there until the second section was about to be closed and the third section was to be opened. With a sudden acceleration, the driver sped forward, made a U-turn, reversed slightly and manoeuvred the vehicle so that the inner gates of the jail could not be closed over. (Although this may seem alarming by today's standards, at the time it would have raised few eyebrows: there was a lack of drivers so the British employed former RAF personnel to drive. They knew how to put the car into gear and get it going, but not much more.)

Two men in the attire of British army officers got out of the armoured car and walked across the courtyard towards the building. Their demeanour did not betray the fact that they, as well as those in the armoured car, were members of the Dublin ASU of the IRA and they were in Mountjoy maximum-security prison to extract one of the organisation's most valuable operatives, Seán MacEoin.

Officially opened in March 1850, Mountjoy Prison, on the north side of Dublin city, was constructed along the same design principles as London's Pentonville Prison. There were four wings, A, B, C and D, each with three tiers (A1, A2, A3, B1, etc.) and the wings radiated like a fan off the 'Circle', the central hub of the prison. From this central position, prison warders could monitor the 496 cells. There were twelve punishment cells for solitary confinement, of which nine were daylight cells and three were in darkness. In 1921 political prisoners were incarcerated in C wing of the prison.[5]

Michael Collins, Director of Republican Intelligence, wanted MacEoin out of Mountjoy. He was an important asset in the war against the British government in Ireland. It was known that MacEoin was held in C wing of the prison along with a number of other political prisoners, but getting in and out of a heavily guarded maximum-security prison would be no easy feat. Collins' network of spies began collecting and collating information about warders, the sequence of military patrols, meal times and relief times for police and Auxiliaries, both inside and outside the prison walls. After reviewing a number of options, the only possible chance to spring MacEoin from Mountjoy was to bluff their way in, get the prisoner and hopefully still be able to bluff their way out or, if that failed, to shoot their way out. To gain access to the prison, a plan was devised to hijack a British armoured car, dress the crew as British soldiers and bluff their way into the prison under the pretence of transferring MacEoin to Dublin Castle. IRA intelligence had been informed of an armoured car crew that regularly breached security protocol by emerging from the vehicle and leaving the door unlocked. Article one of Battalion Standing Orders for Armoured Cars in Ireland stated that:

Every officer, NCO, and private soldier must realise that while on patrol he is liable to sudden attack by armed men when least expected, who will endeavour to overpower him and capture his armoured car, and all ranks, when out on duty on the armoured cars, must not relax their vigilance for one moment, and, in the event of any attempt to attack or rush the car, they will deal with it exactly as if on active service, and without hesitation. The loss of an armoured car will always be a court martial offence.[6]

Early every morning, a British Peerless armoured car accompanied a number of lorries to the Dublin Corporation abattoir on Aughrim Street off the North Circular Road to collect a supply of meat for the Royal Barracks. The military killed their own cattle before loading the meat into the lorries for the return journey. It was noticed that the crew of the armoured car, who were meant to stay inside the vehicle, got restless and were in the habit of leaving the car to talk to fellow soldiers or to go for a cigarette. A recce was conducted and a report submitted to Collins stated that it would be possible to take out the crew and hijack the vehicle. The operation was given the go-ahead.

The man chosen to lead this daring mission was Emmet Dalton, a former British soldier who had served during the Great War and was now part of the Irish Republican Army. Dalton, a recipient of the Military Cross, was considered a dynamic individual capable of handling himself and the job in hand.

The ASU was to seize the armoured car at the abattoir, don the crew's uniforms and proceed towards Mountjoy Prison. MacEoin, who had been informed of an escape attempt, was to get himself into the governor's office at the allotted time and prepare for the arrival of the armoured car. The two operatives would enter the governor's office and serve a bogus Prisoner's Removal Order on the jail authorities. MacEoin would be escorted to the car and they would drive out the same way they had driven in. A small wicket gate in the main gate would be opened on the ruse of letting in visitors to the prison and this gate would be held open, at gunpoint if necessary. Volunteers would then secure this gate enabling the car to exit. While the operation had been planned meticulously by the IRA, they failed to take into account the presence of Auxiliaries within the prison.

'O' Company of the ADRIC, formed in January 1921, had taken up security duties within the prison after a number of escapes had been orchestrated from Mountjoy during the early months of 1921. The authorities believed that some of the prison staff might have colluded with the IRA in assisting these escapes. Security was overhauled and now platoons of Auxiliaries were stationed in the prison and worked shifts alongside the prison warders. Barbed-wire entanglements and machine-gun posts complemented the inside perimeter while outside, the DMP, supported by the British military, patrolled the streets around the prison. Since political prisoners had been incarcerated at Mountjoy, a number of vigils by republican sympathisers had been held in the vicinity, threatening security by the large numbers they attracted. The Cadets within the walls of the prison implemented a stricter regime than the prison officers. Guards were posted at key points throughout the building and sentries patrolled the corridors. The increased security would hinder those trying to get out or in to the prison.

Having seized the armoured car, Dalton and his unit continued their journey to Phibsboro and Mountjoy Prison where they gained entry to the complex.

Once the vehicle was parked in the prison yard, Dalton and Joe Leonard, both dressed as British officers, alighted and entered the prison. The Cadets on duty in the yard were suspicious of the vehicle and how it had parked in the courtyard, blocking the gates.

From the yard, the crew of the armoured car could see Auxiliaries moving around inside the building. In the governor's office, Dalton and Leonard found the Governor, his deputy and the prison medical officer, Dr Hackett, but, to their surprise, there was no sign of MacEoin.

Dalton stated his mission and handed over the typed prisoner-transfer document. The governor of the prison, suspicious of the document and wanting to verify the orders, attempted to telephone Dublin Castle for confirmation. As he lifted the receiver, Leonard sprang forward and knocked the instrument from the official's grasp and held up the staff at gun point. The pair then disconnected the phone and prepared to search for MacEoin.[7]

Unknown to Dalton and Leonard, however, the Auxiliaries had implemented a new system. The officer in charge had ordered a lockdown of C wing that morning and insisted that every prisoner be held in his cell. The officer and his picquet then went to each cell and interviewed the prisoners where notes were taken for identification purposes. This delayed MacEoin's visit to the Governor's office and with the lockdown and shift changeover, the building was full of heavily armed Auxiliaries. Gunfire erupted near the main gate. An alarm rang and the sound of guards running echoed through the building. The plan for holding the main gate open had been foiled.

A small IRA unit had managed to distract and overpower the warder at the wicket gate, enabling the main gate to be opened but a Cadet noticed the group rushing the gate and opened fire, wounding one attacker and raising the alarm. A gun battle ensued between those at the gate and Cadets within the compound. Inside the building, as the alarm bell sounded, Dalton and Leonard abandoned the plan to rescue MacEoin. A squad of Auxiliaries attempted to cut off their retreat but Dalton opened fire, forcing them to retire. A machine gun chattered from the roof as the men rushed back to the armoured car. Several rounds hit the vehicle as the men clambered in. Auxiliaries had taken up positions on the roof and were firing down into the courtyard with rifles and machine guns.

The vehicle drove at speed out through the gates with bullets ricocheting off the car as it careered out onto the road. The group managed to get out of the area before the streets surrounding the prison filled with soldiers. Checkpoints were erected, sealing off the area but Dalton and his group had managed to slip away. The armoured car was later discovered by the authorities in Clontarf where, with the engine overheating, the IRA were forced to abandon it.

On 14 June 1921, MacEoin was tried by court martial and, as expected, was sentenced to death. By this time secret truce negotiations had been under way between the IRA and the British government and one of Michael Collins' terms was that MacEoin be released, which was duly granted by the government.

The attempted escape from Mountjoy Prison was deemed a propaganda coup for the republicans. It was reported across the world, with *The Times* describing the attempted rescue as 'the most daring coup yet effected by Republicans in Dublin'.[8]

While General Macready was forced to review army security, 'O' Company ADRIC had, by tightening security and implementing new measures in Mountjoy Prison, thwarted one of the most daring escapes from an Irish prison in history.

At his court martial in June, three of the Auxiliaries involved in the battle at Clonfin paid tribute to Seán MacEoin for his actions after the battle and he was eventually released under the terms of the truce that came into effect in July 1921.

18

Close-quarter Battle
Urban Combat

Though the Auxiliary Cadets engaged a tough enemy in perilous skirmishes and ambushes in the rugged mountains and countryside, they also fought close-quarter battles with their opponents on city streets. One such battle became known as the Battle of Brunswick Street.

On the evening of 14 March 1921, an IRA Active Service Unit was detailed by their commanding officer, Captain Peadar O'Meara, to attack police and military targets within Dublin city. This action was in retaliation for the execution by Crown forces of six IRA Volunteers, captured in an ambush in Drumcondra two months previously. Bernard Ryan, Thomas Whelan, Patrick Moran, Thomas Bryan, Patrick Doyle and Frank Flood had been tried by a military court, found guilty and sentenced to death.

The men had been hanged and as the news of the executions broke, the Labour movement called a half-day general strike in the city. Many people took part in a day of mourning, with republican forces ensuring that shops and businesses were closed as a mark of respect. British authorities had expected a backlash and patrolled the streets in force as the 21:00 hour curfew came into effect.

An estimated 38 Volunteers, armed with revolvers, automatics and hand grenades, combed the streets looking for suitable targets. Volunteer Seán Dolan's pocket bulged where he held on tightly to a Mills grenade. A weapon of war, the Mills bomb was designed to fragment when exploded, forcing shrapnel up and out, causing destruction, death and injury. Dolan took the bomb from his pocket, pulled the pin and threw the device at the window of College Green Police Station. However, the missile rebounded off the window and came back at Dolan. The bomb exploded, severing his leg. He was taken to Mercer's Hospital where he received medical treatment before being extracted from the building by the IRA as the authorities were searching for a wounded Volunteer. A nurse had alerted the police when she discovered shrapnel in the wound but a cleaning lady overheard her phone call and contacted the IRA before the security forces arrived at the hospital.

'F' Company ADRIC based in Dublin Castle received a call to investigate the explosion. A Rolls-Royce armoured car and two Tenders with sixteen T/Cadets left the Castle yard, their target being the local IRA headquarters of the 3rd Battalion, at St Andrew's Catholic Club, 144 Great Brunswick Street (now Pearse Street). They had received information that insurgents were located within the building.[1] The IRA had a number of operatives providing overwatch on the building and also had a number of men patrolling the area.

A newspaper report from 15 March 1921 described the incident:

> Additional particulars of the fight which took place in Dublin last night between a large number of armed civilians and a party of Auxiliary police show that it was a very desperate affair. It occurred near the Carnegie Library in Great Brunswick Street, which stretches from College Street to the bridge at Ringsend.
>
> When the battle was opened in the Ringsend portion of it, a bomb was exploded at the city end near the college police station and a man's leg was blown off. The explosion diverted the attention of the police and military for a time and it was only when the injured man had been taken to a hospital that the fight at Ringsend became known. Later in the night it was learned that three civilians had been killed, several others wounded, and two

men taken prisoner. Five of the T/Cadets were wounded. One of them, Section Leader O'Farrell, died soon afterwards and Section Leader Beard is so seriously injured that his recovery is doubtful.

To-day the following official report was issued in Dublin: 'Fire was opened on the auxiliaries from four points in the street as well as from a group of men outside St. Andrew's Catholic Club. The driver of the leading lorry, with great presence of mind and without waiting to draw his revolver, drove his car straight at a group of attackers on the street, thus enabling the Cadets to dismount at close quarters on their assailants and rush among them. A hand-to-hand struggle ensued. An officer from an armoured car, having emptied both his revolvers at his assailants, found himself attacked by a civilian who was firing shot after shot at him from a large automatic pistol. Unable to reload, the officer seized the man by the legs, threw him to the ground and made him prisoner. By this time there were five of the attackers lying dead or wounded on the street as well as two cadets seriously wounded and three slightly wounded. Bursts of machine gun fire were maintained from the armoured car on the attackers wherever they could be seen. All four tyres of the car were very cut by the attacker's bullets.

Later several isolated conflicts took place between cadets and civilians who were firing from street corners and from windows of houses. While cadets were standing by their wounded, protecting them from further attack, armed civilians took the opportunity of removing a number of their casualties. Long trails of blood were found afterwards on the streets and side walks indicating the routes on which the dead and wounded had been dragged to places of concealment. Inside St. Andrew's Catholic Club a handbag was found later containing four revolvers and two bombs as well as several bags of revolver ammunition carefully packed and folded in oil rags. The unwounded prisoner told one of his captors that he had taken part in the attack because he had been told he would be shot if he did not.[2]

At his trial, Thomas Traynor, a father of ten and originally from Tullow, County Carlow, stated that he was not an active Volunteer and was only in the vicinity of Brunswick Street as he had been ordered to deliver the weapon he had been caught in possession of. He was tried by military court martial and found guilty of the death of T/Cadet O'Farrell. He was sentenced to death and hanged in Mountjoy Prison on 25 April 1921. Joseph Donnolly, aged seventeen, who was also taken prisoner on that day, was treated for a number of gunshot wounds and held in Mountjoy Prison awaiting sentence. However, the July truce intervened and he was released.

Three civilians were killed in the gun battle. Thomas Asquith, a 68-year-old caretaker, and David Kelly, a prominent Sinn Féin activist and director of the Sinn Féin bank, were both shot dead. Stephen Clarke was a 22-year-old former soldier who was believed to have tipped off the police to the location of the IRA headquarters in Great Brunswick Street.[3]

In total, thirteen people died in Dublin city on 14 March 1921, making it one of the bloodiest days of the Irish War for Independence. They consisted of the six men executed within Mountjoy Prison, two Volunteers killed in action on Brunswick Street, two Auxiliary Cadets killed in the same battle and three civilians caught in the crossfire.

The tally of that March day was not a deterrent and both sides continued their operations and counter-operations with the death toll steadily mounting in the days, weeks and months that followed.

19

Gunned Down
Killings on the Streets

The prisoner escort was a routine assignment. T/Cadets Ernest Bolan and John Bales of 'P' Company ADRIC, stationed at Corofin in County Sligo, would transfer their prisoner from Sligo to Crumlin Road Gaol in Belfast. Though routine, the job would break the monotony of patrolling. Also, Belfast was a popular place with army and police personnel for R & R.

T/Cadet Bales had only recently enlisted in the ADRIC, having served during the Great War in the Norfolk Yeomanry, later transferring to the Royal Flying Corps. Bolan had held the rank of captain during the war and had served in the King's Liverpool Regiment and the Chinese Labour Corps. He had enlisted in the ADRIC in January of 1921.[1]

The train journey was uneventful and on arrival in Belfast, they made their way to Crumlin Road where they signed over their prisoner. As they prepared to return to Sligo, the two men were informed that their return journey was to be delayed owing to the derailment of a train at Glaslough.

This delay, though only for a few hours, would mean that the T/Cadets would be stranded in Belfast and would have to stay overnight at Musgrave Street RIC Barracks, Belfast. Both officers decided to walk into the town to kill some time.

Within the city there were a number of Auxiliaries from another Company, sent to Belfast to collect new transport vehicles. Their distinctive uniform and cap made them stand out from regular soldiers or members of the RIC. Their presence in Belfast was noticed by an ASU of the Irish Republican Army whose O/C, Roger McCorley, addressed his unit, saying they must get in the first blow and 'that we must carry the fight to the enemy at the very first opportunity even at the risk of our lives'.[2] The unit walked the streets, a radius of a mile in each direction, seeking out targets. However, the going was slow as it was the weekend: thousands of Saturday shoppers thronged the streets making the identification and apprehension of potential targets difficult.

> On the 24th April, which was a Saturday, about three o'clock in the afternoon we located five Auxiliaries in the centre of the city. There were only five members of the A.S.U. available at the time – McCorley, Woods, Heron, Murray and myself [Seamus McKenna]. We followed them around the city in the hope that they would break up and that we would thus have an opportunity of attacking two or three of them. They did not do so, however, but continued close together. In fact, when three of them went into the G.P.O. on business, the other two remained outside at the door. We were undecided as to whether to attack these two, or not, but finally ruled against it. We followed them eventually to where they were staying, the Prince of Wales Hotel in Victoria Street.[3]

The ASU kept the hotel under observation but could not decide whether to attack this group or seek out others. An additional unit, armed with revolvers and grenades, would be needed to attack those residents in the hotel. The plan was to find other Auxiliaries on the street and by launching an attack on them to lure the others out of the hotel. However, raising more men would take time. Some of the unit moved off and once again began searching for targets.

T/Cadets Bolan and Bales were walking from the Great Northern Railway Station along Donegall Place when they were spotted. The gunmen shadowed the Auxiliaries in the hope that they would wander into a less-crowded area but the T/Cadets kept to the thoroughfare and did not deviate from the route. With some of the IRA party providing overwatch, Roger McCorley and Seamus Woods approached the officers from behind. They drew their revolvers and opened fire, the echoing gunshots sending hundreds of shoppers fleeing for their lives.[4]

Both men were shot at point-blank range; T/Cadet Bolan was hit in the left side and died immediately. T/Cadet Bales was hit under the left arm and collapsed to the ground, mortally wounded. The IRA unit made their escape amongst the panicked pedestrians who scattered in all directions in an attempt to escape the gunfire. A detective constable of the RIC engaged the attackers and opened fire with an automatic pistol. Some pedestrians attempted to intercept the attackers; two civilians were wounded by shots aimed at the insurgents. Within minutes the area was flooded with soldiers and police who set up a cordon and began a systematic search of people and vehicles in the area. An official police statement read: 'Two temporary Cadets in the Auxiliary Division of the R.I.C. from Sligo were fired at by two men armed with revolvers at Donegall Place, Belfast at 9.15 on Saturday night. One Cadet is dead and the other dangerously wounded in the body. Two civilians named Ruth Galston (44) and Thomas Kennedy (33) were wounded by the fire. There were no arrests.'[5]

The gunmen evaded arrest, having made their escape via Fountain Lane. An IRA unit was near the hotel when the shooting took place but they were not in position to attack when the Auxiliaries came rushing out of the hotel to investigate the gunfire. The republicans withdrew from the scene, leaving the police and military to patrol the streets and seek retribution.

Later that night, two brothers, Patrick and Daniel Duffin, were both shot dead by unknown assailants. It was believed at the time that the brothers were shot as a reprisal for the deaths of the two T/Cadets because Daniel Duffin held the rank of Company Quartermaster of 'B' Company IRA.

On the following day, the Auxiliaries stationed at the Prince of Wales Hotel pulled out and returned to their area of operations.

While many Auxiliaries were killed or injured in ambushes, others were singled out for assassination. On 24 June 1921, Section Leader Leonard Appleford and T/Cadet George Gerald Warnes of 'F' Company had afternoon tea in a restaurant on Grafton Street in Dublin. The two cadets had obtained leave to go shopping and, having finished afternoon tea, were in the fashionable and busy thoroughfare of Grafton Street. As they neared the junction of Chatham Street, a young girl dressed in a dark blue tailor-made costume walked adjacent to the officers and on nearing a group of men shouted, 'There they are,' and pointed out the two officers. She disappeared into the crowd as the two cadets were surrounded and shot from behind. As they lay on the ground, further shots were fired into their bodies. The attackers then made their escape into the side streets.[6]

The IRA operation intended to enclose Grafton Street and shoot any members of the Crown forces that were in the vicinity. The intention went so far as to kill any male fashionably dressed and believed to be an enemy agent. The T/Cadets had been recognised from a marked photograph supplied to republican intelligence by the paid informer and 'F' Company Auxiliary Cadet, Sergeant Reynolds.[7]

Two days later, on 26 June, IRA operatives entered the Mayfair Hotel, Lower Baggot Street, Dublin. Their targets were two off-duty T/Cadets, Platoon Commander William Hunt and Section Leader F. White. Years later, Volunteer James Tully wrote about the operation:

> In June 1921, we were detailed to shoot two Auxiliaries who were staying in the Mayfair Hotel, Baggot Street. The party consisted of Paddy O'Connor, Michael Stack, Peter Larkin, Jack Hanlon, Jim O'Neill and myself. My job was to dismantle the telephone. At about 6.30 on a Sunday evening we entered the hotel. The two Auxiliaries with two women and a child were in a room. O'Connor, Stack, Larkin and O'Toole pushed open the door of the room and fired, killing the two Auxiliaries. O'Connor took their guns. O'Neill was to have the car running in Fitzwilliam

Street to take the guns away. When I came out I put my gun in the car. O'Neill could not get the car started so it had to be abandoned and I lost my gun. The others, living the area, had taken their guns with them.[8]

Unknown to his assassins, T/Cadet White survived the deadly attack but Hunt became one of the many officers killed while on service in Ireland. It is estimated that 60 men of the ADRIC died during the War of Independence, which shows how they managed to survive in a hostile environment. Of these, 44 were killed by the IRA while the others died of suicide or natural causes.

20

Operation Quayside
Attack on 'Q' Company's HQ, April 1921

At 08:00 hours on Monday 11 April 1921, the still morning air was shattered by the sound of gunfire and explosions as the T/Cadets stationed at the red bricked London & North Western Railway Hotel (LNWR) in Dublin came under attack.

Located on the north side of the River Liffey at the North Wall, the LNWR became the operational base for 'Q' Company ADRIC on 21 March 1921. The building gave them an almost impregnable command post from which to launch their operations. Made up of ex-naval, merchant marine and ex-military personnel, 'Q' Company carried out dock and harbour security in order to detect and prevent the shipment of arms and ammunition into the country. It was also tasked with intercepting and capturing insurgents entering or leaving the country via sea transports.

Republican quartermasters were suffering from a lack of arms and ammunition and recent raids by the authorities had captured large supplies of munitions throughout the country. The importation of weapons and ammunition had been severely curtailed since 'Q' Company had taken up position along the quays.

'Q' Company and other Auxiliaries pose for photos after the attack on their base at the London & North Western Railway Hotel, Dublin, 11 April 1921. (National Library of Ireland)

As shift work was about to commence on the docks on 11 April 1921, members of the IRA's 'E' Company, supported by elements of the 2nd Battalion of the Dublin Brigade IRA, under the command of Tom Ennis, mingled with workers as they made their way along the quays. They broke off from the groups of workmen and took up their positions.

Ennis divided his assault force into four groups, each in turn to provide cover while the other advanced to contact. A group of six men would neutralise the sentries guarding the perimeter, enabling a platoon-sized assault on the front and sides of the hotel using grenades and incendiaries. A third group would press home the attack and place a mine in the entrance hall in order to destroy the building. Three squads would be detailed to provide covering fire from surrounding buildings.

The escape plan was for the insurgents simply to go to their places of employment or residence.

The squads covering the attack were armed with rifles while the assault teams carried revolvers, automatics and grenades. While the explosive devices consisted of incendiary and shrapnel bombs, the IRA also carried a new type of weapon. Munitions supplier Volunteer James L. O'Donovan later wrote: 'There were also particular compositions made up for certain jobs; one of these that I remember was quantities of a solution of Phosphorus in Carbon bi-Sulphide. This was packed in small bottles of grenade size, and was used in the attack on the L.N.S. premises [sic] on the North Wall, at that time an enemy outpost.'[1] The use of chemical weapons in the form of gas grenades was innovative for the time.

The fire brigade at Tara Street station was to be held up to prevent it answering any call to the North Wall. Other units would provide overwatch, isolating the target from Spencer Dock, the bridges at the North Wall and Sheriff Street, and Newcomen and Annesley Bridges on the North Strand and East Wall Road respectively. Monday was chosen because it was the only day that no passenger ship was docking at the LNWR landing berth, thereby reducing the number of civilians in the area. Zero hour was 08:00 hours.

Within the hotel, many of the T/Cadets from 'Q' Company had just come off duty, having spent the night patrolling and searching ships that had docked. Some had gone to bed while others relaxed, drank and played cards. Though the building had not been put in a state of defence, a sentry patrolled the perimeter.

A barrage of gunfire erupted at the front of the hotel, hitting and wounding T/Cadet Gerald Alfred Body. Crowds of people on their way to work stampeded along the quays as bullets cut through the air. Body staggered back through the tumult of fire into the hotel. Once inside, he raised the alarm. Shouts of 'Stand to' echoed throughout the building. T/Cadets grabbed their weapons and rushed to the windows, taking up firing positions. Others scaled the staircases and made their way onto the roof, where the tops of the surrounding warehouses and buildings seemed to be alive with enemy fire. Scanning for targets,

Auxiliaries from 'Q' Company clearing up after the attack on their headquarters at the London & North Western Railway Hotel. (National Library of Ireland)

they located enemy positions and engaged. Inside, T/Cadets broke the window panes and opened fire onto the streets below. The Auxiliaries throughout the building soon recovered from their surprise and fought hard to eliminate the enemy's positions.

The main assault teams took cover behind barrels along the quayside, which they then rolled in front of them as they advanced towards the building. When they were within a certain distance, they hurled grenades through the windows. As Volunteer Peter Freyne attempted to lob a bomb, he was shot through the head and killed instantly. A group managed to make their way to the door where they placed the mine and withdrew. The device, like many of the others, failed to detonate.

Within the building, T/Cadets desperately pushed charging clips of five rounds into the magazine wells of their rifles, closed the bolts and, squeezing the triggers, opened fire. Shells casings soon littered the floor as the men moved from window to window, replying to the fire being directed at the building. As 'Q' Company commander, former Major T.P. Ryan, descended the staircase towards the lobby of the hotel, a grenade came through the window, knocking off his cap. The device, however, failed to detonate. Clouds of dust, plaster and gun smoke filled the interior. However, some of the devices did explode, sending noxious smoke wafting through the interior. T/Cadets gasped as they covered their mouths and noses to prevent inhalation of the gas. Faced with being gassed to death or being shot, the Auxiliaries decided to take the fight outside. Under a withering barrage of bullets from enemy small-arms and rifle fire, the Auxies pushed out from the hotel, many of them dressed only in their night attire, firing their weapons. Above their heads, bullets cracked into the hotel walls. The gun teams on the roof kept up a steady stream of fire against the IRA fighting positions.

A sharp whistle blast cut through the cacophony of weapons fire, the signal for the insurgents to break off the engagement. The attackers' fire slackened as the IRA unit broke off their attack, going to ground and breaking up into small groups. In order to cut off any pursuit, the IRA implemented their plan to raise the swing bridges.

Volunteer Gary Holohan was detailed to operate the electric bridge over Spencer Dock. By lifting it, British reinforcements would be prevented from assisting those in the hotel. He recalled:

> I had no key of the cabin, but I entered through a trapdoor I knew was in the floor. We opened one side of the bridge and had the outside gates closed when they started bombing. I went to open the other side, but it would not rise and had to be unlocked by hand. As I turned to do this I nearly fell thirty feet to the ground through the trapdoor. I took all the electric fuses and dumped them into the gully in the street. This had the desired effect, because when the soldiers found the gate shut they were afraid to cross the bridge, as they thought it was mined and they had to have it examined underneath.[2]

Operatives scattered in a number of directions, running through the railway yards pursued by small groups of Auxiliaries. Gun battles erupted in the streets as the insurgents made their escape towards the city or across the Grand Canal. Sweeping through the battle site, the Auxiliaries discovered empty firing positions, brass casings and bloodstains on the ground.

Despite the intensity of the attack, the Auxiliaries had managed to fight off the assault, suffering only one casualty, T/Cadet Body. The IRA had one operative killed in action, while two civilians, Thomas Walsh and James Shaw, were wounded in the crossfire. The entire engagement had lasted twenty minutes.

21

Kill Zone
The Rathcoole Ambush, 16 June 1921

Paddy Byrne, Operations Officer of Cork No. 2 Brigade, Irish Republican Army, opened his pocket watch and looked patiently as the hands approached 18:00 hours. The Auxiliary convoy, 'L' Company, stationed in Rathcoole, County Cork, would be on its return journey and would enter the kill zone within the next 30 minutes.

The railway line west of Banteer station had been rendered impassable a few weeks before, with the burning of the bridge over the River Finnow. The Auxiliaries were now forced to collect their supplies at Banteer railway station. Alternate supply routes were few and with many local businesses boycotting the police and military, the only way to obtain supplies was by road. Though this method made convoys vulnerable to attack, it was, in many cases, the only way rural units could obtain food and fuel.

An IRA observation post was established in Rathcoole Wood and the route was kept under observation for twelve days, revealing that the T/Cadets travelled from their operations base at Mount Leader House in an armed convoy to Banteer via Rathcoole three days one week, two days the next. They made the trip between 11:00 hours and 15:00 hours, making two round trips on Tuesdays: between 09:30 hours

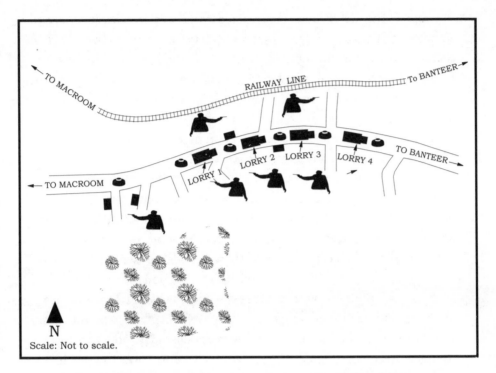

RATHCOOLE AMBUSH AREA 16 JUNE 1921.

and 11:00 hours and then again between 16:30 hours and 18:30 hours. The only anomaly was the strength of the convoys. The most vulnerable consisted of two Tenders with two sections while other convoys were of platoon strength and consisted of Crossley Tenders covered in wire netting and accompanied by armoured Lancias. The vehicles travelled 400 yards apart. The group carried the usual weapons – rifles, revolvers and grenades – but some T/Cadets carried the squad automatic weapon, the Lewis machine gun, giving them a rate of fire equivalent to that of an armoured car.

In order to ambush the convoy and take out the armoured vehicles, especially the Lancia, the insurgents planted a number of IEDs along the route. The IEDs were constructed from cast-iron casings, sealed at both ends by steel plates that were held in position by a ½-inch bolt which passed through the casing. A number of bomb-making factories had been established across Ireland making IED components. Mines were charged with war flour, a home-made explosive substance manufactured by republican bomb makers.

The site chosen for the ambush was on high ground overlooking the Millstreet–Banteer road below the wood, about a mile to the west of Rathcoole. Paddy Byrne assembled his men in Rathcoole Wood. This forest covered several acres and was positioned some 500 yards south of the road. It occupied a slightly elevated position and protected the assembling Volunteers from aircraft and ground observation while enabling them to keep the ambush site under observation. Byrne's force consisted of 140 men divided into 10 sections in which he had 61 riflemen, 50 armed with shotguns, a Hotchkiss machine-gun team of three, and 14 armed engineers who were in charge of the seven landmines. Four battalion staff officers, six signallers and two medics completed the strike force. Eight sections were to cover the south side of the road and the remaining two were located on the north side. Each section was detailed to cover a mine, six on the southern and one, at Drishane Beg, on the northern side. The eastern and western flanks were protected by two squads of five riflemen. Local Volunteers, who knew the ground, were dispersed amongst the various sections in order to coordinate the withdrawal after the ambush. Another group was tasked with erecting barricades on the roads leading to the ambush site as soon as the firing commenced, sealing off the area of operations.

At dawn on 16 June 1921, a practice run of action stations took place. The men took up their posts. Lines of retreat from each position towards the wood were given to the various sections. After the ambush, each section was to retire in order, using three ravines or dried watercourses that ran from the road to the forest as cover. This method of withdrawal provided cover from the road.

The engineers laid the IEDs and with scouts posted for protection purposes, the insurgents withdrew to the nearby forest, where Byrne briefed his section leaders on the plan of attack.

Mines to be numbered one to seven, from west to east. The enemy to be unmolested on the outward journey to Banteer. If this journey took place before 11.00 a.m. – it would indicate a repeat trip in the late afternoon, in which case the attack would be delayed till the homeward journey then. The rear lorry to be attacked first, the mines being so placed that there was little danger of the first lorry being clear of the mined zone by then. A close-up attack would not be practicable and it was explained that the possibility of capturing enemy equipment was slight, and that our main object was to inflict what casualties we could and get away under cover with the least possible loss. Attacking posts were at points varying from forty to one hundred and forty yards from the mines.[1]

Each section was to isolate an enemy lorry, with a view to preventing the Auxiliaries from acting as a cohesive and coordinated force. Throughout the day, the Volunteers rested up under the cover of the wood with local people supplying them with food and tea.

At 16:30 hours the Auxiliaries passed the positions on their outward journey. The convoy consisted of three Tenders and an armoured Lancia, with an estimated 40 T/Cadets. The sections moved into position and prepared for action. At 18:00 hours the supply convoy was sighted and O'Byrne signalled to his men to make ready.

As the last lorry of the four-vehicle convoy crossed over the IED at the eastern end of the ambush site, the engineer detonated the mine. Clouds of dust and debris ascended into the air, momentarily obscuring the vehicle and road. The IRA opened up with rifles and a machine gun from their concealed positions.

The sound of explosions, gunfire and shouting shattered the eerie calm of the summer evening. The T/Cadets who had not been thrown out of the Tender with the force of the explosion took up firing positions in and around the truck. The other three vehicles stopped and the Lancia's driver made a three-point turn in order go back and provide cover for the damaged vehicle. As it drove back another mine was detonated, knocking the Lancia out of action. T/Cadets tumbled from the stricken vehicles, their eardrums ringing from the blast, coughing and gagging on the smell of the explosives and dust that enveloped the road.

The remaining two lorries had stopped between mines so that the mines at the eastern and western ends were the only ones to be exploded to any effect. However, the other two vehicles were trapped in the middle. The IRA had not taken into account the soft, boggy foundation of the road: the soft subsoil absorbed part of the blasts so that the explosions only disabled the vehicles, instead of destroying them and their occupants.[2]

The weight of the incoming fire pinned the Auxiliaries down. Enemy contact was coming from their left and right flanks. Under heavy fire, the T/Cadets tried to determine how many insurgents there were and where they were positioned. The staccato hammering of the ricocheting bullets from the republican Hotchkiss machine gun stopped abruptly as the weapon jammed. This gave the Auxiliaries time to consolidate their precarious position. Many had taken up firing positions in and around their vehicles and though they could not see their attackers, they could hear the pop and splutter of small-arms fire coming from the hillside above them. Two Auxiliaries in the third truck mounted their Lewis machine gun on the side of the vehicle, racked back the bolt and opened fire. Pan after pan of ammunition was discharged at the republican positions. Insurgents attempting to move forward and engage the Auxiliaries were forced to fall back with the intensity of the fire from the Lewis machine gun. T/Cadets taking cover under the trucks racked back the slides of their rifles, chambering rounds and squeezed off shots in an attempt to eliminate enemy shooters. However, the IRA's concealed and well-fortified positions made this difficult. In an attempt to outflank the ambushers, a squad of Auxiliaries jumped up and dashed towards the side of the road. As they ran, another IED was detonated, catching them in the blast. As the smoke cleared, the dead and injured lay where they had fallen, a crumpled heap of charred bodies and broken weapons.

Another Lewis gun was brought into action by the T/Cadets, its withering fire enabling W.E. Crossey, a former lieutenant with the

X regiment, to move up the road at a crouch and take stock of the situation. He realised that the convoy was hemmed in on both sides and that the roads leading in and out of the ambush site were barricaded. He watched as his men returned fire on their attackers while trying to treat the wounded. The suppressive fire from the two Lewis guns had prevented his position from being overrun. The T/Cadets, though shaken by the initial attack, had reacted rapidly and aggressively to the situation. Using the vehicles as cover, they set up dominating fields of fire that gave them control of the space on either side of the road. By fighting together, this strong line of aggressive fire prevented them from being wiped out. A number of insurgents attempted to outflank the Auxiliaries but they were beaten back by the beleaguered T/Cadets.

At the blast of a whistle, republican forces broke off their attacks and fell back, their supply of ammunition expended. They had entered the fight with 40 rounds of .303 per rifle and 250 rounds for the Hotchkiss machine gun. Section leaders directed the men to fall back to the wood, using the ravines as covered routes of retreat. While all the southern sections assembled in the wood, the northern sections withdrew across the River Blackwater to safety. A British airplane was flying near the site but all republican units managed to evade being spotted and withdrew successfully. The firefight had lasted an estimated 50 minutes with no casualties on the republican side and two T/Cadets killed in action with 14 wounded.

The commanding officer of 'L' Company, W.E. Crossey, submitted an After Action Report to his superiors on the day's action:

> 'L' COMPANY AUXILIARY DIVISION, R.I.C. Report on ambush of 'L' Coy: by armed rebels at RATHCOOLE Co. CORK on the 16th instant.
>
> It is my painful duty to report the facts covering the above ambush, in which this unit was trapped on the above mentioned date. At 19.00 hours a convoy was at Banteer station, in order to meet a party returning from Cork, a batch of recruits and the 'runner' returning from Dublin. Thus convoy consisted of 2 open Crossley tenders, 1 armoured Crossley and 1 armoured Lancia with 25 personnel of

the Company. While on column of route the armoured Lancia was leading. The convoy left Banteer and when about four miles from Banteer and half a mile from Rathcoole bridge, it stopped. A reconnoitring party (acting on previous information) left the tenders and proceeded to skirmish the immediate vicinity of the road, to a depth of 400 yards on the left and right flanks. Nothing of importance or of a suspicious character was discovered during the operation. After this, the convoy proceeded over Rathcoole bridge on its homeward journey. When approximately half a mile beyond the bridge, previously referred to and on the Millstreet side of it, the ambush was first encountered. Here, I might point out for your information, in this ambush, the rebels had adopted an entirely new method of attack. Namely, they allowed the 1st, 2nd and 3rd cars to proceed and then exploded an electrically controlled land mine underneath the rear car.

Almost simultaneously with the mining of the rear car, the second leading car was blown up. The leading car (the armoured Lancia) being blown up last of all. The occupants of this vehicle (including myself) on hearing the explosions in the rear were practically blown out of it, when the last mine of all was fired, i.e. after the car had been turned round, in order to go to the assistance of the rest of the convoy.

Therefore it will be easily seen that the only car to escape being mined was the third in column of route. I may say that these mines were timed with the utmost precision. As soon as the mines had been fired, a heavy and concentrated fire was opened up by the insurgents, along a front of ¾ to 1 mile in length. The fire was notably heaviest, from the direction of the thickly wooded hills on our left. A fairly concentrated fire was also opened up from the railway embankment on our right. The range when the attack first commenced, was between two and three hundred yards and gradually increased to about 700 when the fight ended. I should roughly estimate that the strength of the attackers was about 300. From the foregoing it will be easily seen that my party, badly shaken as it was by the explosions, was at a very grave disadvantage to the rebels occupied a position of great natural strength and it was utterly impossible to locate them.

I believe however the rebels sustained severe casualties judging from screams and groans heard coming from their directions. I cannot speak too highly of the way in which my party behaved, out-manoeuvred as they were by twelve to one not overlooking the fact that at the commencement of the action the occupants of each car had to fight as detached groups, until such time as they were able to concentrate. During the whole of the engagement, the discipline of the Cadets was perfect. There was not the slightest sign of panic or nerves as might easily have occurred, owing to the sudden nature of the onslaught.

As soon as I considered it was feasible, I sent to Millstreet for reinforcements. D.I.3 F Scott being the first to go on this errand and the first to arrive at his destination some five miles distant. I cannot find words sufficient to express my appreciation of his hazardous task. He was single handed and under rebel fire for about a mile of his journey and finally arrived in Millstreet without a single round of ammunition; having expended it all on his journey.

This officer gave the alarm and reinforcements were immediately dispatched. Five other members of my party were successful in getting through to Millstreet, but arrived after D.I. Scott. The reinforcements that were dispatched came along at the double. Some in a Ford car and others in commandeered jaunting cars. Unfortunately these were delayed by reason of three trees, which had been felled across the road just outside Millstreet, by the insurgents. A small number of the reinforcements were left at these barriers and the rest proceeded to the scene of the ambush on foot. By the time these had arrived, the rebels (already beaten back) had broken off the fight, which lasted for two hours, the attack itself commencing at about 19.30 hours and ceasing at about 21.45 hours.

Wireless messages were sent out from the billet for assistance and with the utmost dispatch 'J' Company responded to our signals arriving at the scene of the ambush at 00.30 hours on the 17th inst., from Macroom. This unit, with their C.O. (D.I.I.

Williams) in charge did everything possible to assist and help us. After an inspection I found to my regret and sorrow that Cadets Boyd W.A.H. and Shorter F.E. had been killed. Also that S/LDR: Taylor O.C. sustained three wounds. With regards to M.T. which sustained considerable damage, I found that of the four vehicles that were in the convoy, two, the armoured Crossley and the Lancia are severely damaged. In passing, I may state that the armour protecting the engine of this car, was discovered 40 yards away: having been flung that distance by the concussion, that this unit has not suffered the loss of any arms whatsoever, or ammunition, with the exception of the ammunition expended during the engagement. In closing I may state, that I consider the way in which the Cadets under my charge behaved, is worthy of the highest traditions of the Royal Irish Constabulary.

(Sgd.) W.E. Crossey, Lieut., & 1st B.D.L. Commanding 'L' Coy Aux. Div. R.I.C.
17/6/21 Millstreet, Co. Cork.[3]

Though the convoy had managed to fight off their attackers and protect their cargo, the IRA later stated that a republican reconnaissance party returned to the scene of the ambush the following day and collected 1,350 rounds of .303 ammunition that had been discarded by the Auxiliaries during the battle. They also managed to dig up and retrieve the four undetonated IEDs.

In the weeks that followed there were a number of 'round-ups' in the area in a search for the insurgents and their weapons caches. Volunteer Micheal Dineen was apprehended at his brother's house at Ivale, Kilcorney and according to republican sources was tortured before being shot by the Auxiliaries. Bernard Moynihan, a Volunteer from the Kilcorney Company, was also shot dead.

The IRA was planning an all-out assault on 'L' Company of the Auxiliaries when, at 12:00 hours on 11 July 1922, a truce was agreed between British Crown forces in Ireland and the republican command, bringing an end to hostilities.

22

Hit
Engagement at Ardfert Station

Auxiliary officers were often singled out for assassination by the IRA. The commanding officer of 'H' Company, 1st Class District Inspector J.A. MacKinnon DCM, MC, MM, stationed in Tralee, County Kerry, was one such target for elimination. A former major in the Scots/Canadian Regiment, MacKinnon had orchestrated a successful campaign of counter-insurgency against the IRA in Tralee. Through his actions and ruthlessness, he became a priority target and there were a number of attempts on his life but he managed to fight off his attackers. Republican command ordered that MacKinnon be killed as a matter of urgency. Because of this security risk, MacKinnon had an armed guard of Auxiliaries wherever he went and was conscious of his security arrangements.

The republicans established a ten-man team to track MacKinnon and examine all avenues for his assassination. It was suspected that he wore a bulletproof vest under his tunic making it difficult to carry out the usual shoot-and-scoot tactic that had claimed the lives of many police officers. He was found to be vulnerable at the golf links near the town, which he played on frequently. Though he was still accompanied by an armed guard, he could be got. The IRA contacted ex-British soldier and IRA operative Con Healy, who assured his officers that with a rifle he could take out MacKinnon with a shot to the head. On 15 April 1921, Healy and a number of IRA Volunteers took up position on the course. As MacKinnon prepared to tee off on the third green, Healy fired, hitting his target in the forehead. As MacKinnon fell, Healy fired a second shot, hitting the officer again. Healy's accomplices opened fire with shotguns, scattering the district inspector's bodyguard, and allowing the IRA to make their escape.[1]

Reprisals by the ADRIC followed with the burning of houses in Ballymacelligott and the shooting dead of a boy named Reidy. A local paper, *The Liberator,* which refused to carry an obituary for MacKinnon, was wrecked and burned.

Auxiliary Cadets continued their operations in the Kerry area, raiding, arresting suspects and collating information on local IRA units. Three of MacKinnon's officers were to distinguish themselves in action four months later while foiling an attempted hold-up.

Having purchased their rail tickets from the kiosk, the three T/Cadets walked briskly along the station platform towards the first-class carriage on the morning Tralee-to-Dublin train. The officers, George C. Gash, Howard DeCourcey Martelli and H. Bjorkman of 'H' Company ADRIC, stowed their kitbags in the overhead storage compartments before taking their seats.

The train was comprised of a locomotive, a coal tender, four carriages and to the rear a guard van and mail car. Though the officers were heading to Dublin on leave they were in uniform and armed. As the stationmaster signalled the driver, a whistle sounded and the train slowly moved out of the station, heading towards Ardfert.

Bjorkman produced a pipe from his pocket, tapped it on the heel of his boot and, producing a pouch of tobacco, filled the bowl of the pipe. Pressing the tobacco strands into place with his thumb, he lit it with a wooden match. He did not draw deeply on the pipe, merely giving the occasional puff and enjoying the scent and flavour of the quality leaf. T/Cadet Gash perused the morning newspaper while Martelli stretched out along the seat and tried to make himself as comfortable as possible.

The first leg of the journey was uneventful, with the officers discussing their leave and their planned travel arrangements to England.

The train slowed down as it pulled into Ardfert railway station, its brakes hissing and screeching as the engine prepared to stop. The officers in the carriage knew this stop was short and that their journey would resume in a few minutes. Martelli moved to the window and scanned the length of the platform as the train came to a standstill. He heard shouts from further up near the engine. Through the cloud of steam that had engulfed the station platform, Martelli caught sight of twelve armed men partly concealed behind hedging near the last carriages of the train. A number of armed men moved down the platform towards the goods carriages at the rear of the train. The stationmaster was being escorted by two men armed with revolvers, one of which was levelled at his back. Martelli notified his colleagues that the action was a possible IRA attack. The T/Cadets drew their weapons and moved out into the corridor of their carriage and, under the cover of the train, moved towards the engine.

The interception of mail delivery by the Irish Republican Army was a constant source of intelligence as correspondence between informers and the authorities was often sent via the post. Letters destined for the police or other government departments were seized while the mail for civilians was left alone and returned to the post office for delivery. It was during such a raid that the IRA had intercepted a letter addressed to one John O'Reilly in Newmarket-on-Fergus from the RIC. The letter confirmed the suspicions of the local IRA intelligence officer that O'Reilly was a spy and he was executed.

The T/Cadets noted that the two armed men were covered by at least six more armed with rifles who were positioned along the platform. Another seven armed men were overlooking the site from the embankment leading out of the station.

An argument ensued between the stationmaster and his captors over gaining access to the locked goods compartment because the keys were held by the conductor on the train. Vital seconds were gained as the Auxiliaries moved into position.

The three officers made their way through the carriage into the tender and then into the cab where Martelli, with his weapon drawn, ordered the engineer and the fireman 'to put on steam' and drive out of the station. Both men refused and Gash, realising that there were just seconds to spare, decided to drive the engine himself. The former engineer pushed the reverser forward and then opened the cylinder cocks. Releasing the engine brakes, he opened the throttle and the train began to move. The clanking of the couplings as they took up the slack alerted the gunmen on the embankment who shouted a warning to those positioned on the platform. A hail of enemy fire erupted as the train began to move, bullets whining and ricocheting off the boiler and the tender. Martelli returned fire with his .45 Colt automatic while Bjorkman emptied the contents of his Webley revolver at those standing on the platform.

The train gained momentum as the shooting continued between the two groups. The insurgents on the embankment fired on the engine, forcing Gash to take cover. Having reloaded his weapon, Bjorkman hit two Volunteers who had attempted to move down the embankment to get into a better firing position. Leaning from the windows of the carriage, Bjorkman and Martelli continued firing until the train was out of danger. The episode had lasted all of three minutes.

For their action on that day, T/Cadets Gash, Martelli and Bjorkman were awarded the Constabulary Medal on 5 October 1921 for valour and bravery displayed.

23

Black Ops

During a war, both sides often carry out what are known as Black Operations. These are defined as covert missions carried out by a government agency or a military organisation that are not attributable to the group carrying it out. These types of operations are often outside standard military protocol and are also outside the law. The difference between a clandestine operation and a black operation is that the latter involves a significant degree of deception in order to conceal those who planned and executed the mission and in some cases to direct blame onto others.

The Irish Republican Army targeted prominent figures throughout Ireland, assassinating those who threatened the organisation and its members. Many of these men, women and young boys and girls, loyal to the Crown or in receipt of payment from the government, were classed as spies and informers for the British government.

Michael Collins was incensed at the deaths of Commandant Dick McKee and Vice Commandant Peadar Clancy at the hands of the Auxiliaries in Dublin Castle on the evening of 21 November 1920, the day before Bloody Sunday. He ordered an investigation into how both men were compromised and taken into custody from Seán Fitzpatrick's house at Gloucester Street. Evidence was uncovered that revealed that

James 'Shankers' Ryan, a member of the Military Police Corps detailed for intelligence work, had notified the authorities at the Castle by telephone that the two men were in the building. He chalk-marked the house so it would easily recognisable to the raiding party. Having been apprehended and brought to the Castle for interrogation, both IRA officers and Conor Clune, who had been taken by force earlier from Vaughan's Hotel, were subjected to a period of interrogation by two Auxiliary officers, Captain Jocelyn 'Hoppy' Hardy and Major Lorraine 'Tiny' King, and also by Chief of Intelligence, Ormonde de l'Épée Winter. The three men were killed in what the authorities described as an attempt to escape custody. However, this report proved inaccurate as autopsies on the three revealed they had been tortured to extract information before they were shot in what appeared to be execution-style killings.

Having received detailed information on the killing of his men, Collins sanctioned the assassination of 'Shankers' Ryan. On Saturday, 5 February 1921, while sitting in Hynes Public House, Lower Gloucester Place, reading a newspaper at the bar, 'Shankers' Ryan, dressed in mufti, did not notice the three men who entered the bar.

Having identified their target, one gunman approached 'Shankers', drew his revolver and shot him four times in the upper body. He was declared dead on arrival at Jervis Street Hospital.[1]

These hits against informers or government agents created fear amongst the populace, with many losing faith in the security forces. Anti-Sinn Féin societies were organised by loyalists, many of them prominent businessmen, who threatened retaliation for IRA actions in cities and villages throughout the country. One such group, prominent in Cork city, were hunted down by the IRA and killed, one by one.

In recent years research has revealed that a number of groups, comprising regular RIC, Black and Tans, military and Auxiliaries, formed special units to target prominent republicans in response to attacks, kidnappings and executions carried out by IRA operatives. While many of these units acted alone, it is not known if any, all or some were sanctioned by the British government or intelligence agencies.

On Sunday, 14 November 1920, Father Michael Griffin, the curate of St Joseph's Church, Galway, was called out from his house on

Members of 'F' Company, Dublin Castle, outside Hynes Public House in Dublin after the killing of 'Shankers' Ryan in February 1921. (National Library of Ireland)

Montpellier Terrace to attend a sick parishioner and never returned. His disappearance was reported to the police the following day and searches were carried out in the area by locals.

Foul play was suspected and the subject was raised in the House of Commons by an Irish Parliamentary Party MP, Joseph Devlin, when he questioned the Chief Secretary to Ireland, Sir Hamar Greenwood, whether his attention had been called to the case of Rev. Michael Griffin CC of Galway, who was taken from his house by a party of men on Sunday night, since when nothing was heard of him.[2] Devlin accused the security forces of having a hand in the priest's abduction.

The Chief Secretary replied that, 'I do not believe for a moment that this priest has been kidnapped by any armed forces of the Crown.' He continued, 'It is obviously such a stupid thing that no members of the forces of the Crown would do it.' Devlin replied, 'That is why they would do it.'[3]

Father Griffin sympathised with the republican movement and had attended Volunteer Seamus Quirke, a lieutenant in the IRA who had been wounded during a gun battle in the docklands. He also took part in the funeral Mass of Volunteer Michael Walsh who had been killed by a person or persons unknown. His colleague, Father John O'Meehan, was an ardent republican and also lived at Montpellier Terrace.

Six days after his disappearance, the body of Father Griffin was discovered by a local farmer, William Duffy, while out tending his cattle. The body had been buried in a shallow grave in bogland.

It is believed that Father Griffin was lured from the presbytery by British forces or those acting on behalf of the Crown, on the pretence of attending a sick parishioner. He was escorted to Lenaboy Castle, interrogated and then executed by a shot to the head. His body was transported by lorry and buried in an unmarked grave at Cloghscoltia near Barna, County Galway. Three Auxiliaries were suspected of carrying out the killing and Commandant of the Auxiliaries Brigadier General Frank Crozier was dispatched to Galway to investigate the incident. His investigation uncovered that Father Griffin had been murdered and that suspicion fell upon men under his command. Furthermore, his enquiries led him to believe that another black operation was being planned to kill Dr Fogarty, Bishop of Killaloe. Crozier later wrote:

> I found out that the military inquiry into the murder of Father Griffin (held in lieu of an inquest) was fast with a 'frame up' and that a verdict of murder against persons or somebody 'unknown' would result. I told the military commander this and the name of the real murderer but was informed that a senior official from Dublin Castle had been to Galway in front of me to give instructions as to 'procedure' in this murder investigation. At Killaloe the next day I received further evidence that the hidden hand was still at work, and was told in confidence that instructions had been received to kill Dr. Fogerty [sic], R.C. Bishop of Killaloe, by drowning him in a sack from the bridge over the River Shannon, so as to run no further risk of detection by having his body found.[4]

On his return journey to Dublin, Crozier planned to report his findings to General Tudor. However, on reaching Naas, County Kildare, the Crossley Tender in which he was travelling careered off the road and crashed. On regaining consciousness, Crozier discovered his briefcase and pistol had vanished. He suffered a number of injuries and was hospitalised in the Curragh Military Hospital before being transferred to a rest home in Dublin. Brigadier General Wood took command of the ADRIC in his superior's absence.[5]

Dr Fogarty managed to evade his assassins and later wrote to Crozier after reading the officer's book *Impressions and Recollections*, which had a reference to the Bishop. 'A dive for my life was made by four Auxiliaries on the night of December 3rd, 1920, and my escape owing to the fortuitous absence from home on that night was little short of miraculous. Having failed to find me at home two of them, evidently in command, spent about an hour in my library searching papers and drawers in the presence of my housekeeper who had to act as candle-bearer to them.'

From a description given to him by his housekeeper, Dr Fogarty was able to describe the men. 'These two men were of military caste, tall and strong, over six feet high. One of them who was undisguised was fair, almost sandy. The other had his face blackened but when closely examined seemed to be of a naturally black complexion.'

'The other two of the four were one of them low sized, the other a tall brutal black savage, who kicked one of my servants …'

In summing up his letter to Crozier, the Bishop wrote: 'It is not the abandoned creatures like these that are most to blame but the misguided Government who stood over their behaviour and tried to conceal it with wholesale lying.'[6]

The IRA believed that Father Griffin was executed in retaliation for the killing of police officers and informers in the area. However, on examining the operations and the intended targets there may be more to the hit than revenge. The priests were known republican sympathisers and were actively involved with the republican movement, and like other members of religious orders, they may have acted as couriers between local IRA units and republican command in Dublin.

Mystery surrounds the reasons behind the death of Father Griffin with some believing he was not the intended target and that he was shot accidentally while being interrogated. However, the post-mortem results revealed that Father Griffin was shot at close range from behind, the bullet entering the right side of his head and exiting through the left temple.

An IRA intelligence officer, Joseph Togher, later wrote that the man who lured the priest from the house was one William Joyce, later known as Lord Haw Haw who was executed for treason by the British after the Second World War. Joyce was known to have acted as an informant and guide for the security forces in the area. After the death of Father Griffin, a letter was intercepted by republicans that incriminated him, revealing the extent of his relationship with the police. He evaded capture by the IRA and left for England when the truce was declared in July 1921.[7]

After his resignation in February 1921, Crozier stated that he believed Auxiliary Cadets were responsible for the murder of Father Griffin and the targeting of Dr Fogarty, and that these clandestine operations had been covered up by the authorities.[8]

When 'K' Company pulled out of their billets at Dunmanway Workhouse, County Cork, the IRA discovered a notebook listing local informers and loyalists who had provided information to the authorities.[9]

> The Auxiliaries' C.O. [Commanding Officer] was de Havilland and Brownie was the I.O. [Intelligence Officer]. He [Brownie] instituted a very perfect intelligence system and, probably with the help of the local police, drew up lists of all the houses in the Dunmanway Battalion area, both friendly and hostile to the British régime. He also listed every man who was wanted with a description of him in detail, height, looks, voice, manner and so on.[10]

The IRA had a mole within the Workhouse who passed information on the Auxiliaries to local republican forces. Florence J. Crowley was the clerk of the Union and he socialised with the T/Cadets, gleaning information from them on spies and informers in the locality.

Classed as 'helpful citizens' by the Auxiliaries, those whose names appeared in the diary were condemned to death for assisting the authorities. The IRA set about tracking the individuals down and killing them, in an orgy of violence that continued long after the truce came into effect. Many of those targeted were Protestant and their murders led many to believe that the killings were sectarian. Controversy surrounds the origins of the notebook and how it came into the hands of the local IRA unit. Many theories have been put forward by historians over the years. While many believe that the discovery of such documentation was due to an officer's incompetence, perhaps the Auxiliaries planted the notebook for the IRA to discover. By killing those listed, the IRA may have been aiding the ADRIC by tying up their loose ends in relation to incriminating evidence, murder by association and outstanding payments to informants.

The violence continued unabated on both sides. Prominent republicans, municipal politicians and those belonging to republican families were also targeted. On 7 March 1921, between 01:00 hours and 02:00 hours, armed men targeted Councillor Michael O'Callaghan, ex-Mayor of Limerick city, Alderman George Clancy, the serving Mayor of Limerick and a young man named Joseph O'Donoghue, in what became known as the Limerick Curfew Murders.

Councillor O'Callaghan answered a knock on his door and was confronted by three armed men who claimed they were part of a search party. Their faces were partly concealed as they wore driving goggles.

When he challenged them, the men ordered O'Callaghan outside, but he refused and a struggle ensued. His wife came to his assistance but was knocked down in the hallway. The men then opened fire, hitting Mr O'Callaghan who died a quarter of an hour later.

It is believed the same group then travelled to the residence of Alderman Clancy where, having knocked on the door, they were admitted to the house. Mrs Clancy struggled with the assailants but was shot and seriously wounded. Alderman Clancy was then shot several times and died at the scene.

The men moved on to another house where they located Joseph O'Donoghue. He was taken at gunpoint from the residence and executed a few yards from the gates of the house.

In an interview with journalist Richard Bennett for the *New Statesman* in 1961, a former T/Cadet stated that T/Cadet George Nathan, an intelligence officer, had journeyed from Dublin to the Auxiliaries' mess at Killaloe and sought assistance in a mission he was to carry out in Limerick city.

> Nathan, I was told, came down to the Auxiliary mess at Killaloe, a few miles from Limerick, and said he had a job to do that night. He then suggested to my old gentleman that they should drive together into Limerick, have dinner at Kidds and then go on from there. In the end it was another officer from the Auxiliary Company at Killaloe who went with Nathan. They came back to the mess at six o'clock the next morning, 'boozed up and looking like death'. Nathan told the Auxiliaries at breakfast – to their horror – that he had killed Clancy and O'Callaghan.[11]

During the Great War, George Nathan had risen through the ranks of the British army, from private to company sergeant major, to be then commissioned in the field to become the only Jewish officer in the Brigade of Guards. Nathan had served with 'G' Company of the ADRIC and had been stationed in County Clare before transferring to Dublin. He was described by two former colleagues, whom Bennett interviewed, as carrying himself with great panache, being absolutely fearless and 'a roaring homosexual'.[12]

In 1937, during the Spanish Civil War, George Nathan served with the 15th International Brigade on the side of the Republicans. In a conversation with a number of fellow soldiers he remarked that he had served as an intelligence officer for the Crown in the Limerick area during the Irish War of Independence.[13] He was killed in action on 16 July 1937 during the Battle of Brunete.

The former Commandant of the Auxiliaries, Brigadier General F.P. Crozier, wrote in his 1932 book *Ireland Forever*, that: 'After he carried out a personal investigation of the murders in March 1921 he had come to the same conclusion as Mrs O'Callaghan, that is, that her husband, "was murdered by police", acting under orders, as part of a plan to "do away with" Sinn Féin leaders, and put the blame on Sinn Féin.'[14]

Nathan and other Auxiliary Cadets have been accused of being part of what republicans described as a 'Murder Gang' working out of Dublin Castle, carrying out a number of extrajudicial killings during their deployment in Ireland. During the courts of enquiry established to determine the causes of death of these men and others, many people testified that men dressed as Auxiliary Cadets with English accents carried out the killings.[15]

Joseph Kenworthy MP raised the question of such units in Westminster when he questioned the Irish Chief Secretary, Sir Hamar Greenwood: 'Whether the Government have any knowledge of the so-called Anti Sinn Féin Society; whether he is aware that this society boasts of being engaged in an active murder campaign; whether there are any relations between the intelligence service in Ireland and this society; and whether any steps have been taken to suppress this organization.'[16]

Greenwood denied any collusion between the government, the intelligence service and those carrying out extrajudicial killings. A month later in Westminster, Kenworthy said that:

> He had another letter in which it was stated that Forest's draper shop was burned in front of the Cork Examiner office, in full view of the staff, by Black and Tans. They threatened the editor's life if an advertisement was not printed that day. The advertisement said that they had been requested to publish a statement by the Anti-Sinn Fein Society of the Cork District ... The suspicion in Cork and in all parts of Ireland was that they were Auxiliary Police.[17]

Joseph Kenworthy MP and author G.K. Chesterton formed an Anti-Reprisals group in London to lobby politicians and other prominent citizens about the unfolding crisis in Ireland. It was hoped that, through representation, the group would compel Lloyd George and his government to 'abandon a policy, which is as fatuous as it is wicked'.[18] The publicity generated by this group was so adverse that the Director of Sinn Féin's propaganda section declared that it had 'been most damaging to England's prestige'.[19]

As reports filtered in to the security services of republican attacks around Ireland, an unofficial British reprisal campaign commenced, which involved the targeting of prominent republicans and the destruction of buildings associated with Sinn Féin.

Reginald Hanhart Watts, a former Lieutenant in the Royal Marine Light Infantry, enlisted in the ADRIC and was posted to 'M' Company stationed in County Longford. The officer had resigned his commission in the Marines having been court-martialled on a charge of cowardice. However, he was acquitted on this charge but convicted on a charge of 'using words calculated to cause alarm and despondency', the military permitting him to resign on his own request. On a later visit to his former military colleagues at Chatham Army Barracks, Watts revealed the nature of his work within the ADRIC.

> He had joined the Black and Tans [Auxiliaries] and was a member of a murder squad. These squads were given details of about six IRA types of men and, if they managed to kill them, each member of the squad was given a lump sum of money and a passport to go anywhere he wished to go. Unfortunately, Watts himself had become a target for an Irish murder squad and could never sleep more than one night at the same place even in England. His was no job for a coward.'[20]

Incensed at the failure of the judicial system to bring the perpetrators of the killings of their colleagues in the security forces to justice, some took the law into their own hands. Covert squads were raised and carried out operations throughout the country. Whether these had the backing of senior officials is not known but in order to operate in certain areas, these groups had to have the cooperation of the military in order to move undetected in martial-law areas. Otherwise, curfew patrols would have, in many cases, discovered these operatives as they made their way to and from designated targets.

Whether these men were acting out of revenge or on orders from the British administration has never been determined and, to this day, the killings and the alleged police involvement, remain unsolved.

24

Reign of Fire
Final Operations in Ireland

'We have murder by the throat. We had to reorganise the Police. When the Government was ready we struck the terrorists and now the terrorists are complaining of terror.'[1] These words were spoken by British Prime Minister, Lloyd George, at the Mansion House in London in November 1920 in relation to the situation in Ireland. At the same event Winston Churchill included the Auxiliary Division of the RIC in his toast to the armed forces. Both sides were now entering a war of attrition.

On Wednesday, 29 December 1920, a conference was held at 10 Downing Street, London to discuss the present state of affairs in Ireland. Those in attendance included the Prime Minister, General Macready, General Strickland, General Boyd, General Tudor and Sir John Anderson.

> General Strickland, Commanding the Cork area where martial law had been proclaimed, stated that he had not yet received any report regarding the number of arms which had been surrendered. The last day on which they could be handed in was December 27th. His opinion was that the loyalists would fall in with the order, but that the majority of extremists would bury their arms. As time

went on the military might be able to ascertain where these arms had been buried. Referring to the raid by the police at a dance in Limerick, where 138 men had been captured and 5 armed sentries who were standing outside the hall had been shot, General Strickland said that so far he had only received a telegraphic report of what had happened from the Brigadier in charge. As far as he could ascertain there were no women present at the dance, and in all probability it was in reality a conference for future operations. All those captured were now in prison.

General Macready said that, generally speaking, the situation, from a military point of view, was improving. The internment camps were going on satisfactorily, although there was rather a shortage of accommodation. He was convinced that everything was satisfactory in the Cork area, and he had now made an application to the Castle for an extension of the martial law area. He would like Kilkenny, Clare, Waterford and Wexford all under martial law. It would not be necessary to apply martial law to its full effect, but it helped the military in their work and was welcomed in many cases by the inhabitants.

General Tudor said that from the police point of view the position had improved. There were now plenty of men to hold the police barracks. 13 Auxiliary Companies were now formed, and the transport situation was much improved. Further, he hoped to have 80 armoured cars by the end of January. The morale of the Police in the last six months had made a marked advance. Six months ago the Police were living behind sandbags and wire entanglements, they were boycotted, and life altogether was intolerable; but now things were quite different and they could move about freely, and with the exception of ambushes they were practically out of danger.[2]

The meeting continued with the Prime Minister addressing General Tudor in relation to discipline amongst his Auxiliary Police. 'General Tudor admitted that drink was a problem with the Auxiliary Divisions, but his commanding officers were in the opinion they were now getting the men under better control.'[3]

In Ireland the death toll continued to rise as the British government sought a solution to the conflict, and in December 1920, The Government of Ireland Act was put into effect. This provided two separate Irish Parliaments, one sitting in Belfast to govern all of Ulster, the other based in Dublin for the remainder of the country. It was hoped that in time these two parliaments would unite to form a single government for Ireland but both republicans and Unionists objected strongly to what they believed was a flawed solution to a worsening problem.

Unknown to many, during that December 1920, Lloyd George and Arthur Griffith were in secret negotiations to bring an end to the conflict. Initial talks carried out via an intermediary were hampered by Sir Hamar Greenwood, Chief Secretary of Ireland, who refused to enter any discussion unless republican forces decommissioned their weapons. Talks floundered and the war continued.

As the Auxiliaries became more adept at operating in republican-held areas, the IRA intensified its campaign with increased ferocity. The counter-insurgency was as brutal. Official reprisals continued and when the military burnt down the houses of local Irish people, the IRA targeted the property of loyalists. Republican GHQ sanctioned these reprisals in response to police and military actions that saw them burn down several houses after the killing of a prominent British officer.

The IRA decided to extend their campaign to Britain. IRA operative John A. Pinkman wrote:

> The ordinary English people couldn't have cared less about what was happening in Ireland, being unconcerned about these reports of murder and destruction there. IRA headquarters in Dublin wanted to impress upon the English people that a war of terror was being waged in their name against the Irish people, and reluctantly ordered massive reprisals to be carried out in England to show the English the sort of havoc that was being wrought in Ireland.[4]

Since the summer of 1920, the IRA had wanted to launch a terror campaign in Britain but Dáil Éireann had been against this strategy. However, IRA Chief of Staff Cathal Brugha supported the idea as he had in 1918 when he commanded an IRA squad sent to England to assassinate members of the British cabinet in an attempt to prevent conscription being enforced in Ireland. In early November 1920, the Dáil sanctioned operations in England. 'Following the deliberate burnings by the Auxiliaries [in Ireland], the army executive [in Dublin] decided that the Volunteers in the English cities should adopt retaliatory measures in their areas … It was felt that the people in England should be made conscious of what the people in Ireland were suffering as regards depredations carried out by the Crown Forces.'[5]

The initial campaign involved a number of arson attacks on property but orders from republican GHQ requested that a number of high-profile targets, British army and Auxiliary officers, be assassinated. This was met with disapproval by many of the operatives in England who objected to assassination assignments.[6]

Some Auxiliary Cadets were singled out to be hit but last minute changes to republican plans foiled these attempts. However, the houses of fifteen Auxiliary Cadets in London and Liverpool were targeted and on 14 May 1921, their homes were attacked resulting in five relatives being injured and one killed.[7] The police in England retaliated by rounding up suspects, imprisoning some and deporting others to Ireland.[8]

While initial republican attacks in Britain were successful, a change in British military tactics, which saw increased military and police operations, greatly restricted the operational capacity of the IRA both at home and abroad. In a police raid on the house of a Dr Hayes in November 1920, plans taken by Jack Plunkett for the destruction of Liverpool Docks were discovered, forcing the operation to be abandoned.[9]

The British military were optimistic that this new campaign would defeat republican forces. Auxiliary police, supported by the military, launched a number of operations around Ireland in an attempt to capture IRA flying columns. While many of these operations were unsuccessful, they did result in reducing IRA operations as areas were flooded with military personnel, restricting movement or attacking capability. Suspects were interned, many awaiting interrogation or trial.

The capture of arms and ammunition dumps reduced the firepower of republicans as these weapons could not be easily replaced. The interception of a shipment of Thompson submachine guns in New York by American authorities also dealt a blow to the republican armoury. The IRA had purchased 653 submachine guns at £225 per weapon. The consignment also consisted of component parts, instruction manuals and ammunition. The weapons were discovered aboard the freighter *East Side* whose cargo was listed as coal. The ship had been chartered by White Cross, the Irish Relief Organisation, to transport coal to Ireland. A suspicious crew member discovered the weapons cache and contacted the authorities. The cargo was seized and a number of arrests were made. The manufacturers of the weapons disavowed any knowledge of the sale of the guns to the IRA or its inclusion on the shipping manifesto. The gun company claimed that they would not sell weapons to groups that threatened constitutional governments.

As the death toll mounted in Ireland, the British government was faced with a dilemma. It could, as planned, declare an all-out war in Ireland, impose martial law throughout the island, deploy more troops across the country, increase executions and intern suspected republicans. British army commander Nevil Macready was against this policy and wrote, 'There are of course one or two wild people about who still hold the absurd idea that if you go on killing long enough, peace will ensue. I do not believe it for one moment but I do believe that the more people are killed the more difficult a final solution becomes.'[10]

Sir Henry Wilson, Chief of the Imperial General Staff, believed that the declaration of war in Ireland would spread to the colonies, highlighting those seeking independence and escalating the situation, bringing pressure on an already overstretched army that was not capable of fighting a counter-insurgency campaign.

Unknown to many at that time, the IRA were planning their largest operation to date. The attack on the Custom House in Dublin, which involved hundreds of IRA operatives, was seen by many as a daring operation; others believed it was a last throw of the dice in an attempt to gain worldwide recognition for an independent Irish Republic.

On 25 May 1921 at 13:10 hours, an urgent call was put through to Inspector Alexander McCabe of the DMP at Dublin Castle. An Irish civil servant stated that the Custom House had been rushed by approximately 100 civilians.[11] The message was relayed to the Operations Room of 'F' Company ADRIC who immediately grabbed their weapons and mounted three Crossley armoured trucks. Within minutes, the Rapid Response Unit, accompanied by an armoured car, had left Dublin Castle and tore through the streets of Dublin towards their objective.

Unknown to the authorities at that time, the Irish Republican Army had committed its largest force to date in the operation and was utilising every logistical means at its disposal to carry out the mission.

Months previously, at a meeting of the headquarters staff of the IRA, the military situation in Ireland had been discussed. At the meeting it was decided that 'the time had come to deliver a smashing blow to England – some bigger military operation than anything yet attempted.'[12] Two possible operations were discussed: (1) An attack on Beggars Bush Barracks, Depot Headquarters of the Auxiliaries in Dublin, and (2) The destruction of the Custom House, the administrative centre of the British Civil Service in Ireland.

After a detailed reconnaissance of both objectives, it was deemed impossible to launch a surprise attack against the barracks, which was considered too well fortified a position. The Custom House was deemed a better target and after Oscar Traynor, O/C Dublin Brigade, submitted a report to GHQ staff, the operation was given the go-ahead.

The area of operations was the Custom House located on the northern banks of the River Liffey. The building had been designed by James Gandon with construction commencing in 1781 and lasting ten years at a final cost of £600,000.

The following government departments were housed within the Custom House: Inland Revenue, Local Government, Estate Duty Central Registers, Stamp Duty and Income Tax & Joint Stock Company Registers.

The insurgents planned that the destruction of this building would reduce the most important branches of the British Civil Service in

Ireland and would, in addition, inflict a huge financial loss on the exchequer, an estimated £2 million.

The plan took three months to prepare and Commandant Tom Ennis, O/C of the 2nd Battalion, was put in charge of the operation. A force of 120 men, supported by units from other battalions, was to assemble at a staging area near the objective. Once there, weapons and ammunition would be issued. Each raider would be armed with a revolver and six rounds of ammunition. Covering units made up from Collins' 'Squad' and ASU would be armed with automatic pistols. A Lewis machine gun and team would form part of the covering party. Tools needed for the operation were to be picked up on the way to the target.

Main approach routes to the target were to be covered by men from the 1st Battalion. The attacking forces were to approach the target in small groups using the run-up to the lunch-hour rush as cover. Police officers on duty were to be neutralised as were telephone communications. As the target was secured, no persons would be allowed to enter or exit the building. A lorry would pull up to the front of the building and, as each man entered, they were to take two 2-gallon tins of paraffin from the vehicle. Bales of cotton waste were also to be distributed throughout the building. Paperwork was to be scattered on the floors, and offices were to be systematically broken up. Windows were to be closed to prevent air circulation.

Fires were to be started from the upper floors with each unit moving down through the building, setting fire to offices as they withdrew to the entrance hall. In the event of any problems occurring, the O/C would signal a withdrawal by giving a blast on a whistle. Under no circumstances was any other operative to carry or use a whistle during the operation. Egress from the area would be made using the lunchtime rush and the evacuating staff as cover. It was estimated that the operation would take twenty minutes. In order for the fire to catch successfully, members of the 3rd and 4th Battalions would occupy Tara Street Fire Station and Thomas Street Station to prevent or delay any response from the fire brigade. The operation was timed to commence at 13:00 hours.

When such an operation was first proposed, all senior officers connected with its planning understood the great hazards it would entail for those tasked to execute it. The destruction of this building in the city centre would be a *coup de main* operation depending largely on surprise, speed and dash for success. The saboteurs knew from the huge risks being asked of them that their objective was of great importance.

At 13:00 hours on 25 May 1921 the largest operation undertaken by the IRA commenced. On entering the building, Volunteer Jim Conway shot and killed the caretaker, Francis Devine, who attempted to raise the alarm by calling the police. As the gunmen took control of the building, they ushered all the staff at gunpoint into the main hall. The clock was ticking as the demolition teams began moving from office to office and from floor to floor, breaking open doors and scattering papers on the floor before dousing them in paraffin. Within minutes, flames had engulfed many of the offices. A blast on a whistle was heard and many of the men moved down to the main hall. The call was a false alarm and the O/C ordered his men back upstairs to finish the job. As the Volunteers continued with their mission those located in the main hall were surprised by the sound of a motor engine outside. At 13:23 hours an armoured car drove into Beresford Place and pulled up near the entrance to the Custom House. With the engine running, the turret on the vehicle traversed to survey the scene outside. A shot was discharged at the car by a Volunteer who then ran from the building. He was pursued by one of the vehicle's crew. The gunner on the armoured car opened fire at the doors of the Custom House, the bullets ricocheting off the stone façade and sending up plumes of dust. Small-arms fire was directed towards the vehicle, the ping of bullets off metal resonating throughout the streets.

Seconds later, the Auxiliary Crossleys from 'F' Company reached Butt Bridge and the first vehicle was hit by small-arms fire. Volunteer Dan Head pulled the pin from a grenade, flicked off the spoon and pitched the device into the rear of the vehicle; the explosion injured four officers. The armoured truck slewed to a halt. The remaining T/Cadets debussed onto Eden Quay and returned fire. The officers in the second Crossley fired in all directions as the vehicle sped through the streets before coming to a halt on the north side of the building. Covering the

ADRIC in action at the
Custom House, 25 May 1921.
(J. Langton Collection)

main door, the Auxies opened fire as they leapt from the vehicle. The
third Tender screeched to a standstill at Beresford Place. The T/Cadets
engaged the insurgents positioned here and on the bridge overhead.

Noticing the engagement at the bridge, the gunner of the armoured
car traversed the turret and opened fire. The Vickers .303 machine-gun
raked the insurgents' positions, forcing them to take cover behind the
quay wall. Volunteer Dan Head was cut down in this burst of fire and
killed. The suppressive fire from the armoured car and the failure of
the insurgents to bring their machine gun into action (their weapon
jammed) enabled the Auxiliaries to gain a foothold. Working in small
groups, the Auxiliaries, covering each other in fire-and-manoeuvre
drill, advanced towards the Custom House. A fierce gun battle began.
Volunteer William James Stapleton recalled:

> I remember a tender of Auxiliaries coming down the Quay. We
> were at the corner of Marlborough St. Our party moved down
> towards the Custom House and on the way down we heard some
> shooting and I saw an Auxiliary standing beside Liberty Hall with
> a Lewis gun almost on his shoulder and turned in the direction of
> the Custom House, slamming shots from the gun. We fired a few
> shots in their general direction but we could not do very much.[13]

At 13:30 hours, another armoured car, supported by 'Q' Company
ADRIC (stationed within the London North Western Hotel, North
Wall Quay), arrived and covered the eastern side of the Custom House,
preventing any of attackers escaping via the North Wall. As their
vehicles came within range, they were engaged by small-arms fire from
behind the parapet of the railway bridge. The Auxiliaries debussed from
their Tenders and immediately took cover behind an array of barrels

Civilians caught between the gunfire of T/Cadets and insurgents outside the Custom House, May 1921. (J. Langton Collection)

(containing copper sulphate) on the quayside and returned fire. As the Volunteers expended their ammunition, many withdrew across Tara Street.

Hundreds of civilians were caught in the crossfire as both sides fought a running battle in the urban landscape. Men, women and children crouched behind walls and at the corners of buildings to get out of the line of fire. Civilians took refuge in shops and offices while others ran from the scene. Three people, James Connolly, John Byrne, and Mahon Lawless, were shot and killed in the crossfire.

The Auxiliaries edged forward through a withering hail of small-arms fire until they reached the front doors of the Custom House. Flames and smoke poured from the building as they finally breached an entry. Shooting had become sporadic; most of the Volunteers' ammunition was spent. Officers discovered large numbers of paraffin tins and revolvers strewn about the main entrance hall. However, because of the intense heat and flames they were compelled to withdraw. A large number of civilians came out of the Custom House with their hands raised. Panic, confusion and terror reigned as workers and passers-by were rounded up at gunpoint. Senior custom officials were asked to identify their own employees, who were not detained. On completion of identification, about 70 men remained of whom several showed distinct traces of accelerant.

Sections of Auxiliaries continually called for the assistance of the fire brigade but to no avail.

On Wednesday, May 25th, at 1.05p.m. a section of the IRA entered the Central Fire Station. The officer in command said he had orders to 'hold up' the station for one hour. Simultaneously the three sub-stations were raided and the same order given in connection with Thomas Street Station. A party of IRA took the motor engine to Crumlin, and kept it there for about an hour. At 1.45p.m. a telephone message was received notifying occurrence of fire in [the] Custom House. Brigade was still prevented from turning out. At about 1.50 the IRA officer commandeered one of our motor ambulances and drove off with his men, ordering us not to leave the station for ten minutes. The ambulance was later returned by one of our drivers who was compelled to drive. A few minutes before 2.00 p.m. a force of Auxiliaries arrived and directed the attendance of Brigade at outbreak in Custom House.[14]

By the time the fire brigade arrived on the scene, much of the building was ablaze and clouds of smoke billowed upwards into the afternoon sky. Many firemen were members of the IRA or were sympathetic to their cause. Once inside the building, these officers purposely spread the fire into parts that had failed to ignite.[15] The building was soon engulfed by the inferno.

Outside, the Auxiliaries secured the perimeter. However, there were a number of rushes from the building in twos and threes as insurgents tried to fight their way through the cordon and evade capture. Vinny Byrne, a member of the ASU, later wrote:

As I was coming down the stairs, I heard a burst of revolver and rifle fire from inside and outside the building. When I came to the hall, everyone was dashing from place to place. I ran along the corridor towards the docks and, as I came to the end, I could see the Auxies on the quay, firing. I retreated back to the hall. There was not a soul to be seen. I made up my mind to dash out when an Auxie appeared at the door. I opened up and ducked back. At the same time I retraced my steps to the hall.

Having got back to the hall, the next thing I saw approaching the entrance was a Whippet armoured car. As it came to the entrance, it opened a burst of machine gun fire into the hall. I flung myself down on the floor.

I could see the Auxies standing out on the roadway, but yet I had the idea that the Auxie I fired at was still standing beside the building, outside. At this time the whole building was a raging inferno. It meant either being burned or shot. I decided to have another 'go' to get out. The first time I had fired from my Peter [automatic pistol] I did not realise that I had emptied it. I had a look to see how many rounds I had left, and I re-loaded the gun. After firing the second time, my gun went silent – no more ammunition. I said to myself: 'This is where you finish'. I walked out. As I came to the door, I heard a shout, 'Hands up'. I threw up my hands and found myself covered by an Auxie with a rifle. He shouted to me: 'Come over here'. As I came close to him he lowered the rifle to the firing position and struck me a blow in the face, at the same time using some choice language. He ordered me to walk in front of him, over the green patch, to Brooks Thomas' premises. Every minute I was expecting a bullet in the back, which never came. He marched me over to Brooks Thomas' wall and, when another Auxiliary joined him, he remarked: 'This bastard came out of the building'. I got a few more blows on the face and body.[16]

Commandant Tom Ennis, O/C of the 2nd Battalion, brandishing two pistols, was shot and fatally injured as he tried to shoot his way out. He was taken from the scene in a lorry but later died. Sean Doyle also managed to run the gauntlet of fire but was hit and mortally wounded. Others killed in the action included Eddie Dorrins and brothers Paddy and Stephen O'Reilly.

By 14:00 hours British troops from the Wiltshire Regiment had arrived from the Royal Barracks and established a cordon around the area. T/Cadet Robert Stobo Simpson entered the burning building and made his way onto the roof where he secured the large blue ensign of the Custom Services. A British army officer took command of the operation and the Auxiliaries returned to base.

The following day, Volunteer Harry Colley went to receive the remains of IRA Adjutant Paddy O'Reilly at St Agatha's Church, North William Street. He wrote: 'After the majority of the relatives and friends were gone, his brother, Tom, opened the coffin for me and showed me

The rounding-up of suspects after the attack on the Custom House, May 1921. (Allen Library)

where poor Paddy had, apparently, been finished by a bullet through the head. There was a small bullet entrance wound in the side of his nose, which plainly showed scorching, indicating that the gun, presumably an automatic, had been placed right at his head when fired.'[17]

Official reports state that the Auxiliaries of 'F' Company suffered five casualties during the attack, Section Leaders G.H. Lewis and E. Oliver, and T/Cadets A.G.L. Tottenham, H. Beaumont and J.A. Goold.

The use of machine guns, both handheld and those on the armoured cars, enabled the Auxiliaries to regain the initiative. The suppression provided by these weapons eventually gave the British fire superiority over the insurgents.

The outcome of the operation was, and still is, a topic of debate for both sides. While some applauded its success, others stated that it achieved little or nothing.

The Headquarters Command of the Irish Republican Army deemed the operation a success as the target building and its contents were completely destroyed. The contents included all local government records, including those being drawn up for the new Northern Ireland

Parliament as well as all tax files for Ireland. The mission was also a propaganda success for the IRA as the event was broadcast around the world, highlighting the escalating crisis in the country.

The large number of arrests and the cache of weapons seized during the operation led British intelligence at Dublin Castle to believe that the Dublin Brigade of the IRA had been decimated. Charles Dalton, an IRA intelligence officer, wrote:

> The weeks following the destruction of the Custom House were very trying ones for us. Many of our best men had been killed or were in jail and it was necessary for us to conceal our crippled state from the enemy, who might otherwise have taken advantage of it to deal us a decisive blow. Ambushes were, therefore carried out nearly every day by idle Volunteers, or those who could leave their employment for a couple of hours.[18]

In the weeks that followed a number of incendiary attacks were launched at military targets throughout the city, proving that not only was the organisation still viable but that the war was set to continue.

Believing that the IRA would wage a continuous guerrilla war against the Crown, the British government resumed talks with republican forces during the spring of 1921. Severe criticism, both at home and abroad, for police and military operations in Ireland, the rising casualty rate and the increasing pressure on the exchequer were the mitigating factors that brought the British government to the negotiating table. A soldier stationed in Dublin, Major W.E. de B. Whittaker, captured the feeling when he wrote,

> It would be impossible for England to restore peace to Ireland without the employment of an army of at least 200,000 and an expenditure of many millions. Even then it would be an armed occupation. The people would never be sympathetic to English rule. They must shape their own destinies, and if the task is hard it will at least explain to them some of the difficulties which have harassed England in its attempt to govern Ireland.[19]

Increased pressure from Crown forces on the IRA was proving catastrophic for the organisation. In a raid on a safe house belonging to Michael Schweppe, a member of Collins' 'Squad', William James Stapleton, was arrested by the Auxiliaries and escorted to Dublin Castle. On being questioned, Stapleton was shocked at what he saw laid out in one of the rooms. He later recalled: 'We got a great start when we saw on a big table a large pile of small arms and ammunition of all descriptions. To our amazement we recognised most of the squad Armoury. There was a big lanky Auxiliary in the room and he picked up a parabellum which I knew very well and waving it at me called me names and asked me if I knew anything about this weapon.'[20]

With the seizure of weapons in Dublin and elsewhere, Richard Mulcahy, Chief of Staff of the IRA, knew that they could no longer sustain a prolonged guerrilla campaign against Britain.[21] The organisation now possessed only 569 rifles with 20 rounds per weapon and 477 revolvers with a limited supply of ammunition.[22] Across Ireland, there were only 2,000 active personnel and though plans were afoot to import more weapons and ammunition, republican GHQ was sceptical of how long the fight could be continued under such circumstances.

The British government was coming under increased pressure from both domestic and international sources, especially from the United States, to resolve the Irish question, once and for all. Negotiations continued with General Macready and the Under-Secretary of Ireland Andy Cope, meeting secretly with Dáil representatives in order to broker a peace plan. On 6 June 1921, the British government ordered that the burning of houses as reprisals was to be stopped forthwith. At the opening of the Belfast Parliament on 22 June 1921, King George V made an impassioned appeal for peace. The Dublin Parliament convened on 28 June with no royalty attending and only a few MPs assembling, forcing the Parliament to adjourn indefinitely.

The British Prime Minister, Lloyd George, sent a letter to Éamon de Valera suggesting a conference with the intention of a ceasefire and detailed peace negotiations. The British government lifted the prerequisite of a surrender of arms leading intermediaries from both sides to commence negotiations and a ceasefire was suggested. The talks continued with republican representatives and the British military agreeing to an informal ceasefire on 8 July with the terms being signed on 9 July and the truce coming into effect on 11 July 1921.

A republican dispatch sent out to the various commands read, 'In view of the conversations now being entered into by our government with the Government of Great Britain, and in pursuance of mutual conversations, active operations by our forces will be suspended from noon, Monday 11th July.'[23]

Some British officers believed that they were on the verge of victory over the IRA when the truce came into effect. However, others believed that without a defined front and definite targets to engage, there was little the military or police could achieve in the long term. Others, such as Field Marshal Sir Henry Wilson, wanted the country saturated with military. His diary entry for 21 May 1921 stated, 'I said that directly England was safe, every available man should go to Ireland that even four battalions now serving on the Rhine ought also to go to Ireland. I said that the measures taken up to now had been quite inadequate, that I was terrified at the state of the country, and that in my opinion, unless we crushed out the murder gang this summer we shall lose Ireland and the Empire.'[24]

Those on the front line fighting the insurgency were bitterly disappointed at the government's decision to seek a ceasefire. Major General Hawes, Royal Garrison Artillery, noted:

> More and more troops were poured into Ireland until there were some 100,000 of them. Techniques for quelling the rebellion were perfected and the rebellion was being subdued. H.M. Government chose this moment to give in. All the casualties we had suffered were wasted. While it might have been wise to give Southern Ireland independence, I feel this might well have been done earlier or kept until we had made it quite clear that we were acting from a position of strength.[25]

However, neither side could bring the conflict to an end as they lacked the coercive capacity, military hardware and the political will to do so.[26]

In the days and hours leading to the implementation of the truce, republican forces launched a number of attacks against military and police targets. A number of suspected informers were also targeted and executed. Even when the truce came into effect, certain IRA units continued their attacks on British targets, frustrating those on both sides who wanted a cessation to hostilities.

Preliminary discussions began during the summer months, with the official peace negotiations starting in October 1921. During the Treaty talks, republican negotiators insisted that the deployment of military, regular RIC and Auxiliaries was to be stopped. An article in the Treaty refers directly to the Auxiliary police:

> The government of the Irish Free State agree to pay fair compensation on terms not less favourable than those accorded by the Act of 1920 to judges, officials, members of police forces and other public servants who are discharged by it or who retire in consequence of the change of government effected in pursuance of. Provided that this agreement should not apply to members of the Auxiliary Police Force or to persons recruited in Great Britain for the Royal Irish Constabulary during the two years next preceding the date thereof. The British Government will assume responsibility for such compensation or pensions as may be payable to any of these accepted persons.[27]

The Treaty negotiations revolved around three key points:

- The unity of Ireland
- The degree of independence an Irish government would possess
- The relationship Ireland would have with the British Empire.[28]

David Lloyd George refused to compromise on the partition of Northern Ireland and this was left out of the agreement. The Treaty between Britain and Ireland was signed on 6 December 1921, an agreement that provided two political entities in Ireland, an Ulster Unionist-dominated north, consisting of six counties, and a nationalist-dominated Irish Free State comprising 26 counties with a status

T/Cadets loading their personal kit onto lorries as they are demobilised following the Truce, 1922. (Ernest McCall)

deeming it a dominion of the British Empire. Both negotiating parties were forced to compromise but neither was satisfied with the outcome.

Republicans were divided in relation to the contents of the Anglo-Irish Treaty. On 7 January 1922, Dáil Éireann voted, 64 in favour of ratifying the Treaty, 57 against. This action not only divided the Irish government but also the country and a tense stand-off between pro- and anti-Treaty forces began and within six months Ireland was embroiled in a bitter and bloody civil war.

On 13 January 1922 the disbandment of the Auxiliary Division of the RIC commenced. The Auxiliaries were demobilised on the steamer SS *Galteemore,* berthed at Holyhead, which had been temporarily converted into a floating barracks.[29] A sergeant and twelve constables were detailed to process the officers, which involved disarming them and supplying them with civilian attire. As with all military demobilisations, there were problems.

> The terms on which the Auxiliary Division of the R.I.C. was being demobilised provoked that body to make a vigorous protest. A representative committee of 'C' and 'H' and Depot Companies refused to accept final payment or discharge certificates, or demobilisation, until a conference was held to discuss the position arising from the closuring of their contracts without reference to them.[30]

Dispersal terms were drawn up between A.W. Cope, Assistant Under-Secretary to the Lord Lieutenant, acting on behalf of the British government and six members of the Auxiliary Division of the RIC: Wallis Muirhead, B.R. Durlacher, E.M. Nichol, E. Fleming, J.W. Hescroff and R.A. Malony. The terms consisted of the following:

Unexpired Contracts – one pound (£1) per day (or one guinea per day where such is the contracted payment) to be paid in respect of the unexpired portion. Lump-sum settlements to be made as soon as possible and in the case no later than the 31st March 1922.

In the event of any Cadet accepting further employment under the Crown before the expiration of his contract period, an appropriate adjustment to be made in the emoluments due in respect of the unexpired portion of his contract.

Expired contracts. – Payments to be made at the rate of one pound (£1) per a day (or one guinea per day as the case may be) in respect of the period up to 31st March, 1922. This also to apply to contracts terminating before the 31st March 1922.

These arrangements to be regarded as a final settlement covering all emoluments payable both in respect of expired and unexpired contracts and are framed with a view to meeting any possible hardship arising from the promulgation without Government authority or re-engagement of particular Cadets to 31st July 1922, which was subsequently corrected.

An advance of £30 to be made to each Cadet on dispersal, the balance payable under the arrangement for expired contracts to be paid as early as possible, (not later than the 14th February, 1922). Income tax to be charged according to law.[31]

Compensation payments were also paid to officers with those having twelve months' service being paid £200; nine months' being paid £150; six months' service receiving £100.[32]

Many local suppliers were left out of pocket as units pulled out of their areas of operations and there were accusations of the misappropriation of funds, for example, petty cash that each Auxiliary unit possessed for miscellaneous purchases. Many business owners lodged claims against the government for losses they incurred dealing with the Division. While some were successful, others were not, and the attempted balancing of the accounts dragged into 1922, with an estimated £10,000 being written off in total.[33]

On Monday, 16 January 1922, within the grounds of Dublin Castle, the British Viceroy, Lord FitzAlan, relinquished British control of 26 counties to Michael Collins, Chairman of the Provisional Government. Six counties were to remain within British rule. With partition in place, the DMP and the RIC were also preparing to stand down. Two new police forces, the Royal Ulster Constabulary and the Civic Guard (renamed 'Garda Síochána na hÉireann') would govern the north and the south of Ireland respectively.

The majority of the Auxiliary force was disbanded by the end of January but some officers were retained to carry out intelligence and training work for the newly formed government of Northern Ireland.

While some of the Division accepted the unit's disbandment, others could not. The inexorable rush of a firefight, the sudden cataclysms of a reprisal, the havoc and chaos had become a part of everyday life.

As the Auxiliaries stood down, many prepared for their return to England. Others, however, were looking further afield for money, adventure and action. Next stop: the Middle East.

25

The Final Reckoning
Palestine 1922

As the RIC, the Black and Tans and the Auxiliaries were being stood down, the following notice was circulated.

Confidential – Palestine Gendarmerie Royal Irish Constabulary Office, Dublin Castle. 25ᵗʰ January 1922.

There is an opening in the above Force for a limited number of young District Inspectors and Constables, unmarried and under thirty years of age, of superior education and First Class Records. Head Constables and Sergeants up to thirty five years of age would also be considered. The proposed pay of the Force will approximately be:–

Constables 10/-a day, free of income tax; in addition deferred pay of 1/-a day, with Rations, Fuel and Light or allowance in lieu. Officers and N.C.O.'s pay in proportion.

Pensions after ten years service on a scale not less than that of the London Metropolitan Police. Leave, three months every three years, £30, towards the cost of passage.

The matter is not to be circulated generally, but individuals who are known to be suitable should be approached personally. No recruiting will take place in Ireland, but if there are any men who can be personally recommended and who are willing to serve abroad, their names and addresses should be submitted at once in order that they may be brought to the notice of the recruiting officer in London.

Men will not be asked to join this Force until granted pensions and demobilized from the R.I.C. This matter is urgent.

C.A. Walsh. Deputy Inspector General. Issued to C.I.s except in Northern Ireland.

In the aftermath of the Great War and the defeat of the Ottoman Empire in the region, Palestine had been governed by the British military under the authority of the Assistant Provost Marshal who worked alongside the civil administration of Palestine under High Commissioner Sir Herbert Samuel. This relationship was often strained and the garrisoning of Palestine with 7,000 troops was also a considerable burden on the British Exchequer. When Winston Churchill moved from the War Office to the Colonial Office in February 1921, he believed that a British Palestine Gendarmerie was the answer and that the force could be raised by recruiting men from the disbanding Irish police forces.

Trouble in the region stemmed from the fact that Arabs had been promised independence in return for their allegiance during the war, while the Balfour Declaration of 2 November 1917 viewed with favour the establishment of a National Home for the Jews in Palestine.[1] Written by Britain's Foreign Secretary, Arthur James Balfour, the document stated:

His Majesty's government view with favour the establishment in Palestine of a national home for the Jewish people, and will use their best endeavours to facilitate the achievement of this object, it being clearly understood that nothing shall be done which may prejudice the civil and religious rights of existing non-Jewish communities in Palestine, or the rights and political status enjoyed by Jews in any other country.[2]

A former T/Cadet prepares for
deployment to Palestine, 1922.
(G. Burroughs)

The Arab populations were infuriated with the idea that their lands were being given away and clashes between Jewish and Arab Nationalists were becoming increasingly frequent with the under-resourced Palestine Police coming under growing pressure to keep peace in the region.

The recruitment of former officers who had served in Ireland was seen by many as controversial and their recruitment, deployment and costs raised questions in Parliament: 'Mr. Allen Parkinson asked the Secretary for War whether the men who had been serving in Ireland as Black and Tans are being re-engaged for service in Egypt and India at £1 a day and a gratuity on completion of service, amounting to more than £200?'[3]

The War Office was already receiving communiqués from High Commissioner Sir Herbert Samuel, expressing concern over the recruitment of officers who had served in Ireland. Though he had no objection to policemen being recruited who had served in Ireland, he stated that it would be:

most desirable, if it could be avoided, that no public announcement should be made connecting the Black and Tans with our Gendarmerie. Their reputation, as a corps, had not been savoury and if any idea was created in the public mind in England or here that the Black and Tans, or any part of them, were being transferred as a body to Palestine, the new Gendarmerie might be discredited from the outset.[4]

While a government press release stated that it was recruiting a new special force to serve in Palestine, it did not mention that many of them would have served in police units in Ireland. However, the Central News Agency in London stated that they would be recruited from former Irish police units, a statement clarified by the government who issued an official denial that it was 'considering the practicability of employing officers and men of the Auxiliary Division of the Royal Irish Constabulary for Police Duties in Palestine'.[5] To add fuel to the fire, Churchill appointed his old friend and former Auxiliary Commander, Major General Sir Hugh H. Tudor, to the post of General Officer Commanding in Palestine, under the new title of Inspector General of Police and Prisons. Tudor attempted to recommend his friend Brigadier General Ormonde de l'Épée Winter, the former chief of Irish intelligence, for the post of deputy chief of police. However, the War Office deemed Winter unsuitable for the position, possibly for the unorthodox methods he used while in Ireland. Colonel Angus McNeill, a Boer and Great War veteran, was appointed to the position instead.

In England, the secretive and selective recruitment for the Palestine Gendarmerie began at the Air Ministry HQ, Adastral House, London. Temporary Adjutant Captain A. Tyrell Blackett was tasked with sifting through the records of Auxiliary and RIC officers. Potential recruits, some of whom were contacted either verbally or by letter, had to be 'unmarried and under thirty years of age, of superior education and possess first class records'. A one-page application detailing their army and police experience was submitted, along with details of awards and decorations as well as references. Those who met the requirements were sent for medical examination. Contracts were for one year with pay. Platoon Commanders would receive 22 shillings per day and Platoon

Officers 20 shillings per day. While this was considerably less than what Auxiliary Cadets received during their service in Ireland, these rates of pay and employment conditions were considered good for the time. It is estimated that 158 former Auxiliaries served in the Palestine Gendarmerie, which in total numbered in the region of 49 officers and 701 other ranks.[6]

On 12 April 1922, 750 men, many of whom had served in Ireland, sailed from Devonport Dockyard on the steamer *City of Oxford* to Haifa, Palestine. The unit was based at Bir Salem and was equipped with weapons and transport. Model T Ford cars and Rolls-Royce armoured vehicles were the preferred transport for the Gendarmerie but they also maintained a mounted detachment for operations in the hills. Their firepower, speed and mobility gave the unit an advantage over their adversaries.

> According to their own reports, these former 'Black and Tans' were brash and anxious for action. They delighted in skirmishes with bandits in the hills. Four platoons of British Gendarmerie were assigned to Nazareth. After becoming frustrated with their own accommodations there, they took over a floor in the former Russian Hospice, which was used as offices for the staff of the civil governor of Galilee. When a local Palestinian clerk resisted their take over, the gendarmerie tossed his desk, chair, filing cabinet and him out of the second storey window.[7]

The Gendarmerie worked alongside a local police unit which consisted of Jews and Arabs but which remained a separate force.

As was expected, the reputation of the former Auxiliary force preceded them, and many people in Palestine feared their deployment. Helen Bentwich, wife of the Attorney General of Palestine, wrote: 'Our Irish Constabulary have arrived, and a rough looking lot they are. Already it's rumoured they are painting Jaffa red. They don't fit in with our scheme for a moral utopia.'[8]

Within the ranks of the Gendarmerie, there was a macabre element. 'On another occasion in Nabulas, one Gendarme proudly displayed, "an old cigarette-tin containing the brains of a man whose skull he had splintered with his rifle-butt (the smashed weapon was also exhibited)".'⁹

General Tudor left the force in 1924 amid controversy, being described by Angus McNeill as 'dictatorial, capricious, and completely lacking in communication skills'. McNeill also wrote in his diary, 'I never wish again to serve under such a man. He has been no use to us officially or socially since he dropped out of the clouds … 21 months ago.'¹⁰

The Gendarmerie was short-lived and was disbanded in 1926, the government citing financial constraints.

While there were incidents of drunkenness in the ranks, strict discipline was enforced, with the worst offenders being dismissed from the force. There is no direct evidence that the unit acted in a similar vein to the way the Auxiliary Police operated in Ireland. Records and reports are unavailable, either lost or not in the public domain. While their operational deployment in Palestine was regarded as a success by the British authorities, some historians question their conduct.

On the disbandment of the Palestine Gendarmerie in 1926, a number of ex-RIC transferred to the Palestine Police, including Black and Tans and Auxiliary officers. Many, such as Raymond Caffereta, worked their way up the ranks of the British section of the Palestine Police. Caffereta achieved the rank of Superintendent in that force.

During the 1936–39 Arab Revolt in Palestine, Orde Wingate, an intelligence officer in the British army's General Headquarters in Jerusalem, established Special Night Squads (SNS) consisting of British soldiers and Jewish supernumerary police. This force, though initially tasked with securing the Iraq Petroleum Company pipeline from Arab insurgents, evolved into a joint British/Jewish counter-insurgency unit. Amongst its ranks were Yigal Allon and Moshe Dayan, two men trained by the British military who would, in years to come, turn the tables on their former tutors. Training included: 'how to kill without compunction, how to interrogate prisoners by shooting every tenth man to make the rest talk; and how to deter future terrorists by pushing the heads of captured ones into pools of oil and then freeing them to tell their story'.¹¹

A recent study reveals that:

> During the Arab Revolt in Palestine from 1936–1939, when the number of British police swelled and reinforcements from the Army and Royal Air Force were brought in large numbers, brutal tactics were employed, similar to those ones used to put down the Irish Rebellion in 1919 and 1920. These tactics included demolition of homes, or in some cases, entire villages of suspected rebels; arrests and imprisonments without warrant, charges or trials; beatings; and torture. Yet, unlike the media coverage of the Irish Rebellion with its sharp criticism of 'Black and Tan' tactics, the media coverage of the situation in Palestine generally praised the British efforts and villainised the local Arab Palestinian rebels.[12]

The SNS continued to operate until 1939 when a new British policy was implemented that stopped Jewish supernumeraries from participating in offensive operations. However, Jewish groups continued to arm and train themselves against possible attacks by Arab Nationalists, the situation escalating to attacks against the British authorities. The Criminal Investigation Department of the Palestine Police was tasked with investigating attacks and, where possible, apprehending those responsible. The situation escalated with increased attacks against the British administration in Palestine. There was rioting, bombings of police stations and municipal buildings, as well as targeted assassinations, such as the killing of Lord Moyne, the British Resident Minister of State in Cairo. On 22 July 1946, the King David Hotel in Jerusalem was targeted by the Jewish Irgun Zvai Leumi (IZL) or National Military Organisation. Insurgents managed to gain entry into this high-security building, which housed several departments of the secretariat and other government offices. Explosive devices were placed at structural supports, which, when detonated, destroyed the hotel and killed 91 people, both men and women, a considerable number of them Jewish.

Many of those now holding rank amongst the Palestine Police had served in Ireland and in Palestine in the 1920s and were now facing another war of insurgency. In an effort to counteract these paramilitary organisations, the Palestine Police, the military and the British government looked to the past, forming 'Special Squads' as a method of tackling those responsible.

In one case a former Special Air Services (SAS) operative during the Second World War, Major Roy Farran DSO, MC, was seconded to the Palestine Police after the war and tasked with establishing these Special Squads, which would use special-forces methods against the Zionist underground. The Special Squads operated undercover, utilising civilian clothing and civilian vehicles to kill or capture Irgun operatives.

Farran's unit lacked accurate intelligence on those operating against the authorities, leading the group to pick up for questioning, interrogate and detain many people who were inconsequential.

Farran was linked to the murder of a young Jewish activist, Alexander Rubowitz, in May 1947. The sixteen-year-old member of the Jewish Paramilitary group Lehi was picked up for questioning while putting up posters. He disappeared and was never found. Palestine Police investigated the disappearance and were instructed by Henry Gurney, Chief Secretary to Palestine, to proceed with the case as an ordinary criminal offence with the aim of bringing those involved to stand trial. Farran was taken into custody because a hat with his initials on the inside was discovered at the scene of the boy's disappearance. He denied the charges but was arrested and escaped twice from prison before his trial. He believed he was being framed, stating that the Jewish underground was on the brink of defeat when he was accused. He claimed that the British government was making him a scapegoat during a period of tit-for-tat killings in the region. Though he went to trial, he was acquitted and subsequently returned to England. In revenge for his acquittal, underground Israeli forces attempted to assassinate him by sending a bomb through the post. Addressed to R. Farran, the package detonated, killing his brother instead. Farran evaded those trying to kill him and retired to Canada, dying of natural causes in 2006.

Many of those who took part in such clandestine operations in the region believed they had been given carte blanche to operate by those who sanctioned the Squads. Recent research uncovered a statement by Farran claiming that during the course of an interrogation, he had struck the boy with a rock on the head and killed him. The body was mutilated, in order to hinder identification, and disposed of in the desert.[13]

While it is impossible to link former Auxiliary and Black and Tan officers who had served in Ireland directly with these squads, some historians believe that the officers' deployments in Ireland greatly influenced their reaction to the escalating insurgency in 1930s and 1940s Palestine.

While the British administration disavowed Farran's clandestine actions in Palestine in the 1940s, those who had served in the ADRIC, and later the Palestine Gendarmerie, felt let down by a government that initially sanctioned their counter-insurgency tactics, but later sought to criminalise them.

Though these special forces had taken the fight to the enemy, they were deemed by many to have broken the rules of engagement. With the steady decline of the British Empire, MPs were worried about losing their popularity amongst the voters. The former soldiers and police officers who had served in such campaigns were no longer considered of value in a changing world where the ideal of Empire was no longer important amongst a post-war generation.

26

A Very Special Force

Contrary to popular belief, the ADRIC were not guns for hire or mercenaries. Though they were well paid, the T/Cadets were fighting for King and Country as they had done during the Great War. The Irish War of Independence was and often is considered a dirty war of insurgency and counter-insurgency, where a specialist force was recruited and deployed to counteract a terrorist force and bring stability to a country that was spiralling out of control.

Special forces have played an important role throughout history, with specialist units operating covertly and overtly in a number of conflicts. Many modern forces that are recognisable today first emerged in the early twentieth century, with a significant growth of such units during the Second World War. Groups such as the British Commandos or the Special Air Service (SAS) carried out clandestine operations during that war but the idea of such units was conceived much earlier.

However, on closer examination, the term 'specialist' or 'elite' in the military has acquired a number of separate connotations. The traditional and historical meaning may be traced from the Roman Praetorian Guard, Anglo-Saxon Huscarls at the Battle of Hastings, Cromwell's Ironsides, Napoleon's Old Guard or the French Foreign

'I' Company photographed at Beggars Bush Barracks, winter 1920. (R. Porter Collection)

Legion. As centuries progressed and warfare developed, many of these groups were amalgamated into the country's regular forces, but in time of war there was always a need for improvisation.

It was on the North-West Frontier, in India, that the British army first learned how to conduct counter-insurgency warfare. Their opponent's tactics were emulated, with the overall strategy being kill or capture the enemy, the same strategy that is conducted in conventional warfare.

During the Second Boer War (1899–1902), Britain realised the need for more specialised units. It was during this conflict that units such as Lovat's scouts and the Bushveldt Carabineers emerged. Trained for covert operations, reconnaissance and hit-and-run tactics, these groups harried the enemy.

The term 'Commando' originates from that conflict. Having no standing army, the Boers fought a relentless guerrilla campaign against regular British forces. Living off the land, these groups of highly mobile insurgents made lightning strikes on British garrisons and their supply lines, then vanishing into the veldt before the British military could react. Winston Churchill witnessed at first hand this type of operation that left the regular military in disarray. Though the Boers were defeated in the field by 1900, these commando operations dragged the conflict on for a further eighteen months. Churchill was impressed by the advantages of unorthodox warfare and he keenly approved the creation of the British Commandos during the Second World War.

The British army was slow to adapt to such warfare, but there were those who recognised its potential. Within its ranks, the military had a number of men that had earned a reputation for daring, toughness and for the use of unconventional methods. Alongside the relatively large army formations, there was a parallel development of small, unorthodox, intensely self-disciplined, highly motivated and ruthless units who operated covertly behind enemy lines. The success of these specialist units would see them being developed by countries throughout the world.

> The essence of insurgent warfare is the 'hit and run' attack and concealment within the operational environment. T.E. Lawrence described the guerrilla army as resembling a gas – able to disperse as molecules to prevent a counter-strike, but also able to coalesce for its own operations. Yet, guerrilla warfare is like terrorism, actually evidence of comparative weakness: the insurgent lacks the manpower, equipment or support to defeat an enemy in conventional fighting and so turns to an asymmetrical campaign. Guerrilla forces seek to redress the imbalance of power by specific techniques: raids to cripple the capacity to wage war; inflicting casualties to demoralise the enemy; deliberately preventing a conclusion to a campaign in order to conduct a protracted war of attrition to exhaust resistance or rouse civilian opposition; securing external assistance for arms and supplies; focusing on the security of remote and inaccessible mountain or jungle fastnesses; or perhaps by disguising themselves within the fabric of civil society.[1]

It was in this type of warfare that the IRA excelled, turning its smaller and conventionally weaker units into advantages and using methods that struck at the weaknesses of the larger and militarily stronger forces of Britain.

Members of 'Q' Company in action during an attack on their base, April 1921. (National Library of Ireland)

Baden Powell, after a successful military career and his organisation of the South African Constabulary, established the Boy Scout movement in 1910, training youths in a variety of covert skills, including stealth and reconnaissance techniques, skills that were utilised by the military when many of Powell's protégés entered service in the British army.

During the Great War a different type of elite soldier emerged, one that formed ad hoc units to gather information by raiding enemy trenches and capturing prisoners and documentation. It was during this period that T.E. Lawrence and his Arab forces in the Middle East carried out insurgency operations that wreaked havoc behind the Axis lines.

While Winston Churchill has been credited with the concept of special-forces commandos in the Second World War, his support for the formation of the specialist ADRIC and the Palestine Gendarmerie almost two decades previously has been overlooked. As Secretary of War, Churchill was faced with an increasing insurgency in Ireland and Palestine that many feared would spread to Britain's colonies. With the regular forces of law and order overstretched and demoralised, an offensive force was needed to take the fight to the enemy.

He championed the formation of a paramilitary police and the ADRIC may be considered the twentieth century's first anti-terrorist unit. No matter how many regular police officers were on duty or how many soldiers were drafted into Ireland from 1919 to 1921, the British government could not secure every building of significance or ensure the protection of its staff and the Irish population during a war of insurgency.

The ADRIC had a fourfold mission that consisted of conducting special operations, irregular and guerrilla warfare, counter-insurgency and counterterrorist operations against the Irish Republican Army.

Though war was never declared in Ireland, it was considered by some in authority that Ireland was a battlefield and that the security forces could go wherever they pleased and do whatever they wanted, in order to achieve the national security objectives set out by their superiors.

Volunteer Joseph Lawless, a veteran of the 1916 Easter Rising, an IRA operative during the War of Independence and later an officer in the Irish Free State Army, experienced the ADRIC in action. He later wrote:

> ... the first elements of the new enemy force arrived in Dublin, the R.I.C. Auxiliary Division, or as they became popularly known 'The Auxies'. Looking back on it now, one can date the beginning of what was to be the final phase of the struggle from the arrival of this force. The force was organized on the lines of what would have been recognized in the later World War II period as Commando units, the personnel being specially selected and consisting mostly of ex-army officers who on demobilization after the war were ready to take on a well-paid job that offered excitement. The men who composed this force were seasoned and tough fighters, and the particular form of organization was sufficiently loose in its disciplinary code to allow full scope to individual initiative.[2]

All this would open the door for an array of tactics that are familiar in today's world of special operations. Covert actions, Black ops, holding without trial, snatch operations and the assassinations of high-value targets were used by the ADRIC and are tactics and strategies that are still deployed on an unprecedented scale throughout the world today.

The rank and file of the ADRIC were war veterans and on deployment in Ireland conducted high-risk operations within enemy lines, using what was then considered by many as state-of-the-art technology: they had the latest weapons, Tenders (remember: not many people drove back then), use of camera equipment to take photos, film crews for propaganda, etc.

The Auxiliaries, like current special-forces units, were not recruited directly from the public but from former military personnel, which created a *corps d'élite*.

David Neligan, Collins' spy in Dublin Castle, while on a visit to England, witnessed first hand the government's fertile recruiting ground for its new special forces. 'One of the sights I saw when I was there was all the wretched ex-officers begging in the streets. They had their medals pinned on to barrel organs, or they were selling matches and toys along the gutter. This was Lloyd George's "land fit for heroes". It was no wonder so many of them went over to Ireland to join the Auxies.'[3]

Hundreds of these experienced ex-officers enlisted and brought a new dimension to the conflict. Believing themselves to be an elite paramilitary police unit, the Auxiliaries had a special determination that gave them the ability to fight against the odds in an inhospitable environment, carrying out missions against insurgent forces that had many advantages over them.

Like operatives today, they were specially equipped to fight the enemy conventionally, but to do so beyond the front line. Units were provided with the latest weaponry, which included rifles for long-range combat as well as semi-automatics or pistols for close-quarter firefights. Cadets quickly learned that in an ambush, superior firepower is life or death. Using violence of action, attackers must be overwhelmed with sheer force and firepower. Fire support was provided by squad automatic weapons such as the Lewis gun, and armoured cars equipped with Vickers machine guns. Grenades were issued as they provided an effective way of causing substantial damage to pinned-down enemy targets.

Unlike conventional personnel, the personal equipment carried by the Auxiliaries struck a balance between mobility and protection. By wearing the minimum of equipment, the T/Cadets could move fast and silently in order to kill or capture their targets. ADRIC Companies had to enter areas of operations as quickly and effectively as possible. Companies were equipped with Crossley Tenders for speed while some units sought to use bicycles to enter covertly. Like special operatives today, T/Cadets operated in uniform as well as civilian clothing, their distinctive headgear being the only recognisable item of attire that distinguished them from their adversaries.

The formation of a unique specialist unit like the ADRIC was not without its imperfections; mistakes were made as well.

The missions made evident the fact that counter-insurgency operations were high-risk affairs, and the slightest bit of bad luck could, and often did, result in disaster. There was a degree of risk operating in a hostile land, heightened by the lack of understanding of the guerrilla war that they were engaging with. The ADRIC was in its infancy, its personnel untested in guerrilla warfare, their training and techniques not yet perfected. They were tasked with counter-insurgency operations against a force that conducted firefights, ambushes and assassinations both in urban and rural environments. As a result, many died or were seriously wounded while operating in Ireland. The unit had excellent direct assault and finish capabilities but it lacked the 'find and fix' intelligence fusion that is essential to fight a clandestine war.

In October 1920, a special course was devised to train a number of Crown personnel to combat republican tactics.

> A class called the '5th Division Guerrilla Warfare Class' was started under the direction of the General Staff at the Curragh. The course, which lasted for three days, consisted of lectures and practical tactical exercises carried out by the class itself in ambushes on lorry parties and cyclist patrols, and raids by day and night by parties in

lorries or on bicycles. Special attention was also given to instruction in the issue of clear and definite orders. The lessons drawn from these exercises were printed and issued to all in this Division, the RIC and Auxiliaries, and also through GHQ, to other Divisions … Each class consisted of about 40 officers and NCOs drawn from all units in the Divisional area, and later a proportion of the RIC and Auxiliaries were included, many District Inspectors and some County Inspectors attending. In all, 10 courses were held, and 280 officers and NCOs and 125 Auxiliaries and RIC were instructed. The results were excellent, and it was noted that, whenever the lessons inculcated were applied, the enemy failed in his ambush tactics and suffered heavy losses.[4]

The counter-insurgency campaign slowly began to yield results, but with the aggressiveness of many of the operations, Crown forces became increasingly alienated by the Irish population and in some cases, lost the support of those loyal to the Crown.

Aligning them with the RIC instead of with the military greatly hindered their operational capacity. Police rules of engagement and standard operational procedures differed greatly from those of the military, and operations were not exempt from law. Though some Cadets were charged with various offences and were tried by court martial, many were acquitted. Others were prosecuted, fined or imprisoned for breaking the law. However, the group still operated with a certain degree of impunity.

The ADRIC were tasked with operating in a hostile environment that ranged from open countryside to the cities, towns and villages of Ireland. While patrolling in rural Ireland, every bend in the road was a potential ambush site. The urban environment was also difficult to operate in, with an enemy that did not wear uniform or fight pitched battles on defined battlefields, and could disappear as suddenly as they appeared. As a result, the thin line between seeking and destroying an enemy, and protecting the vulnerable and innocent in society became obscured. Vehicle and civilian checkpoints, and house and street clearances were a vital aspect of operating in cities as the gathering of viable intelligence became the main goal for the T/Cadets. In carrying out these operations in order to identify and apprehend insurgents, there was a greater intrusion into the everyday lives of the population, which in turn resulted in the marginalisation of the force.

'The occupants of the house ... were generally terribly frightened, but when they realized the raiders were soldiers, and not the much feared Auxiliaries, they became calmer.'⁵ Extrajudicial killings, aggressive patrolling and the fear and hatred generated by the actions of some T/Cadets created hatred against the British security forces in Ireland with loyalists questioning their actions. The Auxiliaries looked on the majority of the population of Ireland as being hostile and adapted their operational procedures accordingly. The tactic of opening fire while driving through a town, village or the open countryside, which often resulted in the deaths of innocent people, was seen as a deterrent for ambushes and is still used today by armies throughout the world.

Restricted by police doctrine and regulations, the officers' training lacked purpose for the job that they had been given. There were errors on operations that caused the deaths of British soldiers, police officers and innocent civilians. Failing to take into account the proximity of the civil population, even if they were hostile, hindered and greatly reduced the ADRIC's operational capacity. That failure to win hearts and minds would prove detrimental and result in the force continually clashing with the civilian population of Ireland, something that would be reported on by the media, both at national and international level.

Major A.E. Percival, an intelligence officer operating in County Cork, later lectured on his experiences, saying, 'The rebel campaign in Ireland was a national movement backed by a large proportion of the population and was not conducted by a few hired assassins as was often supposed.'⁶

The inherently political nature of the war in Ireland was even more pronounced as this unconventional conflict produced an adversary that was not a state or an army but rather a small irregular force that was difficult to detect yet capable of causing major political and psychological impact. Questions arose in relation to the deployment of such an elite force in Ireland to fight against what was increasingly becoming a popular insurgency against Britain.

This was fundamentally a different type of war for Britain as it was political, more intelligence driven and more psychological than any previous conflict Britain had fought in.

> Historically, the approach to dealing with rebellion was for official forces to crush the insurrection as rapidly as possible. Where an enemy refused to come to battle and deployed tactics of guerrilla warfare, regular armies would often resort to the destruction of crops, livestock and property. With the fabric of their socioeconomic power smashed, the rebels were compelled to gather and confront the State. The combination of military power in the hands of the ruler and this policy of State terror was often very effective.[7]

Today, specialist military units operate domestically and globally with the nominated task of kill or capture of those designated as enemies of the state. These elite soldiers conduct missions in more than 100 countries, engaging in targeted killings, snatch and grab of high-value targets and directing drone and missile strikes. In the past certain governments deployed these ghost militias to operate all over the globe but recent events have seen military commanders being given the support of government ministers to expand operations with unprecedented freedoms.

These specialist forces have to balance their mission statement with gaining the support of the general populace in order to garner a strategy for success. In the long term, the military cannot kill or capture its way to victory but must address the central issue in an insurgency, i.e. gaining (or retaining) political power, with each side vying to get the people to accept its governance as legitimate.

Insurgents will try to win support by employing disorder to undermine or destabilise the current regime, exploiting local grievances or sectarian issues. As they gain the backing of the local populace, insurgents may create a counter-state where local issues that the government have ignored are addressed.

> In unconventional warfare, many people in non-combat roles are part of the clandestine infrastructure of the insurgency; they

shelter and supply the combatants with food, funds and other resources; provide intelligence, lookouts, messengers, weapons caches and transport, safe places, including religious buildings, hospitals and schools. Some activists are women, children, older people and clergy. Without such a supportive covert organization, insurgency is not possible.[8]

Amidst all the military and insurgent operations, the local population carried on with their daily lives as best they could. They suffered the inconvenience of military patrols and vehicle checkpoints, street gun battles and the inevitability of friends or family being killed. Collateral damage, as it has become known, is an outcome accepted by governments and the military because the advantage to the authorities (that of killing insurgents) outweighs the value of civilian lives caught in the crossfire.

The ADRIC, its history and the T/Cadets who served, left an indelible mark in Ireland and on its people. While their deployment did and still does cause controversy, one must examine more closely their formation, their objectives and the failure of the British government to provide a clear and concise directive of what their mission entailed.

While operational mistakes were quickly exploited by republican propagandists, elements of the media demonised the force, marginalising their effectiveness in the battle against the IRA and influencing how the forces were perceived both in Ireland and in Britain. On closer examination, one of the major points of controversy during this period involved decisions made by British politicians and the failure of senior military commanders to deploy their resources strategically and tactically. The ADRIC were left to their own devices, without direction or support from their creators, an error that led to them losing the propaganda war and to condemnation from many of the world's nations.

Major Percival, who had conducted a merciless counter-insurgency campaign in County Cork, was later to lecture on guerrilla warfare using Ireland as his template. He wrote seeking advice from his former colleague, Major (later Field Marshal) Bernard Montgomery, who replied:

My own view is that to win a war of this sort you must be ruthless. Oliver Cromwell, or the Germans, would have settled it in a very short time. Nowadays public opinion precludes such methods, the nation would never allow it, and the politicians would lose their jobs if they sanctioned it. That being so I consider that Lloyd George was really right in what he did, if we had gone on we could probably have squashed the rebellion as a temporary measure, but it would have broken out again like an ulcer the moment we removed the troops. I think the rebels would have probably refused battles, and hidden away their arms etc. until we had gone. The only way therefore was to give them some form of self government, and let them squash the rebellion themselves, they are the only people who could really stamp it out, and they are still trying to do so and as far as one can tell they seem to be having a fair amount of success. I am not however in close touch with the situation over there, but it seems to me that they have had more success than we had. I have arrived at the above conclusion after a great deal of though on the subject. You probably will not agree.

Yours ever,

B.L. Montgomery.[9]

The Irish Civil War that erupted in the aftermath of the British withdrawal was a conflict that divided the population and was witness to some of the fiercest battles and atrocities the nation ever experienced. Extrajudicial killings and government-sanctioned executions enabled the Free State to gain a firm hold, forcing the Republican Army eventually to down arms.

In every war, both sides commit atrocities and in the insurgency and counter-insurgency war in Ireland from 1919 to 1921 many killings took place that still remain unsolved and may never be explained.

The face of war has, through the centuries, changed dramatically. Today, governments everywhere consider it essential to have a standing force prepared to conduct unconventional war primarily because the various skills, especially knowledge of languages and the country where the units will be deployed, take time to acquire, and the special forces must be deployed early in the conflict to ensure maximum effectiveness. Counter-insurgents today reject the kill-or-capture policy that was prevalent during the twentieth century and instead follow a 'win the population strategy' that is directed at creating or stabilising a legitimate political order.

In order to win over the population, government forces must secure the populace, providing essential services, building political and legal institutions and creating a viable economy that is beneficial to all. Counter-insurgency operations must not be counterproductive, causing death or destruction to the population, which is likely to result in a backlash from the people and create support for the insurgency.

While some people regard such units as a necessary military force, others see such clandestine units as a daredevil bunch of cutthroats only to be used in the most extreme of circumstances. Specialist forces in the coming century must be agile, lethal, readily deployable and require the minimum of logistical support. Future wars will be won by forces you do not know about, in actions you will not see and in ways you may not want to know about. The military commanders who had come of age in the shadow of clandestine warfare at the beginning of the twentieth century, and then rose to positions of authority in the decades that followed, established a new precedent in counter-insurgency warfare that is still resonant.

Winston Churchill is credited with the formation of the Commandos during the Second World War, and the successes of these special operators in Europe, North Africa and the Middle East helped turn the tide against Hitler, but some of Churchill's notoriety may also be for the founding of the ADRIC and their controversial deployment in Ireland from 1920 to 1921.

27

Yesterday's Enemies

The signing of the Treaty with Britain and the disbandment of the Auxiliaries were followed by Ireland's descent into a bloody civil war. Those who had served King and Country in the ranks of the ADRIC once again found themselves readjusting to civilian life. After years of violence and death, society in 1920s Britain was also trying to readjust and understand the Great War that had stripped the country of its youth and an insurgency in Ireland that had dehumanised thousands of police, soldiers and civilians. Many of those former T/Cadets locked their experiences away and got back to the daily tasks of living, working and raising families.

Former Chief of Police in Ireland, Lieutenant General Sir Henry Hugh Tudor KCB, CMG served as Director of Public Safety in the Palestine Gendarmerie until his resignation in 1924. He received the Order of the Bath before emigrating to Newfoundland. A story relating to a planned assassination attempt on Tudor by the IRA in the 1950s is unsubstantiated and no documentary proof exists of such an operation. Tudor died of natural causes in St John's, Newfoundland on 25 September 1965.

After his resignation over the Looting of Trim, County Meath, Brigadier General F.P. Crozier continued to defend his tenure as head of the Auxiliary Police as newspapers and magazine articles condemned his failure to control the men under his command. Crozier later wrote a number of books, many on his experiences in the Great War and one in particular telling of his deployment in Ireland. He blamed his superiors and his men, detailing their insubordination and blaming them for escalating the situation. He had made many enemies amongst his former ADRIC colleagues who, it seemed, remembered him in the years that followed. Employment evaded Crozier in England and he applied to the newly formed Irish Provisional Government for a position, pleading past loyalty to Ireland. He offered his services 'in the maintenance of law and order in any capacity,' requesting an interview. The officer was informed that the Minister was unavailable and extremely busy.¹ Crozier became involved in the League of Nations as a speaker and promoted pacifism, which many believed was hypocritical of a man who had served in Ireland as the leader of a special unit. He died peacefully on 31 August 1937.

On retiring from the army in 1924, former Intelligence Chief, Brigadier General Sir Ormonde de l'Épée Winter KBE, CB, CMG, DSO, became involved with the pre-Mosley British fascist movement. It is unknown if Winter continued his cloak-and-dagger career and if his involvement with this group was one of agent provocateur. He was a staunch anti-Bolshevik and in 1940 he offered his services to the Finnish army, in their defence against Communist Russia. He penned his memoirs, entitled *Winter's Tale* and published in 1955. He died peacefully in 1962 aged eighty-seven.

On receiving the Constabulary Medal for his actions in thwarting an attack at Tralee Railway Station, T/Cadet Howard DeCourcey Martelli later joined the Ulster Special Constabulary and became the Commanding Officer of the Governor's Guard.

T/Cadet Gerard John Cullen Tynan O'Mahony (also known as 'Pussy') served with 'N' Company ADRIC. Although little is known of his service in Meath, after he was demobbed from the ADRIC, the Dubliner enlisted in the Palestine Gendarmerie. Working with Major James Monroe MC, another ex-ADRIC officer, he was instrumental in designing and implementing the defence plans for the newly established Jewish colonies and was also responsible for infrastructure projects such as the construction of link roads between Samaria and Jaffa that crossed the Judean Hills. On returning from the Middle East he commenced a career in journalism and later became manager of *The Irish Times*. He was a popular figure on Dublin's social scene, with drinking companions such as Myles na Gopaleen. His aunt, Katherine Tynan, was a renowned author and his son, David Tynan O'Mahony, was better known as the comedian Dave Allen. In 1948, Gerard John Cullen Tynan O'Mahony died peacefully and was buried in Tallaght, Dublin.

Lieutenant Cecil Robert Walter McCammond, a former officer in the Royal Irish Regiment and a T/Cadet in 'G' Company, Auxiliary Division worked as a salesman and caretaker to support his wife and four children. Claims for a pension from the army due to injuries received during the Great War were dismissed.

Lieutenant Colonel John Hendley Morrison Kirkwood DSO died in 1924 soon after leaving the ADRIC. The cause of his death is unknown.

Irishman Major Gerald Vincent Fitzgerald enlisted in the Auxiliary Division having written to the War Office declaring he was unemployed and asking if he was eligible to join the ranks of the ADRIC. He was later struck off the strength of the RIC as an Absentee and was listed as residing in Halifax, Nova Scotia, Canada. He studied agriculture in Winnipeg before returning to England in 1924. In the years that followed, his occupation stated 'retired army officer', and in 1947 he filed an application for temporary employment within the Post Office.

After disbandment, T/Cadet John Edward Workman continued his police career enlisting in the Special Ulster Constabulary before taking up positions in the Gold Coast Police, Fijian Police and the Constabulary of Northern Rhodesia before retiring in 1951.

Three officers within the ADRIC are listed as having won the esteemed Victoria Cross during the Great War. T/Cadet James Leach VC enlisted in the ADRIC in January 1921 and was initially stationed at Glengarriff in County Cork.[2] His family lived within the police barracks and moved as Leach moved between Companies before his departure from the force in July 1921. T/Cadet George Onions VC served in 'C' Company until disbandment. T/Cadet James Johnston VC is listed as an absentee within two months of enlisting in the ADRIC. This record usually means that a T/Cadet did not return to duty after leave and therefore did not see out his contract. The guerrilla warfare experienced by these men was vastly different than what they had experienced on the Western Front and this may have affected their service in the force.

Many ex-T/Cadets travelled abroad seeking their fortune. They made new lives for themselves, settling down, marrying and in many cases living ordinary lives.

Former T/Cadet Edwin Barrows of 'B' Company joined the Palestine Gendarmerie before returning to England and marrying in 1926. The following year, Edwin, his wife and young son left England for New Zealand. However, like many countries at this time, New Zealand faced a depression and employment was difficult to find. Edwin was involved in building bridges and erecting fencing in rural New Zealand before finding work in Wellington. He later became the National Secretary of the New Zealand Fruit and Produce Association until his death in 1968. Edwin Barrows, like many former Auxiliaries, never spoke of his deployment in Ireland.

Like all T/Cadets, Major James Carey Fillery had served in the army during the war. He enlisted in the ADRIC in November 1920 and served in 'J', Depot, 'M' and 'R' Companies, until finally taking up a post with 'S' Company. After disbandment, Fillery emigrated to New Zealand where he later married and had two children. The family lived in the farming community of Te Pahu, located between the city of Hamilton and the coastal town of Raglan in the Waikato region. He died peacefully in 1955 aged 74.

George 'Hori' Morse trained as a pilot with the Canterbury Flying School in New Zealand but the war ended before he saw action. He joined the ADRIC in November 1920, serving with 'H' Company stationed in Tralee, County Kerry. While on deployment he became romantically involved with a married woman named as Mrs Hilda Hunter. After the Truce they both left for Sydney, Australia, where their relationship floundered. She left and travelled to Adelaide by ship but he followed her and confronted her on the quayside. An argument ensued and he shot her with his service revolver. He then tried unsuccessfully to commit suicide. He was tried for her murder and served ten years in prison. After his release he returned to New Zealand, married, had a family and settled down and died in Auckland in 1983. A street, Hori

'Q' Company Cadet outside the London & North Western Railway Hotel, Dublin, May 1921. (R. Porter Collection)

Morse, is named after him in Wigram, Christchurch, as he was one of the first pilots to graduate from the Canterbury Flying School.

Though T/Cadet Charles Henry Williams and his wife, Amelia, resided in Dublin when he was in the ADRIC, they spoke little to their family about their time in Ireland. Amid the turmoil of the war in Ireland, their second child, Honor, was born at No. 11 Leeson Street, Dublin. On disbandment, Williams moved back to England and worked in the motor and haulage businesses that were becoming prevalent in the 1920s. He became a civil servant working as a driving examiner before his retirement. He died in 1965.

Having evaded prison and numerous attempts by the IRA to kill him, Major William Lorraine 'Tiny' King returned to England and continued his career in the military. During the Second World War, King was stationed in Gaza where he was posted to the Corps of Military Police. He died in 1942, aged 57, and is interred within the Gaza War Cemetery.

Captain Jocelyn Lee Hardy, Major King's accomplice in interrogating prisoners, retired to Norfolk in England and became a writer after the disbandment of the force. He penned a number of books, including *Escape, The Key, Never in Vain, Recoil, The Stroke of Eight, Pawn in the Game* and *Everything is Thunder*. His work *Never in Vain* is a semi-autobiographical account of his exploits in Ireland. In it, the author also attempts to justify the extrajudicial killings he carried out as a member of the ADRIC. Some believe his inclusion of the deaths of Clancy and McKee in the novel is an admission to the killings.

He named his seventeenth-century residence 'Kilcoroon', an Irish version of the Norse Valhalla or Hall of the Slain. On 30 May 1958, Hardy died peacefully in Hammersmith, London, aged 63. An obituary written by a family friend, Norman Edwards, reads: 'Hardy was not only a gallant soldier: he was a rare bird, a writer of good and simple prose. A pity he did not write more. But, above all, Hardy was a man.'[3]

Many former Cadets of the ADRIC never spoke of their service in Ireland. Official records are difficult to locate, with many historians believing that they were either destroyed or have been filed or hidden away in order to avoid controversy, and registers are illegible and incomplete. Official British histories of the period fail to provide details of British military, Auxiliary and intelligence operations in any detail, choosing to keep secret both their covert and overt missions. Individual police or military officers who acted on their own initiative and worked their own intelligence-gathering operations never recorded their experiences, leaving a substantial void of such undercover operations.

Personal testimonies that are held by families and relations are, in many cases, inaccessible due to the fear of reprisals for having had a family member serve as a T/Cadet during the Irish War of Independence, even to this day.

Depot Commandant and ADRIC Adjutant W.F. Martinson, C/O of 'L' Company ADRIC, later to become Adjutant of the Palestine Police, photographed in April 1921. (R. Porter Collection)

While some IRA members had their actions recorded by the Bureau of Military History, set up in the 1940s with the aim of recording the experiences of activists during the period from 1913 to 1923, the ADRIC were not granted that same courtesy by either the Irish or British authorities and so many of their personal testimonies have been lost, leaving a great vacuum in this period of world history.

Little is known of what happened to the majority of officers that served in the ADRIC after their contracts in Ireland ended. Those who fought in the Irish War of Independence, on both sides, sustained wounds, if not to their body then to their soul. Like all men brutalised by war, some were locked in worlds of fear and anger, some lashed out at their families, others tried to drown their feelings in a sea of alcohol, a few possibly became homeless and others just disappeared into an unforgiving world, their service for their King and Country forgotten.

Conclusion

The Auxiliaries were a specialist force tasked by the British government to 'terrorise the terrorists'. While they carried out their mission to the best of their capabilities, that same government disavowed knowledge of their orders, operations and clandestine activities. The omission by Winston Churchill to establish their role officially, the failure of the unit's commanding officers to seek a clear mandate of their assignment and the remissness of the authorities to support the force's actions in Ireland proved detrimental.

The formation of the ADRIC was in response to the growing insurgency in Ireland. By 1920 a state of undeclared war existed between the British Crown and the Irish Republican Army. Britain was embroiled in an unconventional war and, though it had experienced similar insurgencies in some of its colonies, Ireland was nearer to home and for many people, Ireland was home.

The Division operated with impunity in Ireland, leaving death, havoc and chaos in their wake. Their deployment reveals the lengths to which the British government was prepared to go in the war with the IRA: the killings, the assassinations, the destruction of property and the terror inflicted on a population with the sanction of the authorities.

State agents killed and were protected in many sanctioned killings organised by men who were meant to protect the populace and solve murders, not commit them. Their strategies and tactics adapted to a new type of warfare that is still current today.

All the T/Cadets who operated in Ireland were killers; they had fought in a war where killing was an everyday occurrence. Others were killers by association, not only partaking in the act but directing murder and, in many cases, covering it up. No action was taken against those suspected of carrying out extrajudicial killings except for the odd reprimand. Those responsible knew that no action would be taken against them. The British government assigned the men, operations and history of the ADRIC to the dusty, bloody and controversial annals of British imperial history. Political constraints against the ADRIC hampered their operational capacity as did their link to the police force rather than the military.

In hindsight it is easy to sit in judgment on the ADRIC and their deployment in Ireland. Yet little is still known of this force as two states, England and Ireland, want to consign the insurgency, or at least elements of it, to history. As long as the T/Cadets, their operations, their After Action reports and their personnel records remain hidden or lost, their legacy will continue to be mired in controversy and hearsay. Their service has been erased and their dead forgotten, buried in the hope that generations to come will forget about their past in Ireland.

Republican commanders considered the Auxiliaries more ruthless, more dangerous and far more intelligent than the other branches of the Crown security forces.

It is perhaps fitting to leave the last words for the ADRIC's greatest adversary. Referring to the Auxiliary Division, Michael Collins, on a visit to the constituency of Armagh in September 1921, is quoted as saying, 'Wherever they appeared it was because the men of the place had put up a good fight. The Volunteers knew generally they were the best fighters they had to meet.'[1]

Appendix

Locations of ADRIC Companies for the dates of actions described in this book

While deployed in Ireland, Temporary Cadets often transferred between Companies. The following list gives the date of the actions described in the text and where the Companies were stationed at that time.

Depot	19 September 1920	Kilmashogue, Dublin
'A' Company	December 1920	Kilkenny
'B' Company	22 May 1921	Upperchurch, County Tipperary
'C' Company	28 November 1920	Kilmichael, Cork
'D' Company	18 January 1921	Kilroe, County Galway
'E' Company	25 October 1920	Sligo
'F' Company	25 May 1921	Custom House, Dublin
'G' Company	9 June 1921	Darragh, County Clare
'H' Company	2 July 1921	Ardfert Station, Kerry
'I' Company	30 June 1921	Keady, County Armagh
'J' Company	25 February 1921	Coolavokig, County Cork
'K' Company	11 December 1920	Dillon's Cross
'L' Company	16 June 1921	Rathcoole, County Cork
'M' Company	2 February 1921	Clonfin, County Longford
'N' Company	9 February 1921	Trim, County Meath
'O' Company	14 May 1921	Mountjoy Prison, Dublin
'P' Company	24 April 1921	Belfast, County Antrim
'Q' Company	11 April 1921	London & North Western Railway Hotel, Dublin
'R' Company	31 May 1921	Blackrock College, Dublin
'S' Company	18 February 1921	Dublin Castle
'Z' Company	April 1921	Dublin Castle

Endnotes

INTRODUCTION

1 Walsh, M., *The News from Ireland* (London, I.B. Tauris & Co., 2008), p. 70.
2 Jeffrey, K., *Field Marshal Sir Henry Wilson* (Oxford, Oxford University Press, 2006), p. 300.
3 Griffith, K., & O'Grady, T.E., *Curious Journey* (London, Hutchinson & Co., 1982), p. 154.

1. A POLICEMAN'S LOT: LAW ENFORCEMENT IN IRELAND

1 *Collins Dictonary & Thesaurus* (Glasgow, HarperCollins Publishers, 2005).
2 Cowley, R., *A History of the British Police* (London, The History Press, 2011).
3 Walsh, M., *The News from Ireland* (London, I.B. Tauris & Co., 2008).
4 Herlihy, J., *The Royal Irish Constabulary: A Short History & Genealogical Guide* (Dublin, Four Courts Press, 1997), pp. 44–60.
5 Connolly, S.J., *The Oxford Companion to Irish History* (Oxford University Press, 2002).

2. A SITUATION REPORT FROM IRELAND

1 Parliamentary Papers, House of Commons & Command 1799.
2 O'Brien, W., Witness Statement WS 1766 (Bureau of Military History 1913–21, Dublin, hereafter BMH).
3 *A Gallant Gunner General – The Life and Times of Sir H. Tudor, KCB, CMG,* together with an edited version of his 1914–1918 War Diary. Tudor's Papers. Imperial War Museum, London.
4 'Record of the Rebellion In Ireland in 1920–21 and the part played by the army in Dealing with it, Vol I: Operations', papers of Lieutenant General Sir Hugh Jeudwine, Imperial War Museum, London, Box 78/82/2/ p. 4.
5 House of Commons debate, January 1920.

3. THE AFTERMATH OF WAR: THE RETURN HOME

1 Gleeson, J., *Bloody Sunday* (London, Peter Davis Ltd, 1962).
2 Bennett, R., *The Black and Tans* (London, E. Hulton & Co. Ltd, 1964).
3 Holmes, R., *Tommy, The British Soldier on the Western Front 1914–1918* (London, Harper Perennial, 2005), p. 621.
4 *Ibid.*, p. 623.
5 *Ibid.*, p. 623.

6   Townsend, C., 'Policing insurgency in Ireland', in David M. Anderson and David Killingray (eds), *Policing and Decolonisation: Politics, Nationalism and the Police 1917–65* (Manchester, Manchester University Press, 1992), p. 36.

7   Figgis, D., *Recollections of the Irish War* (London, Ernest Benn, 1927), p. 282.

8   McCall, E., *Tudor's Toughs* (Newtownards, Red Coat Publishing, 2010), p. 33.

9   Laffan, M., *The Resurrection of Ireland: The Sinn Féin Party 1916–23* (Cambridge, Cambridge University Press, 1999), p. 292.

10 MacArdle, D., *The Irish Republic* (London, Corgi, 1968).

11 Hawkins, R., 'Dublin Castle and the Royal Irish Constabulary', in T. Desmond Williams (ed.), *The Irish Struggle 1916–1926* (London, Routledge and Kegan Paul, 1966), p. 180.

12 O'Shea, P., *Voices and the Sound of Drums* (Belfast, 1981), quoted in Peter Somerville-Large, *Irish Voice: An Informal History 1916–1966*, 2nd. Edn (London: Pimlico, 2000), pp. 38–39.

13 PRO HO 351/63.

14 Low, W.J., *The War Against the R.I.C. 1919–21*, Journal of Irish Studies Fall–Winter (2002).

4. THE DOGS OF WAR: RECRUITING A NEW FORCE

1   Abbott, R., *Police Casualties in Ireland 1919–1922* (Cork, Mercier Press, 2000), p. 107.

2   www.theauxiliaries.com/index.html

3   *Ibid.*

4   Messenger, C., *Broken Sword, The Tumultous life of General Frank Crozier 1879–1937* (South Yorkshire, The Praetorian Press, 2013), p. 103.

5   *Ibid.*, p. 118.

6   Gleeson, J., *Bloody Sunday* (London, Peter Davis Ltd, 1962).

7   Crozier, F., *Impressions and Recollections* (London, Werner Laurie, 1930), p. 131.

8   McCall, E., *Tudor's Toughs* (Newtownards, Red Coat Publishing, 2010), p. 59.

9   www.theauxiliaries.com/index.html

10 BMH/CD/227/23/03.

11 Lycett, E., www.theauxiliaries.com/index.html

12 House of Commons debate, September 1920.

13 *Ibid.*

14 www.theauxiliaries.com/index.html

15 Gleeson, J., *Bloody Sunday* (London, Peter Davis Ltd, 1962).

16 Martin, K., *Irish Army Vehicles* (Dublin, Cahill Printing, 2002).

17 Allen, M.S., *The Pioneer Policewomen* (London, Chatto & Windus, 1925), p. 60.

18 *Ibid.*

19 *The Weekly Summary*, 27 August 1920.

6. CHASING SHADOWS: COMMENCING COUNTER-INSURGENCY OPERATIONS

1   *An t-Óglach* (BMH).

2   O'Donoghue, F., *No Other Law* (Dublin, Anvil Press, 1954), p. 49.

3   McCannon, P., Witness Statement 1383 (BMH).

4   Abbott, R., *Police Casualties in Ireland 1919–1922* (Cork, Mercier Press, 2000), p. 139.

5   Farry, M., *The Irish Revolution 1912–23 Sligo* (Dublin, Four Courts Press, 2012).

6   CI Sligo Oct, Nov, Dec. 1920 (TNA, CO 904/113).

7   Dalton, C., Witness Statement 434 (BMH).

8   BMH/CD/227/23/5.

9   'Record of the Rebellion In Ireland in 1920–21 and the part played by the army in Dealing with it, Vol I: Operations', papers of Lieutenant General Sir Hugh Jeudwine, Imperial War, London, Museum, Box 78/82/2/.

10 Leeson, D.M., *The Black & Tans* (Oxford, Oxford University Press, 2011).

11 Martial Law Declaration printed in the *Cork Examiner,* 11 December 1920, *The Irish Times,* 14 December 1920.

12 GHQ, the Forces in Ireland, 'Record of the Rebellion in Ireland in 1920–21, VOL I: Operations', Jeudwine Papers, IWM, London, Box 78/82/2, p. 22.

13 Brennan, M., *The War in Clare* (Dublin, Four Courts Press), pp. 70–71.

14 County Inspector's Report, C.I.F. Whyte, 30 September 1921, CO 904/116.

15 Matthews, A., *Renegades; Irish Republican Women 1900–1922* (Cork, Mercier Press, 2010), p. 268.

16 House of Commons debates, 21 Feb. 1921. www.parliament.uk/hansard

17 PRO, CO904/168.

18 Cork R.I.C. County Inspector's Report, June 1920.

7. Extreme Prejudice: The Kilmichael Ambush, 28 November 1920

1   Gleeson, J., *Bloody Sunday* (London, Peter Davis Ltd, 1962), p. 70.

2   Barry, T., *Guerrilla Days in Ireland* (Dublin, Anvil Books, 1989).

3   Hennessy, J., Witness Statement 1234 (BMH).

4   Leeson, D.M., *The Black & Tans* (Oxford University Press, 2011), p. 152.

5   McCall, E., *Tudor's Toughs* (Newtownards, Red Coat Publishing, 2010).

8. Shadow Warriors: The Intelligence War

1   Hart, Peter Ed., *British Intelligence in Ireland 1920–21 the Final Reports* (Cork, Cork University Press, 2003).

2   McMahon, P., *British Spies & Irish Rebels, British Intelligence and Ireland 1916–1945* (Woodbridge, Boydell Press, 2008)

3   *Ibid.*

4   Sheehan, W., *British Voices from the Irish War of Independence 1918–1921* (Cork, The Collins Press, 2005), p. 84.

5   Kennedy, P., Witness Statement 499 (BMH).

6   Gleeson, J., *Bloody Sunday* (London, Peter Davis Ltd, 1962).

7   McMahon, P., *British Spies & Irish Rebels, British Intelligence and Ireland 1916–1945* (Boydell Press, Woodbridge, 2008), p. 41.

8   McCall, E., *Tudor's Toughs* (Newtownards, Red Coat Publishing, 2010), p. 74.

9   Hart, Peter (ed.), *British Intelligence in Ireland 1920–21 the Final Reports* (Cork, Cork University Press, 2003), p. 67.

10 *Ibid.*, p. 28.

11 *Ibid.*, p. 43.

12 www.theauxiliaries.com/index.html
13 H.O. 184/226–229.
14 PRO, CO904/177 (2).
15 Hart, Peter Ed., *British Intelligence in Ireland 1920–21 the Final Reports* (Cork, Cork University Press, 2003), p. 63.
16 Mhairtin, B.B.U., Witness Statement 398 (BMH).
17 Kennedy, P., Witness Statement 499 (BMH).
18 Neligan, D., *The Spy in the Castle* (London, Macgibbon & Kee, 1968).
19 Neligan D., Witness Statement 380 (BMH).
20 Broy, E., Witness Statement 1280 (BMH).
21 Hopkinson, M., *The Last Days of Dublin Castle, The diaries of Mark Sturgis* (Dublin, Irish Academic Press, 1999).
22 McCall, E., *Tudor's Toughs* (Newtownards, Red Coat Publishing, 2010), p. 87.
23 O'Malley, E., *On Another Man's Wound* (Cork, Mercier Press, 2013).
24 www.theauxiliaries.com/index.html
25 McMahon, P., *British Spies & Irish Rebels, British Intelligence and Ireland 1916–1945* (Woodbridge, Boydell Press, 2008), p. 41.
26 McCall, E., *Tudor's Toughs* (Newtownards, Red Coat Publishing, 2010), p. 165.

9. MASTERS OF CHAOS: ERRORS & RETRIBUTION

1   Bacon, F., *The Essays of Francis Bacon* (Everyman Library, 1623 edition).
2   GHQ, the Forces in Ireland, 'Record of the Rebellion in Ireland in 1920–21, VOL 1: Operations', Jeudwine Papers, IWM, Box78/82/2, p. 22.
3   Augusteijn, J., *From Public Defiance to Guerrilla Warfare* (Dublin, Irish Academic Press, 1996), p. 270.
4   House of Commons debate, 22 April 1921.
5   Grey, R.C., *The Auxiliary Police* (Romer C, 1920).
6   McCall, E., *Tudor's Toughs* (Newtownards, Red Coat Publishing, 2010).
7   www.theauxiliaries.com/index.html
8   House of Commons debate, February 1921.
9   *Ibid.*
10 www.theauxiliaries.com/index.html
11 McInerney, T., Witness Statement 1150 (BMH).
12 Ó Fathaigh, P., Witness Statement 1517 (BMH).
13 *Ibid.*
14 Kennedy, P., Witness Statement 499 (BMH).
15 House of Commons debate, 24 November 1921.
16 Sheehan, W., *British Voices from the Irish War of Independence 1918–1921* (Cork, The Collins Press, 2005), p. 187.
17 RIC Reports January–May 1921, C.O. 904 114–15.
18 House of Commons debate, 1 June 1921.
19 Jon Lawrence, 'Forging a peaceable kingdom: war, violence, and fear of brutalization in post-First World War Britain', *Journal of Modern History*, 75 (September 2003), p. 557.

20 Bennett, R., *The Black and Tans* (London, E. Hulton & Co. Ltd, 1964), pp. 95–96.
21 BMH/CD/227/16/06.
22 Dublin District Historical Record. NA WO 141/93, vol 1 pt 1.
23 Borgonovo, J., *Spies, Informers & the Anti Sinn Féin Society* (Dublin, Irish Academic Press, 2007).
24 White, G., O'Shea, B., *The Burning of Cork* (Cork, Mercier Press, 2006).
25 *Belfast Telegraph* (1920–22).
26 Labour Party, *Report of the Labour Commission to Ireland* (London, 1921), Part II p. 6.
27 *Ibid.*, p. 7.
28 O'Neill, T., *The Battle of Clonmult, The IRA'S Worse Defeat* (Dublin, Nonsuch Press, 2006).

10. Requital: Dillon's Cross & The Burning of Cork, December 1920

1 Healy, S., Witness Statement 1339 (BMH).
2 *Ibid.*
3 White, G., O'Shea, B., *The Burning of Cork* (Cork, Mercier Press, 2006).
4 *Ibid.*, p. 113
5 O'Donoghue, M., Witness Statement 1741 (BMH).
6 White, G., O'Shea, B., *The Burning of Cork* (Cork, Mercier Press, 2006), p 126.
7 Ellis, Alan J., *The Burning of Cork: An Eyewitness Account by Alan J. Ellis* (Cork, Aubane Historical Society, 2004), p. 9.
8 Anon., *Who Burnt Cork City?* (Dublin, Irish Labour and Trade Union Congress, 1921), p. 65.
9 White, G., O'Shea, B., *The Burning of Cork* (Cork, Mercier Press, 2006), p. 139.
10 BMH/CD/006/09/16(e).
11 Crozier, F., *Ireland for Ever* (London, Jonathan Cape Ltd, 1932).
12 McCall, E., *Tudor's Toughs* (Newtownards, Red Coat Publishing, 2010).

11. The Force of the Crown: Waging war in Ireland 1919–21

1 Kautt, W.H., *Ground Truths, British Army Operations in the Irish War of Independence* (Kildare, Irish Academic Press, 2014), p. 126.
2 Sheehan, W., *Fighting for Dublin* (Cork, The Collins Press, 2007), p. 135.
3 Sheehan, W., *Hearts and Mines, The British 5th Division in Ireland 1920–1922* (Cork, The Collins Press, 2009), p. 281.
4 Griffith, K., & O'Grady, T.E., *Curious Journey* (London, Hutchinson & Co., 1982), p. 193.
5 Crozier, F., *Impressions and Recollections* (London, Werner Laurie, 1930), p. 134.
6 Sheehan, W., *Fighting for Dublin* (Cork, The Collins Press, 2007), p. 125.
7 Gleeson, J., *Bloody Sunday* (London, Peter Davis Ltd, 1962), p. 68.
8 Augusteijn, J., *From Public Defiance to Guerrilla Warfare* (Dublin, Irish Academic Press, 1996), p. 93.
9 Yeates, P., *A City in Turmoil Dublin 1919–21* (Dublin, Gill & Macmillan, 2012), p. 256.

10 *The Capuchin Annual* (1970), p. 463.
11 Sheehan, W., *Hearts and Mines, The British 5ᵗʰ Division in Ireland 1920–1922* (Cork, The Collins Press, 2009), p. 285.
12 Ó Súilleabháin, M., *Where Mountainy Men have Sown* (Cork, Mercier Press, 2013), p. 90.
13 Barry, T., *Guerrilla Days in Ireland* (Dublin, Anvil Books, 1989), p. 41.
14 O'Casey, S., 'Inishfallen, Fare thee Well' in *Autobiographies* 2 (London, 1980), pp. 40–41.

12. INTERNAL AFFAIRS: DISCIPLINE IN THE RANKS

1   Cabinet, 2 June 1921, Jones, Whitehall Diary, Vol III, p. 73; Townsend, *British Campaign In Ireland*, p. 184.
2   Crozier, F., *Impressions and Recollections* (London, Werner Laurie, 1930), p. 133.
3   McCall, E., *Tudor's Toughs* (Newtownards, Red Coat Publishing, 2010), p. 90.
4   House of Commons debate, April 1921.
5   National Archives, CO904/168.
6   *The Weekly Summary* 27 August 1920, TNA CO 906/33.
7   Crozier, F., *Impressions and Recollections* (London,Werner Laurie, 1930), p. 259–260.
8   Messenger, C., *Broken Sword, The Tumultuous Life of General Frank Crozier 1879–1937* (South Yorkshire, Praetorian Press, 2013), p. 143.
9   *The Times*, 11 March 1921.
10 Bratton, E., Witness Statement 467 (BMH).
11 McCall, E., *Tudor's Toughs* (Newtownards, Red Coat Publishing, 2010), p. 83.
12 www.theauxiliaries.com/index.html
13 McCall, E., *Tudor's Toughs* (Newtownards, Red Coat Publishing, 2010), p. 93.
14 Extract 2. Military Appreciations, in Macready to Francis Stevenson, 20 June 1921. Lloyd George papers F/36/2/19.
15 The London Magazine (1921).
16 Courtney, U., *The Blinding Light* (Kilmainhamwood, Ulltan Courtney Publishing, 2014).
17 Sheehan, W., *British Voices from the Irish War of Independence 1918–1921* (Cork, The Collins Press, 2005), p. 187.
18 Philips, W.A., *The Revolution in Ireland 1906–23* (London, Longmans, 1923).
19 Duffy, P., Witness Statement 237 (BMH).
20 O'Sullivan, T., Witness Statement 1478 (BMH).
21 Sheehan, W., *British Voices from the Irish War of Independence 1918–1921* (Cork, The Collins Press, 2005), p. 187.
22 McCall, E., *Tudor's Toughs* (Newtownards, Red Coat Publishing, 2010), p. 98.
23 *Ibid.*, p. 98.
24 Coogan T.P. (ed.), *Caroline Woodcock; Experiences of An Officer's Wife in Ireland* (London & Dublin, Parkgate Publications, 1994), pp. 48–50.
25 Sheehan, W., *British Voices from the Irish War of Independence 1918–1921* (Cork, The Collins Press, 2005).

26 'The Irish Rebellion in the 6th Divisional Area from after the 1916 Rebellion to December 1921' Compiled by the General Staff, 6th Division. EPS/2/2; Imperial War Museum.

27 PRO CO904/188.

13. A Chance in Hell: The Arrest of Ernie O'Malley, December 1920

1 O'Malley. E., *On Another Man's Wound* (Cork, Mercier Press, 2013), pp. 279–291.

2 *Ibid.*

3 McCall, E., *Tudor's Toughs* (Newtownards, Red Coat Publishing, 2010), p. 136.

14. A Toss of the Coin: Counter-insurgency Warfare

1 Johnson, R., Whitby, M., France, J. (eds), *How to Win on the Battlefield* (London, Thames & Hudson, 2010).

2 Sitaraman, G., *Counterinsurgency, the War on Terror and the Laws of War* (Virginia Law Review, 2009), p. 16.

3 Hogan, S., *The Black & Tans in North Tipperary* (Dublin, Untold Stories Publishers, 2013).

4 Kinnane, P., Witness Statement 1475 (BMH).

5 Hogan, S., *The Black & Tans in North Tipperary* (Dublin, Untold Stories Publishers, 2013).

15. Making the Rounds: Patrols & Raids

1 Barrett, J., Witness Statement 1324 (BMH).

2 Carragher T., Witness Statement 681 (BMH).

3 Sherry, E., Witness Statement 576 (BMH).

16. Harbingers of Death: The Coolavokig Ambush, 18 January 1921

1 Duggan, J., Witness Statement 875 (BMH).

2 PRO, HO 351/73.

3 www.theauxiliaries.com/index.html

4 O'Reilly, T. (ed.), *Our Struggle for Independence, Eye Witness accounts from the pages of An Cosantóir* (Cork, Mercier Press, 2009), pp. 40–44.

5 'The Irish Rebellion in the 6th Divisional Area from after the 1916 Rebellion to December 1921' Compiled by the General Staff, 6th Division. EPS/2/2; Imperial War Museum.

6 *The Times,* 23 April 1922.

17. Fighting for your life: The Clonfin Ambush, 2 February 1921

1 Gleeson, J., *Bloody Sunday* (London, Peter Davis Ltd, 1962).

2 MacEoin, S., Witness Statement 1716 (BMH).

3 *Ibid.*

4 House of Commons debate, February 1921.

5 Conway, E., *The Joy, A Brief History of Mountjoy Prison* (Dublin, Arbour Hill Print Unit, 2002).

6   Sheehan, W., *Fighting for Dublin* (Cork, The Collins Press, 2007).
7   Dalton, C., *With the Dublin Brigade* (Cork, Mercier Press, 2014), p. 51.
8   *Ibid.*, p. 67.

18. CLOSE-QUARTER BATTLE: URBAN COMBAT
1   Noyk, M., Witness Statement 707 (BMH).
2   *The Irish Times* 15 March 1921.
3   *Ibid.*

19. GUNNED DOWN: KILLINGS ON THE STREETS
1   Abbott, R., *Police Casualties in Ireland 1919–1922* (Cork, Mercier Press, 2000).
2   McCorley, R., Witness Statement 389 (BMH).
3   McKenna, S., Witness Statement 1016 (BMH).
4   *Ibid.*
5   *The Freeman's Journal*, 25 April 1921.
6   www.theauxiliaries.com/index.html
7   Dalton, C., Witness Statement 434 (BMH).
8   Tully, J., Witness Statement 628 (BMH).

20. OPERATION QUAYSIDE: ATTACK ON 'Q' COMPANY'S HQ, APRIL 1921
1   O'Donovan, J., Witness Statement 1713 (BMH).
2   Holohan, G., Witness Statement 328 (BMH).

21. KILL ZONE: THE RATHCOOLE AMBUSH, 16 JUNE 1921
1   Byrne, P., Witness Statement (BMH).
2   Doherty, G., Intro., *With the IRA in their Fight for Freedom* (Cork, Mercier Press, 2010), p. 434.
3   www.theauxiliaries.com/index.html

22. HIT: ENGAGEMENT AT ARDFERT STATION
1   O'Riordan, J., Witness Statement 1117 (BMH).

23. BLACK OPS
1   Breen, D., *My Fight for Irish Freedom* (Dublin, Anvil Books,1978).
2   *The Times*, 20 November 1920.
3   *Manchester Guardian*, 20 November 1920, 13.
4   Crozier, F., *Ireland for Ever* (London, Jonathan Cape Ltd, 1932), p. 107.
5   Messenger, C., *Broken Sword, The Tumultous life of General Frank Crozier 1879–1937* (South Yorkshire, The Praetorian Press, 2013), p. 138.
6   Crozier, F., *Ireland for Ever* (London, Jonathan Cape Ltd, 1932), p. 300.
7   Togher, J., Witness Statement 1729 (BMH).
8   *Daily News* 24 May 1921.
9   O'Brien, P., Witness Statement 812 (BMH).
10 *Ibid.*

11   Bennett, R., 'Portrait of a Killer' (*New Statesman*, 1961), p. 471.

12   Leeson, D.M., *The Black & Tans, British Police and Auxiliaries in the Irish War of Independence* (Oxford, Oxford University Press, 2011).

13   McLoughlin, B., *Fighting for Republican Spain* (Dublin, B. McLoughlin Publishing, 2014).

14   Crozier, F., *Ireland for Ever* (London, Jonathan Cape Ltd, 1932).

15   Leeson, D.M., *The Black & Tans, British Police and Auxiliaries in the Irish War of Independence* (Oxford, Oxford University Press, 2011), pp. 187–188.

16   House of Commons Debates, 25 November 1920, Vol. 135, c.645.

17   House of Commons Debates, 13 December 1920, Vol. 136, c.1136.

18   Circular from the Anti-Reprisals Association, November 1920, Bonar Law Papers HLRO 102/6/10.

19   Fanning, R. (ed.), *Documents on Irish Foreign Policy, Vol: I 1919–1922* (Dublin, Royal Irish Academy, 1998), pp. 106–107.

20   Bentinck, V.M., *Mutiny in Murmansk*, 'The Hidden Shame', the Royal Marines Historical Society, Special publication No. 21.

24. Reign of Fire: Final Operations in Ireland

1   *Irish Independent*, 10 November 1920.

2   Cabinet Office Papers (CAB) 23/23/337.

3   *Ibid.*

4   Pinkman, J.A., *In the Legion of the Vanguard* (Cork, Mercier Press, 1998), pp. 32–33.

5   *Ibid.*, p. 54.

6   *Ibid.*, p. 87.

7   McMahon, P., *British Spies & Irish Rebels, British Intelligence and Ireland 1916–1945* (Woodbridge, Boydell Press, 2008), p. 99.

8   Bennett, R., *The Black and Tans* (London, E. Hulton & Co. Ltd, 1964), p. 172.

9   Pinkman, J.A., *In the Legion of the Vanguard* (Cork, Mercier Press, 1998), p. 33–34.

10   Hopkinson, M., *The Irish War of Independence* (Dublin, Gill & Macmillan, 2002), p. 183.

11   Neligan, D., *The Spy in the Castle* (London, Macgibbon & Kee, 1968), p. 147.

12   Ferriter, D., *Dublin's Fighting Story 1916–21* (Cork, Mercier Press, 2009) p. 313.

13   Stapleton, W., Witness Statement 822 (BMH).

14   Fallon, L., *Dublin Fire Brigade and the Irish Revolution* (Dublin, South Dublin Libraries, 2012), p. 77.

15   *Ibid.*, p. 78.

16   Byrne, V., Witness Statement 425 (BMH).

17   Corry, H., Witness Statement 1687 (BMH).

18   Dalton, C., *With the Dublin Brigade* (Cork, Mercier Press, 2014), p. 183.

19   Situation in Ireland Report, Major Whittaker, CAB 24/139.

20   Stapleton, W.J., Witness Statement 08022 (BMH).

21   Cottrell, P., *The War for Ireland* (Oxford, Osprey Publishing, 2009), p. 123.

22   McMahon, P., *British Spies & Irish Rebels, British Intelligence and Ireland 1916–1945* (Woodbridge, Boydell Press, 2008), p. 46.

23 O'Malley, E., *On Another Man's Wound* (Cork, Mercier Press, 2013), pp. 380–381.

24 Jeffrey, K., *Field Marshal Sir Henry Wilson* (Oxford, Oxford University Press, 2006).

25 Sheehan, W., *British Voices from the Irish War of Independence 1918–1921* (Cork, The Collins Press, 2005), p. 71.

26 HLRO F36/2/19.

27 CAB 24/31.

28 Dorrney, J., *Peace After the Final Battle, The Story of the Irish Revolution 1912–24* (Dublin, New Island Press, 2014).

29 *Independent*, 16 January 1922.

30 *Irish Independent* 16 January 1922.

31 BMH/CD/227/23/03.

32 McCall, E., *Tudor's Toughs* (Newtownards, Red Coat Publishing, 2010), p. 157.

33 Messenger, C., *Broken Sword, The Tumultuous Life of General Frank Crozier 1879–1937* (South Yorkshire Praetorian Press, 2013), p. 150.

25. The Final Reckoning: Palestine 1922

1 Horne, E., *A Job Well Done, A History of the Palestine Police 1920–1948* (London, The Anchor Press Ltd, 1982).

2 Yapp, M.E., *The Making of the Modern Near East 1792–1923* (Harlow, Longman, 1988), p. 290.

3 www.theauxiliaries.com/index.html

4 Gannon, S.W., 'The formation, composition and conduct of the British Section of the Palestine Gendarmerie, 1922–26' published in *The Historical Journal*, vol. 54, no. 4 (2013).

5 *The Irish Times* 18, 20 January 1922.

6 www.theauxiliaries.com/index.html

7 *Ibid.*

8 Horne, E., *A Job Well Done, A History of the Palestine Police 1920–1948* (London, The Anchor Press Ltd, 1982).

9 Duff, D.V., *Bailing with a Teaspoon* (London, John Long, 1953), p. 46.

10 Sean William Gannon, '"Sure it's only a holiday": The Irish contingent of the British (Palestine), Gendarmerie, 1922–26' in *Australasian Journal of Irish Studies*, vol. 13 (2013).

11 van Creveld, M., *Moshe Dayan* (London, Weidenfeld & Nicolson, 2004).

12 Cahill, R.A., *Going Beserk: Black and Tans in Palestine* (Jerusalem Quarterly 38).

13 Cesarani, D., *Major Farran's Hat* (London, William Heinemann, 2009).

26. A Very Special Force

1 Becket, I.W.F., *Modern Insurgencies and Counter-insurgencies: Guerrillas and their Opponents since 1750* (London & New York, 2001).

2 Lawless, J., Witness Statement 1043 (BMH).

3 Griffith, K., & O'Grady, T.E., *Curious Journey* (London, Hutchinson & Co., 1982), p. 246.

4   Sheehan, W., *Hearts and Mines, The British 5th Division in Ireland 1920–1922* (Cork, The Collins Press, 2009), p. 129/130.

5   Coogan, T.P. (ed.), *Caroline Woodcock; Experiences of An Officer's Wife in Ireland* (London & Dublin, Parkgate Publications, 1994), pp. 48–50.

6   Sheehan, W., *British Voices from the Irish War of Independence 1918–1921* (Cork, The Collins Press, 2005), p. 100.

7   Becket, I.W.F., *Modern Insurgencies and Counter-insurgencies: Guerrillas and their Opponents since 1750* (London & New York, 2001).

8   Sitaraman, G., *Counterinsurgency, the War on Terror and the Laws of War* (Virginia Law Review, 2009), p. 30.

9   Sheehan, W., *British Voices from the Irish War of Independence 1918–1921* (Cork, The Collins Press, 2005), p. 151.

27. YESTERDAY'S ENEMIES

1   Correspondence 1 Jan–8 April. 1922 National Archive H99/2.

2   Bonner, R., *'Stand To', James Leach VC* (The Journal of the Western Front Association, No. 87).

3   www.theauxiliaries.com/index.html

28. CONCLUSION

1   *The Irish Times* September 1921.

Bibliography

Abbott, R., *Police Casualties in Ireland 1919–1922* (Cork, Mercier Press, 2000)

Allen, M.S., *The Pioneer Policewomen* (London, Chatto & Windus, 1925)

Augusteijn, J., *From Public Defiance to Guerrilla Warfare* (Dublin, Irish Academic Press, 1996)

Bennett, R., *The Black and Tans* (London, E. Hulton & Co. Ltd, 1964)

Borgonovo, J., *Spies, Informers & the Anti Sinn Féin Society* (Dublin, Irish Academic Press, 2007)

Breen, D., *My Fight for Irish Freedom* (Dublin, Anvil Books, 1978)

Brennan, M., *The War in Clare* (Dublin, Four Courts Press, 1980)

Dalton, C. *With the Dublin Brigade* (Cork, Mercier Press, 2014)

Connolly, S.J. (ed.), *The Oxford Companion to Irish History* (Oxford, Oxford University Press, 2002)

Conway, E., *The Joy, A Brief History of Mountjoy Prison* (Dublin, Arbour Hill Print Unit, 2002)

Courtney, U., *The Blinding Light* (Kilmainhamwood, Ulltan Courtney Publishing, 2014)

Coogan, T.P. (ed.), *Caroline Woodcock; Experiences of An Officer's Wife in Ireland* (London & Dublin, Parkgate Publications, 1994)

Crozier, F., *Impressions and Recollections* (London, Werner Laurie, 1930)

Crozier, F., *Ireland for Ever* (London, Jonathan Cape Ltd, 1932)

Doherty, G., Intro., *With the IRA in their Fight for Freedom* (Cork, Mercier Press, 2010)

Fallon, L., *Dublin Fire Brigade and the Irish Revolution* (Dublin, South Dublin Libraries, 2012)

Gleeson, J., *Bloody Sunday* (London, Peter Davis Ltd, 1962)

Griffith, K., & O'Grady, T.E., *Curious Journey* (London, Hutchinson & Co., 1982)

Hart, Peter (ed.), *British Intelligence in Ireland 1920–21 the Final Reports* (Cork, Cork University Press, 2003)

Herlihy, J., *The Royal Irish Constabulary: A Short History & Genealogical Guide* (Dublin, Four Courts Press, 1997)

Hopkinson, M., *The Last Days of Dublin Castle, The diaries of Mark Sturgis* (Dublin, Irish Academic Press, 1999)

BIBLIOGRAPHY

Horne, E., *A Job Well Done, A History of the Palestine Police 1920–1948* (London, The Anchor Press Ltd, 1982)

Holmes, R., *Tommy, The British Soldier on the Western Front 1914–1918* (London, Harper Perennial, 2005)

Hogan, S., *The Black &Tans in North Tipperary* (Dublin, Untold Stories Publishers, 2013)

Jeffrey, K., *Field Marshal Sir Henry Wilson* (Oxford, Oxford University Press, 2006)

Kautt, W.H., *Ground Truths, British Army Operations in the Irish War of Independence* (Kildare, Irish Academic Press, 2014)

Laffan, M., *The Resurrection of Ireland: The Sinn Féin Party 1916–23* (Cambridge, Cambridge University Press, 1999)

Leeson, D.M., *The Black & Tans* (Oxford, Oxford University Press, 2011)

Martin, K., *Irish Army Vehicles* (Dublin, Cahill Printing, 2002)

Messenger, C., *Broken Sword, The Tumultuous Life of General Frank Crozier 1879–1937* (Praetorian Press, South Yorkshire, 2013)

McCall, E., *Tudors Toughs* (Newtownards, Red Coat Publishing, 2010)

McMahon, P., *British Spies & Irish Rebels, British Intelligence and Ireland 1916–1945* (South Yorkshire, Boydell Press, Woodbridge, 2008)

MacArdle, D., *The Irish Republic* (London, Corgi, 1968)

Matthews, A., *Renegades; Irish Republican Women 1900–1922* (Cork, Mercier Press, 2010)

Neligan, D., *The Spy in the Castle* (London, Macgibbon & Kee, 1968)

O'Donoghue, F., *No Other Law* (Dublin, Anvil Press, 1954)

O'Donoghue, F. (ed.), *Rebel Cork's Fighting Story* (Tralee, Anvil Books, 1961)

O'Malley, E., *On Another Man's Wound* (Cork, Mercier Press, 2013)

O'Neill, T., *The Battle of Clonmult, The IRA'S Worse Defeat* (Dublin, Nonsuch Press, 2006)

O Reilly, T., (ed.), *Our Struggle for Independence, Eye Witness accounts from the pages of An Cosantóir* (Cork, Mercier Press, 2009)

Ó Súilleabháin, M., *Where Mountainy Men have Sown* (Cork, Mercier Press, 2013)

Philips, W.A., *The Revolution in Ireland 1906–23* (London, Longmans, 1923)

Reynolds, J., *46 Men Dead: The Royal Irish Constabulary in County Tipperary, 1919–22* (Cork, The Collins Press, 2016)

Sheehan, W., *Fighting for Dublin* (Cork, The Collins Press, 2007)

Sheehan, W., *Hearts and Mines, The British 5th Division in Ireland 1920–1922* (Cork, The Collins Press, 2009)

Walsh, M., *The News from Ireland* (London, I.B. Tauris & Co., 2008)

White, G., O'Shea, B., *The Burning of Cork* (Cork, Mercier Press, 2006)

Acknowledgements

Without the assistance of historian and author Ernest McCall I would never have been able to relate the history of the Auxiliary Force and those who served within its ranks. His insight and encouragement have been inspiring and for that, I am truly grateful.

David Grant has been a wealth of information on the subject and I thank him most sincerely for sharing his research with me and many others through his website.

For their professional advice and for reading the initial drafts, I would like to thank Dr Mary Montaut, Barrister John McGuiggan and Sergeant Wayne Fitzgerald.

I am most grateful to Commandant Padraic Kennedy, Lisa Dolan, Noelle Grothier and all the staff of Military Archives in Dublin.

I am indebted to Sue Sutton for her research in the British Military Archives at Kew in London and to Liz Gillis for her research into the Irish Republican Army 1919–22.

I would like to express my thanks to Nuala Canny of the Library of the Office of Public Works, the staff at the National Library, the National Archives, the Capuchin Archives and the staff of Kilmainham Gaol Archives.

Many thanks to Desmond Braden who provided detailed accounts of ADRIC operations, and to Gerald Burroughs for filling in the gaps about General Tudor. For information on the Palestine Gendarmerie I am indebted to Seán Gannon for sharing his research. All three responded to my queries, telephone calls and correspondence with frankness and courtesy.

I wish to acknowledge the assistance of Peter McGoldrick and all those at Irishconstabulary.com. This facility has enabled me to amplify details, seek opinions, and relate the history of the force and of the individuals who served in its ranks.

For information on individual T/Cadets I would like to thank Simon Pile, Manus O'Riordan and Lorna Keane. I would also like to thank the following for information, their assistance, encouragement and advice: James Langton, Michael Curran, Las Fallon, Ronnie Daly, Darren O'Brien, Mick Cahill, Johnny Doyle, James Fogarty, the staff of *An Cosantóir*, all my colleagues in the OPW, Darren O'Brien, Tommy Galvin, Micheál O'Doibhlín, Dr Padraig Óg Ó Ruairc and to my parents, Thomas and Rita O'Brien.

Thanks to cartographer Gerry Woods for once again bringing the battlefield to life with his amazing maps.

Credit is also due to historian and author William Sheehan for his invaluable work on the British Security Forces in Ireland during this period.

Many thanks to all at The Collins Press for their support with this project.

This book could not have been written without the love, patience and support of my amazing wife Marian and our daughter Bláthnaid. I am very lucky to have these two wonderful women in my life and they know first hand the importance of our nation's history and how rewarding it is to document and write on the subject.

Material in this book has been sourced through archives, electronic sources and private collections, and through interviews with relatives of those that served within the ADRIC, many of whom have requested to remain anonymous. To them all I offer my gratitude for their willing, often enthusiastic, help.

There are many people who helped with this book and in naming some of them I can only apologize to those who I fear I may have indirectly forgotten and I would like to invite them to make me aware of any omissions or relevant information that may be included in any future updated edition.

I would also like to hear from those whose relatives served within the ADRIC and I assure them that the information they may provide will be treated confidentially.

Index